D0303863

DISRUPTING EARLY CHILDHOOD EDUCATION RESEARCH

Recent and increasing efforts to standardize young children's academic performance have shifted the emphases of education toward normative practices and away from qualitative, substantive intentions. Connection to human experience, compassion for societal ailments, and the joys of learning are straining under the pressure of quantitative research, competition, and test scores, exemplified by federal funding competitions and policymaking.

Disrupting Early Childhood Education Research critically interrogates the traditional foundations of early childhood research practices to disrupt the status quo through imaginative, cutting-edge research in diverse U.S. and international contexts. Its chapters are driven by empirical data derived from unique research projects and a variety of contemporary methodologies that include phenomenological studies, autoethnographic writings, action-oriented studies, arts-based methodologies, and other innovative approaches. By giving voice to marginalized social science researchers who are active in learning, school, and early education sectors, this volume explores the meanings of actionable and everyday approaches based on the experiences of young children, their families, and educators.

Will Parnell is Associate Professor of Education and a pedagogical liaison to the Helen Gordon Child Development Center at Portland State University, USA. He also coordinates the master's in early childhood education for the Graduate School of Education's Curriculum and Instruction Department.

Jeanne Marie Iorio is a Senior Lecturer in Early Childhood Education at Victoria University, Melbourne, Australia.

Changing Images of Early Childhood

Series Editor: Nicola Yelland

Books in this forward-thinking series challenge existing practices in early childhood education and reflect the changing images of the field. The series enables readers to engage with contemporary ideas and practices of alternative perspectives which deviate from those theories traditionally associated with the education of young children and their families. Not only do these books make complex theory accessible, they provide early childhood educators with the tools to ensure their practices are backed by appropriate theoretical frameworks and strong empirical evidence.

Titles in the *Changing Images of Early Childhood* series include:

Shift to the Future
Rethinking Learning with New Technologies in Education
Nicola Yelland

Playing It Straight
Uncovering Gender Discourse in the Early Childhood Classroom
Mindy Blaise

Childhood and Postcolonization
Power, Education, and Contemporary Practice
Gaile S. Cannella and Radhika Viruru

Rethinking Parent and Child Conflict
Susan Grieshaber

DISRUPTING EARLY CHILDHOOD EDUCATION RESEARCH

Imagining New Possibilities

Edited by
Will Parnell and Jeanne Marie Iorio

Routledge
Taylor & Francis Group

NEW YORK AND LONDON

First published 2016
by Routledge
711 Third Avenue, New York, NY 10017

and by Routledge
2 Park Square, Milton Park, Abingdon, Oxon OX14 4RN

Routledge is an imprint of the Taylor & Francis Group, an informa business

Library of Congress Cataloging-in-Publication Data
Disrupting early childhood education research : imagining new
    possibilities / edited by Will Parnell and Jeanne Marie Iorio.
        pages cm.— (Changing images of early childhood)
    Includes bibliographical references and index.
  1. Early childhood education—Research. I. Parnell, Will,
1968– II. Iorio, Jeanne Marie.
    LB1139.23.D57   2016
    372.21—dc23
    2015027369

ISBN: 978-1-138-83910-6 (hbk)
ISBN: 978-1-138-83911-3 (pbk)
ISBN: 978-1-315-73362-3 (ebk)

Typeset in Bembo
by Apex CoVantage, LLC

For Helen Gordon Child Development Center,
For Lucia Kai
and
For all of the children who contributed in these stories

CONTENTS

SERIES EDITOR INTRODUCTION

The books in *Changing Images of Early Childhood* consider contemporary and alternative theoretical perspectives in the domain of early childhood education. The topics span classroom, family, and community settings and provide readers with *rich* descriptions of everyday lives. These include classrooms, teachers' experiences and the decision-making process in which they are involved, the multifaceted lifeworlds of children, the ways in which parents interact with children, and new insights into routine practices from different theoretical perspectives. The books engage us in deep conversations around intricate and complex sets of circumstances in the early childhood years. Their relevance to the lived experiences and everyday practices of adults who interact with young children in a myriad of environs is continually highlighted, thus enabling educators to create learning environments that are underpinned by a respect for all participants, equity, and social justice.

The *Changing Images of Early Childhood* books challenge and confront educators with a wide range of topics. They reflect the *complex* nature of our lives in a postmodern world where issues around globalism, capitalism, democracy, and the multifaceted nature of our contemporary experiences are not easily resolved. They have been created to bring to the forefront the issues faced by marginalized groups so that they might be interrogated with *respect* and from perspectives that are relevant to the nature and culture of those groups and individuals.

In this volume, *Disrupting Early Childhood Education Research: Imagining New Possibilities*, the authors ask us to contest the *status quo* and also suggest alternative ways of seeing, doing, and thinking about key issues in the early years of children's lives. The book is organized around three key ideas: new theoretical and methodological imaginings, democratizing the research process, and critical issues in ECE research from new perspectives. The chapters in the first two sections challenge us to consider the ways in which we theorize and conduct research with young children and their families, interrogate our roles as researchers in the research process in classrooms, and ask us to think differently about the ways in which we do things both with children and their parents. The final section presents topics that are of contemporary importance in the field: transition to school, play, surviving the test culture, creating contexts for learning that recognize diversity, and especially how economic adversity impacts on the lives of the children in our classes. These are important and powerful topics and ones that teachers, parents, and administrators face every day. They have been significant issues for some time, and it is relevant to revisit them in the context of twenty-first-century lives, which have become increasingly complex as economic adversity is having a huge impact globally. These topics need to be addressed, researched, and theorized in order for early childhood educators to understand and act in viable and relevant ways so that young children are respected and given opportunities to participate in society. The underlying theme of the book reflects the overall aim of the *Changing Images* series. That is, to deconstruct and reconstruct ideas and practices in early childhood education with the goal to encouraging educators to recognize the challenges faced by many young children and their families and to support them to reach their full potential.

Nicola Yelland
Professor of Education
College of Education
Victoria University
Melbourne
Australia

FOREWORD

Peter Moss

> *There is still a continued reliance [in early childhood education] on positivist empirical research and psychological perspectives in a journey to knowledge . . . We see these unnecessarily narrow approaches as problematic insofar as they tend to dominate the sector, capture the discourse and garner privileged access to government funding. The combined effect is to perpetuate the status quo, and construct a particular, perhaps even binding, paradigm readily appropriated by ministries and governments to promote efficiency frameworks of standards, outcomes and policies.*
>
> (Farquhar & White, 2014, p. 824)

Early childhood education today is dominated by a particularly narrow, instrumental, and outmoded idea of research, what Sarah Farquhar and Elizabeth White refer to in the opening quotation as "positive empirical research" and Patti Lather (2006) terms neoliberal "repositivisation." It is a research of numbers and variables, the former to be manipulated and the latter controlled, in the interest of achieving a false and reductive certainty enacted through standardized and prescribed methods and outcomes. (Which is not to say that numbers have no place in research, the question being rather what that place should be.) And it is a research that provides embellishment to the dominant but stultifying narrative in today's early childhood education, a narrative I have termed elsewhere the story of quality and high returns (Moss, 2014). This is a story about how early intervention, including early childhood education, offers an excellent investment, for individuals and society alike—if only the correct human technologies ('quality') can be identified, applied, and assessed by courtesy of scientific research. Invest early and invest smartly, using 'evidence-based' programs, or so the story goes, and you will realize human capital to the full, enabling flexible and compliant lifelong learners to navigate the endlessly changing currents of hyper-market capitalism and nations to compete successfully in the never-ending and perilous global race. In this story, research has been suborned as one of the technologies needed for our emerging "societies of control" (Deleuze, 1992); it is a technical practice for improving technical practice.

I say that early childhood education today is dominated by a particularly narrow, instrumental, and outmoded idea of research, but this assertion needs clarifying. Such positivistic research, focused on numbers and facts rather than meaning, is dominant in a very particular sense—in that it has a privileged position within circles of political and economic power, garnering (as Farquhar and White put it) "privileged access to government funding"—and is complicit in the capture of government action by a particular pedagogical narrative, that story of quality and high returns. Read any national or international policy paper and you will come across the same recurring research references, the same "iconic studies" (NESSE, 2009, p. 29), which have been, in Helen Penn's words, "endlessly recycled in the literature" (2011, p. 39). These are the kind of studies that get funded, these are the kind of studies that get included by academic gatekeepers when asked to review the literature, these are the kind of studies that are used to rationalize increased public spending on early childhood education—spending that is used to impose increasingly powerful technologies in the interests of more tightly governing the child to maximize the extraction of human capital.

But such research is not dominant viewed from another perspective. It has not succeeded in suppressing diversity; it has not eradicated other types of research, research that is situated in different paradigms, works with different theories, and contributes to other stories about early childhood education (including, but not only, what I have termed the "story of democracy, experimentation and potentiality" [Moss, 2014]). It is not dominant in the sense of having achieved a position of unassailable authority, placing it beyond question and without alternative. One of the pleasures of this book is to see such a rich medley of researchers working with a wealth and diversity of ideas, sensibilities, and questions, and doing so in most cases in schools or nurseries; they are, as the subtitle puts it, "imagining new possibilities," and not just imagining new possibilities but putting them to work.

Their research is not about finding better ways to attain the predetermined. It does not adopt the programmatic ethos of repositivization, with its will to achieve more efficiently the already foreseen and prescribed. This, instead, is research that allows for, indeed desires, wonder and surprise, new thinking and new understandings, research that is suffused with a relational ethos, an ethics of care, encounter, and hospitality.

Nor is this book an isolated example of research that imagines and enacts new possibilities in early childhood education. Whether in pedagogical networks (such as those associated with the Reconceptualizing Early Childhood Education conferences or the municipal schools of Reggio Emilia), or journal articles, or other books (for example, the *Contesting Early Childhood* series that I have co-edited with Gunilla Dahlberg), or doctoral theses, the vitality and diversity of research in early childhood education is everywhere to be found, shouting loud and clear that there are alternatives. So if this book, as its title claims, is 'disrupting early childhood education research,' it is doing so in good company and in a particular sense: of confronting one particular idea of research, one that is influential, one that makes assertive truth claims, but still one—and not the one and only, but the one among many.

This book can be seen as part of a swelling movement of people telling different stories about early childhood education, who attribute different meanings to the concept of research. It also raises important questions about the identity—or identities—of researchers. Is or should this role be confined to a certain academic caste, or is it more inclusive, entailing an attitude of mind and an approach to work that can be inhabited by many others—educators, parents, and children included? The authors in this volume are more of the latter view, echoing the *cri de coeur* of Carlina Rinaldi, from Reggio Emilia: "We want our research, as teachers, to be recognised. And to recognise research as a way of thinking, of approaching life, of negotiating, of documenting" (Rinaldi, 2006, p. 192).

The authors, too, raise important questions about the responsibilities of researchers, especially in the face of a world of increasing inequality and decreasing democracy, where increasingly powerful economic and political forces seek to impose ever more control and conformity. Is it the job of researchers to offer further tools to aid the exercise of such elite power, or to help disrupt it? How, for example, does a researcher avoid colluding with the divisive and oppressive effects of austerity policies on children and their families alike?

This book will bring comfort and renewed hope to those who believe that a different world is possible, with a different early childhood education infused by a different sort of early childhood research. It relativizes the dominant mode of research that amplifies the voice of those telling the dominant story of early childhood education. Rather than an exercise in measuring, controlling, and extracting, this volume shows how research can be participatory, emancipatory, and emergent, a means of listening to and seeing what has not been heard or viewed before.

Such research, it seems to me, has an important role to play in a democratic politics of education—if we can any longer imagine such a thing. In such a case, no research and no researchers, no matter what kind, would adopt an epistemic position, laying claim to discovering universal and objective laws or supplying evidential certainty, nor would any lay claim to a privileged position on account of special scientific authority. Rather, all would adopt what Bent Flyvbjerg calls a "phronetic" position, which recognizes certainties and generalizations are impossible in the social sciences "because the phenomena modelled are social, and thus 'answer back' in ways natural phenomena do not" (Flyvbjerg, 2006, p. 39). All would assume, too, the importance of perspective and context, and the inescapability of interpretation and uncertainty, and thus adopt a democratic approach of *modus vivendi*, which acknowledges that their interpretation is only one of many that are possible and should as such be considered along with others in democratic processes of public deliberation. Flyvbjerg, a proponent of a phronetic role for the social sciences, concludes:

> Though imperfect, no better device than public deliberation following the rules of constitutional democracy has been arrived at for settling social issues . . . Social science must therefore play into this device if it is to be useful . . . No one voice, including that of the researcher, may claim final authority . . . [P]hronetic social science explicitly sees itself as not having a privileged position from which the final truth can be told and further discussion arrested . . . To the phronetic researcher, this is the reality of social science, in contrast to researchers who act as if validity claims can and should be given final grounding (and with it, total acceptance). By substituting phronesis for episteme, phronetic social scientists avoid trying to lift this impossible burden.
>
> *(ibid., pp. 39, 41)*

In a democratic politics of education, there are a polyphony of voices engaged in dialogue, contestation, and negotiation. Researchers would be just some of these voices, just some of the actors engaged in democratic argumentation and deliberation. That research contribution to the polyphony of voices is prefigured in the chapters that follow.

References

Deleuze, G. (1992). Postscript on the societies of control. *October, 59*, 3–7.

Farquhar, S., & White, E.J. (2014). Philosophy and pedagogy of early childhood. *Educational Philosophy and Theory, 46*(8), 821–832.

Flyvbjerg, B. (2006). Social science that matters. *Foresight Europe* (October 2005–March 2006), 38–42.

Lather, P. (2006). Foucauldian scientificity: Rethinking the nexus of qualitative research and education policy analysis. *International Journal of Qualitative Studies in Education, 19*(6), 782–791.

Moss, P. (2014). *Transformative change and real utopias in early childhood education: A story of democracy, experimentation and potentiality*. London: Routledge.

NESSE (2009). *Early childhood education and care: Key lessons from research for policy makers.* Retrieved from http://www.nesse.fr/nesse/activities/reports/ecec-report-pdf

Penn, H. (2011). *Quality in early childhood services: An international perspective*. Maidenhead, UK: Open University Press.

Rinaldi, C. (2006). *In dialogue with Reggio Emilia: Listening, researching and learning*. London: Routledge.

1

REACHING TOWARD THE POSSIBLE

Jeanne Marie Iorio and Will Parnell

The current climate of education is excessively concerned and dominated with quantitative statistical analyses of children, in both the short term and via longitudinal data collections and 'valued-added' standardized assessments (Chetty, Friedman, & Rockoff, 2012; Iorio & Adler, 2013; Kumashiro, 2012). This reductionist approach produces an oversimplified view of children and their educational experience and masks the complexities of the diverse practices that exist internationally.

The chapters in this text are designed to act as a counter-narrative to disrupt dogmas around the quantitative and reductionist frameworks and in response to our own choices as researchers. For example, in our search for non-traditional ways of understanding the questions we pose to ourselves, in particular related to early childhood education, the view of the child, and the image of the teacher, we embrace arts-based methodologies. These methods create a space for us to intertwine our education and experiences within the arts and in early childhood. Curiously, our backgrounds—Jeanne's in dance and Will's in romance languages—include studying in the arts while working in early childhood education settings, thus causing a co-mingling of ideas to emerge for us.

This collaborative view across the arts and education has framed our practice as a combination circulating around the abstract and concrete, pushing at the tension between expected early childhood practices, disrupting traditional perspectives on early childhood, and rethinking through an artistic vision. This perspective is clear as we borrow from the arts to articulate how we understand child-adult conversations as aesthetic experiences (Iorio, 2008); seek meaning in early childhood studio, Reggio-study tour, and classroom experiences (Parnell, 2012; 2011a; 2011b; 2011c); or use arts-based methodologies to document children's and families' viewpoints (Iorio & Visweswaraiah, 2012; Parnell, 2011b). Our choices are further evidenced in one of our research projects using collage to understand action research processes. This research centers on our own experience teaching action research as a means to empower emerging teachers with the tools to continually reflect and enact change in their practices.

As an example, when we talk about action research with our students, we move through our usual elements of action research—reflecting, questioning, collecting baseline data, reviewing the literature, analyzing, changing, considering the change, more data collecting, more analyzing, more developing questions—yet we begin to wonder how we have really understood the action research process. Using an arts-based methodology, in particular collage, we begin our own action research project focused on how we understand action research. For our purposes, we both utilize collage, bringing together small parts to create a whole, in order to see how we understand the process of action research. As we move through our collaging experiences of action research, we find Leavy's (2009) sentiments important to our work. We are moved and wholeheartedly agree when we encounter her thinking, "Visual art can jar people into seeing something differently" (p. 220). Since we are so embedded in action research process as we teach and discuss it for a majority of our teaching, we want to see action research from a new perspective, and collage seems to be a vehicle to jolt us into seeing anew, allowing alternative perspectives to come to the fore.

For us as scholars, these inquiry and research experiences create a space to document and bring to light a variety of contemporary researches in early childhood, especially those taking on alternative viewpoints to traditional research in the field. As editors, finding other research-disrupters, we have invited early childhood scholars to contribute research that identifies strongly as fringe qualitative researches enacted in contemporary and global early childhood settings; we want to offer a way to consider research beyond the reductionist frames so prevalent in early childhood currently.

The perspectives offered in this volume attempt to illumine some of these multifaceted issues of revealing ideas and experiences from the field through story, narration, and sharing voices—unmasking the complex nature of connecting with the human story rather than with numbers, facts, and figures. We recognize that this unmasking and revealing can only be achieved with new approaches and ways of considering the generation and proliferation of data that requires alternative readings of the lives of young children, their families, and the communities in which they live, move, and have being.

In coming to know children, families, and our related early childhood classroom practices through alternative research methodologies, new perspectives emerge and contribute to making meanings about classroom learning that attach to the heart and the head simultaneously. This becomes an alchemist's point of view. Our intent is to offer illustrations of alternative qualitative research practices that disrupt the expected research paradigms in order to create spaces for new conversations about early childhood education.

This edited collection describes research practices that represent alternative means of conducting research projects, asking enduring questions, making initial attempts at new meanings with existing findings, gathering and interpreting data, as well as discussing and sharing understandings and initiating new lines of inquiry. Each chapter depicts a research project conducted in an early childhood setting and includes either a description of the researchers' entire process or focus on one particular aspect that highlights their way. Critical descriptions of projects take on many different frames including, but not limited to, narratives, modes of inquiry, photography study of the visual field, pedagogical documentation, (re)positioning protagonists, children's ethnography, playworld research, and many researchers in action. This text is open to the creativity of the contributing authors. All chapters come together to provide an overarching discussion about what can be possible through imagination and disrupting early childhood education research. This first chapter leads the way by exploring the arch across the book and diving into a few details of each of the chapters across the three sections of the book.

In section 1, we intentionally provoke an ever-widening eye toward *new theoretical and methodological imaginings*. Chapters 2–5 engage the bleeding edges of marginalized and extreme qualitative researches. Giamminuti shares experiences from Reggio Emilia's Arcobaleno infant-toddler center and Scuola Pablo Neruda in chapter 2. Engaging pedagogical documentation and constructing together meaning in the lives of those inhabiting school, she illumines "an ethic of welcome and relationships" where research is enacted and lived from hospitality. Projecting forward and reflecting back supports the living documents as "instruments for collegiality" among educators, children, and parents in school. Giamminuti locates the value in education and research as "a public good." Her chapter gives rise to the notion that making visible the *now* lives of children (the culture of childhood) is a way to improve the *now* lives of adults (the culture of adulthood).

In chapter 3, Farquhar and Tesar theorize what it means to be pedagogical in (the) early years (of) teaching in Aotearoa. Their work engages philosophically through narrative to develop "an organic and unpredictable mode of inquiry." Thus, their methodological substances develop from those involved in their project. Farquhar and Tesar look more deeply into the complexities of their unique place by briefly outlining and playing with the "curriculum strands" of *Te Whāriki*. They find a provisional attitude toward research attempting to deconstruct and reconstruct anew as an emerging paradigm of post-approaches. Further, they contribute to alternative conceptualizations dehomogenizing colonial paradigms and staying open to participant contributions.

Johnson's chapter 4 critiques colonialism in teacher education through visual culture analyses. Declaring particular personal and professional concerns (and those we—Iorio and Parnell—share closely), Johnson traverses the halls of his own teacher education program as well as spaces where educators and children find themselves. Through his revelations of looking in on the photographs, images, and words (values and ideals), he brings to light a certain dominant visual field.

He uncovers what is in plain sight for most, a rubric-laden "imperialism of traditional discourses in early childhood education." He reasons that our subjectivity is co-defined by the culture surrounding us and that we are steeped in this educational cultural interpretation of standards, values, and highly politicized and monetized discourse. He shows us that this sameness is found in syllabi, on the walls, and in government documents and governing associations and guidelines. Beyond rereading these pervasive messages, Johnson suggests teacher education programs redefine and reimagine the system in its entirety before it turns to a stone relic through irrelevancy.

In chapter 5, Bray and Kenney thoroughly explore co-protagonism between parents-as-researchers in the lives of children and respective education researchers. Parents are placed in front of the researchers in this project and elevated to a level of respect not conceived of in most early childhood researches. Dismantling the traditional paradigm of colonial educational research *on* parents, Bray and Kenney develop enduring knowledge through inquiry by listening to and working from a place alongside parents of young children. Through this project, parents become analytical leaders who own the data they find, listen more thoughtfully for community needs, make data-driven decisions, and take action for community-based outcomes.

Section 2 centers on *democratizing the research process*. Chapters 6–8 demonstrate novel and alternative researches, approaches, and interpretations in the early childhood field. Henward's chapter 6 asks, "Is 'helping' hurting research?" Henward relocates herself as a co-player in the art of playing and the playful lives of children in pre-primary school. She attempts to lessen adult roles in research with children and more intentionally level the playing field by entering into the lifeworld of play, playing—in the play—with children.

In chapter 7, Fincham enters the world of toddler's words and bodies to (re) imagine narrative data. Letting go of the verbal developmental "push" opens a surprising lens to bodily performance. Fincham states that this is a "quite powerful, site of understanding and meaning making." Fincham displays episode examples that re-center the focus from texts and logos to words and bodies together, found in children's experiences. She explores their subjective meanings and finds that new unbounded and expanded strands of consideration—cross-hatching of ideas—appear as non-traditional resultants.

Axelrod's chapter 8 pushes to the edge new ideas in rethinking children's roles in ethnographic research. Axelrod's work with four-year-olds in a bilingual Head Start classroom explores how children negotiated between their languages and their emerging languages. Taking a strong stance of listening and writing observational records and field notes, Axelrod locates important stories of children's language learning: On day one, Javier wants his "j" returned to him from her journal. Then, a story emerges about the way Soraya explores writing notes as a researcher does. In addition, children want to read the research field notes as time goes by in Axelrod's 10-month study. Ethnography changes Axelrod in depth.

In section 3, authors lay out *critical issues in early childhood research from new perspectives*. Chapters 9–12 powerfully explore, examine, and break through barriers in the critical realm. In chapter 9, Ferholt, Nilsson, Jansson, and Alnervik journey into playworlds research in Sweden. Taking a participant stance, these re-searching-educators enact a reconceptualized study, asking teachers and children to study their own meaning-making about play, teaching, and learning. This research process moved the researchers to focus on the relationships between children and teachers disrupting the "doing" of research as the usual concern of researchers. The shift in perspective positions the work to contribute to theory and practice as well as the critical connection between practice, theory, and research.

In Chapter 10, Dockett and Perry reimagine children's strengths as they start school. Defining transitions to school in the early years, they research children's strengths as children begin school. Dockett and Perry ask children to respond directly to their own perspectives of starting school. The research unfolds to demonstrate children's conceptions about starting school in narration and drawing. Some children share their ideas, such as that there will be "lots of children at big school" and "You go to school to learn stuff. At school. It's a beautiful day." They conclude by reminding us that children start school with a wide array of "skills, knowledge, and understanding."

Sánchez-Blanco's chapter 11 steers us directly into an action research where she and a classroom teacher in Galicia Spain study children's perceptions of news articles and clippings. This chapter carries a poignant argument about consumerism, capitalism, and the need for strong educators' activism undertakings in classroom settings. Sharing personal accounts from the families struggling to fulfill the capitalist dream while being in poverty, Sánchez-Blanco takes us through twists and turns, the ethical dilemmas of the teacher and families—all the while reminding us how children are affected. This chapter pushes us to reconsider social capital and human rights and responsibilities in early childhood education settings and teaching and learning.

In our closing chapter 12, *One Test Is Not Enough*, we follow second grade children into their bilingual classroom as the author and teacher, Osorio, shares her own experience as teacher and researcher hoping to disrupt traditional perspectives on what knowledge is valued within school and the classroom experience. "Meaningful and detailed conversations" around text highlight children's lived experiences and knowledge of the world and are the crux of this research. Osorio illustrates how locating the curriculum of a classroom within the stories of children and their native languages can be a rich source of knowledge and a foundation for inspiring strong readers.

Every chapter in our text offers another way to imagine and reimagine research in early childhood education. Considering new theoretical and methodological imaginings of research, the implications of democratizing the research process, and viewing critical issues in early childhood from new perspectives contribute to how research can be rethought outside reductionist approaches and detail the richness of young children, teachers, and researchers. Reading research in these manners opens up possibilities of what could be imagined in research methodologies and reveals stories, discoveries, and understandings within the field of early childhood education and beyond.

References

Chetty, R., Friedman, J., & Rockoff, J. (2012). The long term impacts of teachers: Teacher value-added and student outcomes in adulthood. Retrieved from http://obs.rc.fas.har vard.edu/chetty/value_added.html

Iorio, J.M. (2008). Conversation as a work of art: Will it hang in a museum? *Contemporary Issues in Early Childhood, 7*(3), 297–305.

Iorio, J.M., & Adler, S.M. (2013). Take a number, stand in line, better yet, be a number get tracked: The assault of longitudinal data systems on teaching and learning. *Teachers College Record*, March 8, 2013. Retrieved from http://www.tcrecord.org, ID number: 17051.

Iorio, J.M., & Visweswaraiah, H. (2012). Crossing boundaries: A variety of perspectives on preschool stories. *Indo-Pacific Journal of Phenomenology, 12* (Special Edition), 1–13.

Kumashiro, K. (2012). *Bad teacher! How blaming teachers distorts the bigger picture (Teaching for Social Justice)*. New York: Teacher's College Press.

Leavy, P. (2009). *Method meets art*. New York: Guilford Press.

Parnell, W. (2011a). Experiences of teacher reflection in the studio: Reggio inspired practices. *Journal of Early Childhood Research, 10*(2), 117–133, doi: 10.1177/1476718X11407982.

Parnell, W. (2011b). Revealing the experience of children and teachers even in their absence: Documenting in the early childhood studio. *Journal of Early Childhood Research, 9*(3), 291–309, doi: 10.1177/1476718X10397903.

Parnell, W. (2011c, Nov.). Teacher collaboration experiences: Finding the extraordinary in the everyday moment. *Early Childhood Research and Practice, 13*(2).

Parnell, W. (2012, July). Investigating the Reggio Emilia study tour experience: From conversation to insights. *Networks: An Online Journal for Teacher Research, 14*(1), 1–18.

New Theoretical and Methodological Imaginings

2

RESEARCH AS AN ETHIC OF WELCOME AND RELATIONSHIP

Pedagogical Documentation in Reggio Emilia, Italy

Stefania Giamminuti

Introduction

Indeed, education without research or innovation is education without interest.
(Malaguzzi, in Gandini, 2012, p. 49)

This chapter charts my personal experience in Reggio Emilia as a bilingual and multicultural teacher/researcher and traces the narrative of being welcomed and the discovery of a shared research identity with participants—a turning point in the development of research relationships. The research framework for the study is explored from the perspective of the possibility it offered to mirror the ways of doing research that belonged to the shared culture of the research context. The chapter thus looks at the significance of adopting tools for research that are coherent and consistent with—and familiar to—the culture of the place the researcher encounters. It also highlights the significance of documentation in creating a culture of research (Rinaldi, 2006) that is welcoming and hospitable to "strangers" (Dahlberg, Moss, & Pence, 2007; Levinas, 1998).

The chapter aims to honor pedagogical documentation as a 'legitimate' research tool—a place and space for disrupting normalized discourses (Dahlberg & Moss, 2005; Dahlberg et al., 2007) and a tool for rethinking research as "a call to a more human dimension, one that is more open to investigating the sense and meaning of things, of events, of connections and relationships, especially interhuman ones" (Malaguzzi, cited in Reggio Children, n.d.). The intent is to contribute to the discourses surrounding professionalism of early childhood educators (Balduzzi & Manini, 2013; Moss, 2010; Urban, Vandenbroeck, Van Laere, Lazzari, & Peeters, 2012) by legitimizing their research identities in ways that are not imposed from existing frameworks of power; the aspect of 'dwelling together' as researchers is explored—creating a space for new conversations around what constitutes research and who owns research. Research is theorized as a place of "hospitality" (Dahlberg et al., 2007), an ethic of welcome and relationship.

Background and Context

I begin here by briefly tracing the history of the educational project of Reggio Emilia and its commitment to activating research through documentation of young children's learning. I then situate these historical reflections within the current debate on professionalism of early childhood teachers, creating a connection between the philosophical stance of Loris Malaguzzi and the provocations of contemporary theorists and researchers who invite educators to become collegial activists and inventors—researchers.

The Reggio Emilia Educational Project

In spring of 1945 in a village called Villa Cella, a few miles from the town of Reggio Emilia, the people sell an abandoned German war tank and a few of the retreating soldiers' trucks and horses, and with this money they decide to build and run a school for young children (Malaguzzi, 1998a); through this extraordinary beginning the ground was laid for a unique educational project. In 1963, the first municipal school of Reggio Emilia, the Robinson school, came to life, and for the first time in Italy the citizens affirmed a right to establish a secular school for young children (Malaguzzi, 1998a). As Malaguzzi acknowledges, those who played the greatest role of all in constructing the new experience were the children: "A simple, liberating thought came to our aid, namely that things about children and for children are only learned from children" (Malaguzzi, 1998a, p. 51). Their approach was undeniably a challenge to prevalent ideas on education; it was a courageous, progressive provocation influenced by the thought and practice of many international thinkers, leading the educators to gain "a sense of the versatility of theory and research" (Malaguzzi, 1998a, p. 60) and further to successfully engage in their own ongoing research in practice. Malaguzzi attributes the enduring nature of the educational project to the shared aspirations of parents and educators, which he called "collective wisdom" (1998a, p. 58). This collective wisdom is a fundamental strategy for activating research:

> Our goal is to build an amiable school, where children teachers and families feel at home . . . It must embody ways of getting along together, of intensifying relationships among the three central protagonists, of assuring fullness of attention to the problems of educating, and of activating participation and research.
>
> *(Malaguzzi, in Gandini, 2012, p. 43)*

In an amiable school research is a place of welcome and relationship, a stance for being together; during the time I spent in Reggio Emilia, I belonged to amiable schools, and I was welcomed. The invitation begins by conceiving of school as a place that speaks and then helping it to speak.

Pedagogical Documentation: The School's Voice

> One thing is a school that speaks; another a school that is silent.
> If it is a school that speaks we have to consider and help it to speak.
> *(Malaguzzi, 1992, cited in Gandini, 1998, pp. 175–176)*

Documentation makes individual and group learning visible (Giudici, Rinaldi, & Krechevsky, 2001); it allows all participants in the school community and beyond to listen for, observe, interpret, and reflect upon the processes of learning. Documentation is a pedagogical tool, but also a social and cultural tool; it is viewed in Reggio Emilia as a "democratic possibility to inform the public of the contents of the schools" (Vecchi, 1998, p. 141), as a way of communicating with parents (Malaguzzi, 1998a), as a way to "construct the meaning of school" (Rinaldi, 2001, p. 79), and, furthermore, as an instrument for collegiality among teachers.

Pedagogical documentation encompasses process and visible products. Documentation as a process features: the careful observation and interpretation of teaching and learning processes; an attitude of listening; a democratic way of being with children; a way of making meaning and encountering each other through dialogue. Documentation as a visible product can take the form of notes, wall displays, journals, publications, presentations, exhibitions, and video recordings, which are shared in order to promote democratic dialogue on pedagogical, social, and cultural issues. Documentation is "a way of living and reliving learning experiences and making meaning of life" (Parnell, Cullen, & Downs, 2016), it is "a relationship" (Rinaldi, 2005). Documentation is not an isolated and objective act, rather it occurs in the context of relationships between human beings, and therefore it is an act of ethics and values (Giamminuti, 2013).

Professionalism?

> It is a great effort, a brave act of honesty towards herself, an exhausting autonomous desecration of things in which until now she has in good faith believed in, that which we ask of the teacher so that together with children and then with young people and families and citizens she may participate in the construction of school as a lively center of open and democratic culture, that she may be enriched and nurtured by those roles and those social exchanges that will not only allow her to overcome her false and equivocal autonomy and her historic detachment but will enable her to finally be free of ideological leanings and authoritative indoctrination.
> *(Malaguzzi, 1971, p. 149, my translation)*

Malaguzzi's vision for teachers, his invitation to brave acts of honesty in the early years of the educational project, was hopeful and radical, and echoes may be found in more recent theorizations of professionalism of early childhood teachers. For example, both Balduzzi's (2013) call to a "collegial dimension" as an "inalienable quality of teacher professionalism" (p. 111) and Lazzari's (2012b) reinterpretation of Fielding's *radical collegiality* echo Malaguzzi's invitation to overcome "false and equivocal autonomy." Furthermore, Panciroli's (2013, p. 190) view of "competent interpersonal relationship" as fundamental for professionalism carries forth Malaguzzi's vision of honoring children, families, and citizens as competent interlocutors in matters relating to education and care. The study on "competence requirements in early childhood education and care" (CoRe; see Urban et al., 2012) offers insights into how "competent systems" offer "true possibility for a radical *democratic* and *epistemological* renewal of public education" (p. 253), echoing Malaguzzi's tireless call to democracy and renewal. Groundwater-Smith and Mockler's (2006; 2007) "ethical guidelines for practitioner research" are a further invitation to abandon ideological leanings and authoritative indoctrination in favor of ethical processes, transparency, collaboration, transformation, and participation in communities of practice. Fenech, Sumsion, and Shepherd's (2010) exhortation to reimagine early childhood educators as "activist professionals" engaged in "resistance-based professionalism" furthers Malaguzzi's invitation to teachers to overcome "historic detachment" through an "exhausting autonomous desecration of things in which until now [they have] in good faith believed in" (1971, p. 149).

Finally, Moss's (2010) image of the educator as needing "a certain attitude of mind that desires to research and experiment" (p. 16) and his invitation to embrace a "pedagogy of invention" (p. 16) align with Malaguzzi's radical hopes for teachers. However, mindful that Moss himself struggled with the theme of professionalism and was "left wondering what we gain by the focus on professionalism" (2010, p. 17), I acknowledge with him that "the worker as researcher may choose not to take 'professional' as an identity and not to participate in the discourse of professionalism" because "the bordered and exclusionary condition of professionalism is at odds with the values and desires of the worker as researcher: border crossing, uncertainty, subjectivity, and inclusionary democratic practice" (Moss, 2006, p. 38). In fact, a research identity may reveal itself to be the key to freedom from the boundaries and exclusions of all professions—teacher, architect, engineer, and so forth. Research thus becomes a connecting element rather than an instrument of separation: research as "the pattern which connects" (Bateson, 1979, p. 7). This leaves professionalism as a question rather than an answer, a construct to be engaged with and debated as part of a research identity, but in the spirit of "honesty towards oneself" that Malaguzzi so forcefully advocated. My experience in Reggio Emilia is a narrative of border-crossing, primarily for myself as a teacher, learner, and researcher. So I narrate my experiences and recall who I was at that time of belonging . . .

Research Identities: Many Outfits

One fresh morning in April I was walking the familiar route from my apartment in suburban Reggio Emilia to Scuola Pablo Neruda. I had arrived in Reggio Emilia during a snowy January, a 'familiar stranger'—an Italian from Rome living in Australia and returning to Italy to encounter this world-renowned educational project. I had spent one month in Arcobaleno infant-toddler center and was due to remain at Neruda until June. My research question had to do with how pedagogical documentation enables the construction of communities of learners. What I had failed to do until then was to see myself as part of that community of learners. An outsider, perhaps, but carefully and empathetically—albeit until that point unconsciously—adopting for my research the ways of researching that were familiar to the everyday lives of the children and educators I spent my time among. What I had failed to see was that I had been welcomed into a hospitable place by hospitable people to share an identity and construct a relationship—not simply to investigate questions.

That morning, as I tried to find a breakthrough, I thought back to my early months in Reggio Emilia and I revisited the ongoing struggle to own my identity as a novice researcher. I was expected to be a researcher when I first arrived: an outsider coming to observe and investigate. I was unable to claim that sole identity. Having only recently left my role as a classroom teacher in Rome to move to Australia and work full-time on a doctorate of philosophy, I came to Reggio Emilia as a teacher, and my extended presence in the place generated the relationships expected of a teacher—the children crawling to me, learning to walk, drawing me into dramatic play, the stories to be read, the lunch to be shared, the sleep to be enticed. Who am I? A researcher? A teacher? A learner? I was in fact a participant in a culture—though I still failed to see it—and most emphatically a participant in a culture where it was impossible to claim a 'sole' identity or, in the words of Balduzzi (2013), only one outfit:

> Only one traceable culture could not exist . . . in infant-toddler centers or schools of childhood, only one outfit with which to dress the role of the educator or teacher, but instead multiple cultures in relation to how a specific institution has learnt to respond to the problems arising from everyday practice.
>
> *(p. 105; my translation)*

Looking back several years later, I can picture myself as I stopped in my tracks that April morning and wrote in my notebook: *It is through the metaphor of teacher as researcher that communities of learners are constructed.* And so began my deeper encounter with the people who had invited me among them to learn: my ability to "understand their understanding" (Uhrmacher, 1991, pp. 29–30) was enhanced, but most of all I became at peace with my own identity. In a place where all children and adults are teachers, learners, and researchers, I could claim all those identities too; I could have many outfits and belong to many cultures. And so emerged my awareness of how strongly my methods for generating data had grown to mirror those of the people whom I had spent my life among for some months.

Upon my return to Australia to complete the doctorate and commence an academic career, my encounter with Reggio Emilia informed my own struggle with the conceptualization of 'research' as something with defined boundaries and protocols, something 'owned' as a profession rather than constructed in encounters. I could argue with Moss (2010) that the bordered and exclusionary conditions of being a professional researcher do not sit well with my desire—nurtured through my encounter with Reggio—for border-crossing, uncertainty, subjectivity, and inclusionary democratic practice; indeed, you can embrace a pedagogy of invention as a researcher, distancing yourself from the bordered and exclusionary culture of a professionalism of research, caught as it is in "quality standards that are neither enabling nor appropriate" (Groundwater-Smith & Mockler, 2006, p. 105). Professionalism as a question extends from the teacher in school to the researcher in academia. The story in this chapter is that of my own becoming a 'professional?' researcher: a story of blurring boundaries and dwelling together in research, legitimizing each other and disrupting truths to reimagine research as an ethic of welcome and relationship. As Giudici suggests in an interview with Cavallini (2011, p. 196), I experienced "boundary-crossing":

> This approach, this boundary-crossing, which does not separate subjects or languages, does not separate those doing the daily action of teaching from those doing the pedagogical research, recurs as innovation and resource in [our] research projects.

As one researcher among many, I did not feel or experience separateness; rather, I was invited into relatedness.

The Research Framework: Relatedness

I spent six months observing and living in Reggio Emilia, and during this time I interviewed children, parents, teachers, atelieriste (educators with a background in the visual or expressive arts, in charge of the atelier), pedagogiste (pedagogical coordinators), and the psychologist Ivana Soncini. I experienced—or "appreciated" (Eisner, 1991)—the breadth of daily life in Reggio Emilia: from early mornings welcoming the children to late night meetings with families; from the many visits of international network groups to large international conferences; from celebrations in infant-toddler centers and schools to events and exhibitions in the city. This wide choice of contexts to observe reflects the connection of all things in Reggio Emilia and the strong links between the educational project and the city. Given that my focus was documentation, this breadth of experiences also highlights the notion that pedagogical documentation is a way of being with children, rather than something that is 'done' at segmented times and with prescribed tools. You do not 'do' documentation; instead, it becomes something you are: Educators approach their relationships with children, each day and during every moment of the day, with an eye that observes, senses that listen, and a mind that records.

Karen Martin, an Australian Aboriginal researcher and teacher, developed *Ways of Knowing, Being, and Doing* as a theoretical framework and methods for indigenous and indigenist research that conceptualizes research as ceremony and encompasses relatedness as an "ontological premise" (Martin, 2003; 2008). I take inspiration from Martin's framework; within this research I too move between identities, not an Outsider or Other, but Another (Martin, 2008). Italian and Australian, an educator, learner, and researcher—I moved within spaces and places as 'Another' with relatedness as my premise. I will explain this with the story of my arrival in Reggio Emilia:

> On my first morning, I met Marina Castagnetti at the Centre for Documentation and Educational Research. Marina called Nido Arcobaleno to inform them that I had arrived. She spoke with Francesca, teacher of the 'Grandi,' then passed me the handset. I spoke with Francesca and perceived some hesitation on the other side of the line. Some months later Francesca and I remembered this moment. She told me that after she had hung up the phone she turned to the other teachers in the room and said, with great surprise: "That was the Australian intern—she speaks Italian with a Roman accent!" Indeed, the teachers were expecting an Australian—my perfect Italian, which revealed my Roman heritage, was a surprise. The Outsider, the Other, revealed herself in fact to be Another.

Relatedness—"a particular manner of connectedness" (Martin, 2008, p. 69)—is the ontological premise of Martin's framework; it is also at the core of the Reggio Emilia pedagogy of relationships and listening (Rinaldi, 2006). Relatedness with people (adults and children) and place (school and city) was at the forefront of my experience and became an ontological premise for my study. As Martin (2003) argues, a framework of relatedness "requires fieldwork that immerses the researcher in the contexts of the Entities and to watch, listen, wait, learn, and repeat those methods for data collection" (p. 213); this perspective honors the role of participants as informed researchers, best placed to contribute to the stock of knowledge about themselves, and positions researchers as learners whose primary role is to dwell, listen, and relate. Repeating the methods for data collection was a necessary and inevitable step for me: As I researched pedagogical documentation I dwelt in pedagogical documentation and became a documenter alongside the children and adults who welcomed me—their tools became my tools and their glance informed my glance, our ways were mirrored. I learned the ways in which the teachers documented, and I welcomed multiple tools, as advocated by Rinaldi (1982) in early work on observation: "It is through the use of multiple tools (audio-recordings, notes, video-recordings, etc.) that we obtain the most complete and effective documentations" (p. 93; my translation). In fact, in Reggio Emilia children are viewed as possessing "a hundred languages" (Cavallini, Filippini, Vecchi, & Trancossi, 2011; Edwards, Gandini, & Forman, 1998; 2012; Malaguzzi, 1998b), which require "a hundred ways of listening" and narrating:

> We have always believed that beauty, joy, humor, and poetry are an integral and important part of knowledge-building, and thus that learning should be experienced in daily life through multiple languages (verbal, written, musical, visual, dance, and so on) and it can and should be narrated by means of many languages.
>
> *(Vecchi, 2001, p. 160)*

The alignment between social semiotics (Hodge & Kress, 1988; Van Leeuwen, 2005), poststructuralist semiotics (Chandler, 2002)—my key frameworks for data analysis—and the theory of the hundred languages allowed me to dwell fully in these rich contexts, and I became a user of a language of joy, poetry, and humor alongside the children and adults who welcomed me; relatedness is enabled by a shared language, and a shared language grows through relatedness (Giamminuti, 2013). Vecchi (2006) further states that "it is not possible to understand the philosophy and practice of the schools in Reggio without an understanding of the contribution of the dimension of aesthetics"; it was not possible in fact for me to mirror ways of knowing, being, and doing without embracing the dimension of aesthetics, for I was welcomed into an aesthetic community, where beauty is a value (Giamminuti, 2013). My experience in Reggio Emilia was thus informed by an "artistic approach to research," framed as "educational connoisseurship and criticism" (Eisner 1991). Connoisseurship is "the art of appreciation" (Eisner, 1991); to make "vicarious participation" (Eisner, 1991) possible is one of the aims of educational connoisseurship—an aesthetic aim. Similarly, Carla Rinaldi (2006) refers to the research that occurs in the schools of Reggio Emilia in daily life as "art," and she puts forth an invitation to create a "culture of research":

> A new concept of research, more contemporary and alive, can emerge if we legitimate the use of this term to describe the cognitive tension that is created whenever authentic learning and knowledge-building processes take place. "Research" used to describe the individual and common paths leading in the direction of a new universe of possibility . . . Research as art: research exists, as in art, within the search for the being, the essence, the meaning . . . We need to create a culture of research . . . The word research, in this sense, leaves—or rather demands to come out of—the scientific laboratories, thus ceasing to be a privilege of the few (in universities and other

designated places) to become the stance, the attitude with which teachers approach the sense and meaning of life.

(pp. 101, 148)

The Teachers: A Lively Culture of Research

Toward the end of my time in Reggio Emilia, and following the epiphany of my April morning walk, the image of the teacher as researcher increasingly became a focus of my observations and interviews. I scheduled an interview with three teachers from Arcobaleno infant-toddler center: Giuliana, who had been at Arcobaleno since it opened 30 years earlier; Silvia, who had been there for a few years; and Marica, who was in her first year of teaching. I asked the question of what it means to be a teacher as researcher and whether they could see themselves in this image. The ensuing dialogue between the educators at different levels of experience shows that, even in Reggio Emilia where a lively culture of research is nurtured, the separation from the academy and the ivory towers of research is a risk:

> Personally I don't see myself as a researcher . . . I think it's a term that is a bit removed from the world of children, too technical and rigid in relation to daily life in the infant-toddler center . . . I think rather of an adult that is personally and deeply involved in the discoveries and research of the children . . . an adult that researches together with children, who challenges herself in daily life together with children. I personally don't feel that I can use the term 'researcher' . . . the adult and the child research together every day. I refer therefore to that empathetic listening, to sharing and being available to welcome the needs and requests without positioning yourself as an expert—I associate the term 'researcher' to a detached expert, perhaps incorrectly. Instead, we create a context in which it is possible to dialogue and research together.
>
> *(Silvia, interview with Stefania Giamminuti, 2006)*

Silvia struggles with owning the identity of researcher because she feels close to the children; in the early years of her professional career, she sees the ivory towers as a threat to her relationship with children. Given our often misguided focus on a particular kind of research, and the question of the "research that counts" (Groundwater-Smith & Mockler, 2006), perhaps her attitude of caution is wise. With this premise, it is also very clear to Silvia that research is something that occurs in a relationship; her research with children, though she will not own the term 'researcher,' occurs within an ethic of welcome and relationship. Her hesitancy in owning the term 'researcher' and making it part of her identity has to do with an image of the lonely expert in the ivory tower. Silvia does not want to be lonely; rather she recognizes the value of what in Reggio Emilia is defined as "co-participated research":

Co-participated research between children and adults is a priority of daily life, an existential and ethical attitude that is necessary to interpret the complexity of the world, of phenomena, of systems of shared living; it is a potent instrument of renewal in education.

(Scuole e Nidi D'Infanzia Istituzione del Comune di Reggio Emilia, 2009, pp. 11–12; my translation)

Giuliana instead feels far more comfortable with the term, her confidence reflecting her more than 30 years within the educational project:

I am really comfortable with the term 'researcher,' because it gives me the sense of abandoning stereotypes, therefore an image of researching and a research that is never actually completed, where you always have to open your ideas up for debate . . . researching constantly and continuously does not mean that you don't have competencies or experiences, but rather it means putting those competencies and experiences on the line in order to go and search for that which you do not know . . . it helps to have an interpretative glance on what [children] are understanding, what they are trying to elaborate, throughout the day, in all contexts. For example I had a child who was very strong in mathematics and once at lunch she takes a fork and tries to balance it on the chair. If you had expected to see that event in another situation it would have been a notable thing—observing it then and there you can connect it to the research that child is engaged in, and so that gesture is no longer banal and your response isn't "turn around, put your fork in its place, sit nicely it's time for lunch now."

(Giuliana, interview with Stefania Giamminuti, 2006)

Giuliana's experience highlights the lively exchange between research and practice and the energy this gives to her daily work. Having worked closely with Carla Rinaldi as her pedagogista for many years, she does not see research as the privilege of the few, but rather as a stance and attitude—leading to new universes of possibility for children and to a lively culture of research for all.

The Children: "Stimulating Solidarity"

Documentation . . . we stick the work on the walls and then we have to look at it otherwise we stick it up and why do we have it if we don't do anything with it.

(Lucia, 5.9 years old, Scuola Pablo Neruda)

The issue of dissemination, or "transparency of process" (Groundwater-Smith & Mockler, 2006) in research, is nicely captured by Lucia's words; pedagogical documentation, situated within its democratic history and ethical responsibility toward open debate, dialogue, and experimentation, demands to earn the right to be viewed as research. I asked the children of Scuola Neruda why their teachers write notes and take photos all the time. Their most common reply was: "as a memory." They were quite convinced that they said "interesting things" and that their teachers would want to keep a memory "forever" of those "interesting things." After years in the municipal infant-toddler centers and schools, these children recognize that their voice has value and that they have a right to be heard. To further understand their theories, Antonia—their teacher—and I asked the children: "What is memory for?" Federico (six years old) wonderfully replied, "To tell a story"—or rather, as conveyed in the Organisation for Economic Co-operation and Development's (OECD) definition of research, "To increase the stock of knowledge" (Groundwater-Smith & Mockler, 2006).

In Neruda, where the walls are graced with beautiful panels that tell stories of experiences long in the past, I decided to ask the children why these panels are still there:

Stefania: "Other children made these things [the clay seats represented in the panel]. Why are they here if they were made by other children?"
Rebecca: "As a memory."
Stefania: "And how can you use this memory of the other children?"
Rebecca: "To see how other children built these things [the seats made in clay] that they can't show us now."
Stefania: "How is it helpful for you to see things other children have made?"
Rebecca: "To build something . . . something different of course, with the help of these things."

Rebecca (six years old) acknowledges that the panels show you not just *what* children make but *how* they make it; whilst they can't show you the real chairs now because they might have taken them home, you can have a memory of how they did it so that if you want to you can build something like it with the help of the narrative of how they did it. Thus memory can be transformed to create possibilities for the present; in fact, the children said to me about another panel, "it gave me the idea." The children suggest we can harness ideas to build something different—this is the essence of research. In the words of the OECD, in fact, a purpose of research is to "use of the stock of knowledge to devise new applications" (Groundwater-Smith & Mockler, 2006). These are all examples of a context of "stimulating solidarity":

> The child 'feels' this new life condition: it is through the work 'together' with adults—teachers, auxiliary staff, parents and other men and women of the neighborhood—that he [sic] gathers the first concrete models for *living together*; it is by perceiving how his own interests and those of his family and his environment become topics of attention and care for adults that he experiences the **stimulating solidarity** that surrounds him . . . it is through these events and through the teacher's behavior that he experiences

a very important feeling: *that he counts not only for the present but also for the future and that his becoming is a topic of great interest and preoccupation for adults.*
(Malaguzzi, 1971, pp. 149–150;
my translation—bold and italics in the original)

The Families: Expanding the Boundaries of Adult Imaginations

At the time of my experience in Reggio Emilia, the educators in Arcobaleno were documenting the children's growing interest in narrative, particularly their desire to tell stories about their drawings. The 'Narration Group'—a research group investigating narrative that meets a few evenings a year and includes parents of children frequenting the center, educators, and at times even parents whose children have left the center but wish to continue learning—chose to research children's narratives by sharing the documentation. They decided to create a new 'story' based on the children's drawings. Their story, entitled "The Last Paratrooper to Land," was presented to children, educators, and families at the end of year celebration, which I was privileged to attend:

> It's a warm evening in June in Reggio Emilia; it's still bright at 8 pm as the party begins and families arrive in the nido's park. Suddenly we are all called into the building. We all noisily gather in the piazza, children of all ages sitting together at the front, adults standing at the back. The chorus is introduced—a group of educators and parents who have been rehearsing for months. A 'real' conductor stands in front of them and as he waves his arms, the chorus begins to sing. The children's eyes grow wide as the sound of singing fills the silent piazza. A child lifts his arms and sways them gently, following the movements of the conductor. Other children move slowly as if they were dancing in their seats. Others sit very still, eyes wide with wonder . . .
>
> As the singing ends, we exit into the now dark and silent park. In the darkness, we notice a large luminous screen and hiding behind the screen a small group of educators and parents sit expectantly, with sound equipment and a guitar. The air of excitement rises as children, families, educators, and friends take place in the many seats facing the screen. We are welcomed to the show: "L'ultimo Paracadutista Atterrato" ["The Last Paratrooper to Land"]. A strong voice resounds from the darkness: "This is the story of the fantastic journey that a little boy named Martino took aboard a special airplane . . . Children, come aboard and be passengers on this airplane with Martino . . . Are you ready to fly? What a terrible sound . . . what a noise! The engine is warming up!"
>
> Young children's drawings appear on the screen: faces, objects and signs with identities and stories. These are the drawings that the educators have collected throughout the year, along with the children's words about their drawings.

The voice continues from behind the screen: "Tower control here, we are about to announce departure. The airplane is about to take off, the sky is blue, the sun is shining . . . But there are some clouds here and there . . . Three two one blast off!"

And so Martino flies across starry skies on an adventure that will bring him to encounter planets of dancing dinosaurs, elephants making bubbles, a snoring shell planet, a guitar planet, and the airplane planet, inhabited by many paratroopers . . . Until The Last Paratrooper to Land comes up to him in great haste and wakes him up, it's time to go to school! It was all a wonderful dream . . .

(Giamminuti, 2013)

The children lived the experience of seeing their drawings and characters as onscreen protagonists of a wonderful story, in front of a large audience, during an important celebration. "The Last Paratrooper to Land" is not the first of such stories. "The Story of Scapiglino, Messy-haired Child" was created and performed in Arcobaleno in 2003 and became a book. At the end of the book, the educators and parents give a background to their experience of creating the story, discussing how the nature of their research is always connected to the children's daily life, and adding, "The observations we shared during the research process allowed us, as adults, to interpret the signs, traces, and drawings of children with greater sensibility" (Nido Arcobaleno, 2003). It is significant to note that they use the term 'research' to describe their experience together and furthermore that they recognize the 'shared' nature of their research and the opportunities it has created for them to encounter each other and the children. In fact, most importantly, they write:

> We believe this experience has *enriched and expanded the boundaries of our adult imagination*: we interpreted and gave value to the children's work, but above all *we gave it back to them* through the use of dramatic and narrative modes.
>
> *(Nido Arcobaleno, 2003, my italics)*

Sensitive observation and documentation of ordinary, rich events such as telling stories about drawings allowed teachers and parents to expand the boundaries of their imaginations and give a gift to their children. 'Giving back' is inherent to stories and narratives; it is inherent to documentation, which for its nature strives toward visibility, share-ability, and democracy. It is also essential to research. This 'giving back' is experienced by parents as a gift that brings them closer to their children: Paola, a parent at Neruda, told me that she sees documentation as "that tool which supports you in reaching the children." 'Giving back' is an ethical and democratic process that respects the gifts that children offer us daily with their work and words and honors the rights of all participants in a learning community. Loris Malaguzzi developed a "charter of rights" (Reggio Children, 1996, pp. 212–213), and of the rights of parents he states:

> It is the right of parents to participate actively . . . in the growth, education, care and development of their children . . . When school and parents are able to converge toward a cooperative experience . . . then it is easy to see how hostile and mistaken is the pedagogy of self-sufficiency and prescription, and how friendly and fertile is the strategy of participation and shared research.

"The Last Paratrooper to Land" and Scapiglino are cooperative, interactive experiences and spaces for shared research—these spaces were created through documentation of children's learning processes.

An Amiable Research Community: An Ethic of Welcome and Relationship

Malaguzzi's vision for an amiable school has indeed made possible the creation of an amiable research community, one that welcomes its members—children and adults—into a culture of invention far removed from the dominant voices, distancing itself from "education without interest" (Malaguzzi, in Gandini, 2012, p. 49). It requires those who wish to take part to accept a call to a more human dimension, to welcome an invitation to boundary-cross, and to participate in a brave act of honesty in order to finally be free of temples and false cultures:

> A *project* of this kind is founded on a new concept of education, free of preconceptions. [An education] which, relieved of its temples, its destinations and selections, its organic fragmentations and false cultures, is able to re-formulate and re-invent itself in a dynamic of open time and open space where the process of learning and educating—which goes from birth to death of an individual—belongs to everyone and anyone, thus overcoming that fixedness of roles and that separation and classification of institutions and individual destinies which represent the moment of most evident distortion and failure of the school and educational system.
>
> *(Malaguzzi, 1971, p. 140; my translation)*

Documentation as research is an ethic of welcome and relationship—a place of shared invention for children and adults—where education and research are valued as "the public good" (Groundwater-Smith & Mockler, 2006; Lazzari, 2012a) and where the debate about what is "good" continues lively and hopeful, rich in the voices of children and teachers.

Acknowledgments

This chapter narrates my story of becoming one among many. As such, it is those many researchers—adults and children—whom I thank for their generosity. I am grateful to the citizens of Reggio Emilia of all ages, and to its educational project, for their welcome and hospitality—for making me a part of their amiable research community, giving me the courage to nurture . . .

> a critical attitude towards those things that are given to our present experi-
> ence as if they were timeless, natural, unquestionable: to stand against the
> maxims of one's time, against the spirit of one's age, against the current of
> received wisdom. It is a matter of introducing a kind of awkwardness into
> the fabric of one's experience, of interrupting the fluency of the narratives
> that encode that experience and making them stutter.
>
> *(Rose, 1999, p. 20)*

References

Balduzzi, L. (2013). Lavoro di gruppo e accoglienza. Strategie per lo sviluppo nella profes-sionalita' in campo educativo. In L. Balduzzi & M. Manini (Eds.), *Professionalita' e servizi per l'infanzia* (97–132). Roma: Carocci.

Balduzzi, L., & Manini, M. (Eds.). (2013). *Professionalita' e servizi per l'infanzia*. Roma: Carocci.

Bateson, G. (1979). *Mind and nature: A necessary unity*. Cresskill, NJ: Hampton Press.

Cavallini, I. (2011). For schools of research: Interview with Paola Cagliari and with Claudia Giudici. In I. Cavallini, V. Vecchi, T. Filippini, & L. Trancossi (Eds.), *The wonder of learning: The hundred languages of children* (pp. 194–197). Reggio Emilia, Italy: Reggio Children.

Cavallini, I., Filippini, T., Vecchi, V., & Trancossi, L. (Eds.). (2011). *The wonder of learning: The hundred languages of children*. Reggio Emilia, Italy: Reggio Children.

Chandler, D. (2002). *Semiotics: The basics*. London: Routledge.

Dahlberg, G., & Moss, P. (2005). *Ethics and politics in early childhood education*. Abingdon, UK: RoutledgeFalmer.

Dahlberg, G., Moss, P., & Pence, A. (2007). *Beyond quality in early childhood education and care: Languages of evaluation* (2nd ed.). Abingdon, UK: Routledge.

Edwards, C., Gandini, L., & Forman, G. (Eds.). (1998). *The hundred languages of children: The Reggio Emilia approach—advanced reflections*. Westport, CT: Ablex.

Edwards, C., Gandini, L., & Forman, G. (Eds.). (2012). *The hundred languages of children: The Reggio Emilia experience in transformation*. Santa Barbara, CA: Praeger.

Eisner, E.W. (1991). *The enlightened eye: Qualitative enquiry and the enhancement of educational practice*. New York: Macmillan.

Fenech, M., Sumsion, J., & Shepherd, W. (2010). Promoting early childhood teacher profes-sionalism in the Australian context: The place of resistance. *Contemporary Issues in Early Childhood, 11*(1), 89–105.

Gandini, L. (1998). Educational and caring spaces. In C. Edwards, L. Gandini, & E. Forman (Eds.), *The hundred languages of children: The Reggio Emilia approach—advanced reflections*. Westport, CT: Ablex.

Gandini, L. (2012). History, ideas, and basic principles: An interview with Loris Malaguzzi. In C. Edwards, L. Gandini, & G. Forman (Eds.), *The hundred languages of children: The Reggio Emilia experience in transformation*. Santa Barbara, CA: Praeger.

Giamminuti, S. (2013). *Dancing with Reggio Emilia: Metaphors for quality*. Mt. Victoria, NSW, Australia: Pademelon Press.

Giudici, C., Rinaldi, C., & Krechevsky, M. (2001). *Making learning visible: Children as individual and group learners*. Reggio Emilia, Italy: Reggio Children.

Groundwater-Smith, S., & Mockler, N. (2006). Research that counts: Practitioner research and the academy. *Review of Australian Research in Education, 6*, 105–118.

Groundwater-Smith, S., & Mockler, N. (2007). Ethics in practitioner research: An issue of quality. *Research Papers in Education, 22*(2), 199–211.

Hodge, R., & Kress, G. (1988). *Social semiotics*. Cambridge: Polity Press.

Lazzari, A. (2012a). The public good. Historical and political roots of municipal preschools in Emilia Romagna. *European Journal of Education, 47*(4), 556–568.

Lazzari, A. (2012b). Reconceptualising professionalism in early childhood education: Insights from a study carried out in Bologna. *Early Years: An International Research Journal, 32*(3), 252–265.

Levinas, E. (1998). *Otherwise than being: Or beyond essence*. Pittsburgh, PA: Duquesne University Press.

Malaguzzi, L. (1971). *La nuova socialita' del bambini e dell'insegnante attraverso la esperienza della gestione sociale nelle scuole dell'infanzia*. Paper presented at the La gestione sociale nella scuola dell'infanzia, Modena.

Malaguzzi, L. (1998a). History, ideas, and basic philosophy: An interview with Lella Gandini. In C. Edwards, L. Gandini, & G. Forman (Eds.), *The hundred languages of children: The Reggio Emilia approach—advanced reflections*. Westport, CT: Ablex.

Malaguzzi, L. (1998b). No way. The hundred is there. In C. Edwards, L. Gandini, & G. Forman (Eds.), *The hundred languages of children: The Reggio Emilia approach—advanced reflections*. Westport, CT: Ablex Publishing.

Martin, K.L. (2003). Ways of knowing, being, and doing: A theoretical framework and methods for indigenous and indigenist research. *Journal of Australian Studies* (76), 203–214.

Martin, K.L. (2008). *Please knock before you enter: Aboriginal regulations of outsiders and the implications for researchers*. Teneriffe, QLD, Australia: Post Pressed.

Moss, P. (2006). Structures, understandings and discourses: Possibilities for re-envisioning the early childhood worker. *Contemporary Issues in Early Childhood, 7*(1), 30–40.

Moss, P. (2010). We cannot continue as we are: The educator in an education for survival. *Contemporary Issues in Early Childhood, 11*(1), 8–19.

Nido Arcobaleno. (2003). *The story of Scapiglino*. Reggio Emilia, Italy: Author.

Panciroli, C. (2013). La formazione nello sviluppo professionale delle insegnanti. In L. Balduzzi & M. Manini (Eds.), *Professionalita' e servizi per l'infanzia*. Roma: Carocci.

Parnell, W., Cullen, J., & Downs, C. (2016). Fostering intelligent moderation in the next generation: Insights from Remida-inspired reuse materials education. *New Educator*.

Reggio Children. (1996). *I cento linguaggi dei bambini: Narrative del possibile. [The hundred languages of children: Narratives of the possible]. New extended exhibit catalogue*. Reggio Emilia, Italy: Author.

Reggio Children. (n.d.). Reggio Children Centro Internazionale per la difesa e la promozione dei diritti e delle potenzialita' dei bambini e dele bambine. Retrieved from http://www.reggiochildren.it/?lang=en

Rinaldi, C. (1982). Per una corretta operativita' nell'osservazione. In L. Benigni, M.P., Casali, E. Catarsi, A.L. Galardini, R. Gay, L. Malaguzzi, S. Mantovani, M. Mattesini, R. Perani, & C. Rinaldi (Eds.), *Un nido educativo*. Milano: Gruppo editoriale Fabbri.

Rinaldi, C. (2001). Documentation and assessment: What is the relationship? In C. Giudici, C. Rinaldi, & M. Krechevsky (Eds.), *Making learning visible: Children as individual and group learners*. Reggio Emilia, Italy: Reggio Children.

Rinaldi, C. (2005, July). *Pedagogical documentation*. Paper presented at the Biennial Conference of the Reggio Emilia Australia Information Exchange, Landscapes of Listening, Melbourne, VIC, Australia.

Rinaldi, C. (2006). *In dialogue with Reggio Emilia: Listening, researching and learning*. Abingdon, UK: Routledge.

Rose, N. (1999). *Powers of freedom: Reframing political thought*. Cambridge: Cambridge University Press.

Scuole e Nidi D'Infanzia Istituzione del Comune di Reggio Emilia. (2009). *Regolamento Scuole e Nidi D'Infanzia del Comune di Reggio Emilia*. Reggio Emilia, Italy: Author.

Uhrmacher, P.B. (1991). *Waldorf schools marching quietly unheard* (Ph.D.), Stanford University. Retrieved from http://search.proquest.com.dbgw.lis.curtin.edu.au/docview/3039611 09?accountid=10382

Urban, M., Vandenbroeck, M., Van Laere, K., Lazzari, A., & Peeters, J. (2012). Toward competent systems in early childhood education and care. Implications of policy and practice. *European Journal of Education, 47*(4), 508–526.

Van Leeuwen, T. (2005). *Introducing social semiotics*. London: Routledge.

Vecchi, V. (1998). The role of the atelierista: An interview with Lella Gandini. In C. Edwards, L. Gandini, & E. Forman (Eds.), *The hundred languages of children: The Reggio Emilia approach—advanced reflections*. Westport, CT: Ablex.

Vecchi, V. (2001). The curiosity to understand. In C. Giudici, C. Rinaldi, & M. Krechevsky (Eds.), *Making learning visible: Children as individual and group learners*. Reggio Emilia, Italy: Reggio Children.

Vecchi, V. (2006, January). *Estetica e apprendimento [Aesthetics and learning]*. Paper presented at the Winter Institute, Reggio Emilia, Italy.

3

THEORIZING WHAT IT MEANS TO BE PEDAGOGICAL IN (THE) EARLY YEARS (OF) TEACHING

Sandy Farquhar and Marek Tesar

Problematizing a Research Project

A traditional way of writing up research is to outline the concerns and the literature, describe the methodology, and present and analyze the findings. In this chapter, however, we focus on the 'how' of a research project. We do this in the context of an emerging research practice with newly qualified early childhood teachers in Auckland in Aotearoa. (Aotearoa is the Māori name for New Zealand. Frequently, Aotearoa and New Zealand are used in conjunction. We use just the Māori name—Aotearoa—in this chapter.) Our research aim is to explore what it means to be pedagogical in diverse social and political early childhood contexts. In the project we will be asking newly qualified teachers to share their experiences with us and to engage in reflective and challenging thinking, to question and evaluate their own, and other more established, practices. In this evolving project, they will share their unique experiences of their workplace relationships and question their own pedagogies.

The focus of the chapter is to report on how we are working in a philosophical way through narrative to develop an organic and unpredictable mode of inquiry, in which the methodology and analysis emerge from the action/people/events involved in the project. Promoting an organic mode of narrative and discovering methodological and analytical insights within teachers' narratives is, in short, not always an easy task, when educational discourses are heavily laden with the expectations of traditional research outcomes. We outline some conceptual thinking about how we put together existing scholarship in a playful way, to set about considering the literature and what might be useful thinking as we embark on this project of theorizing pedagogy. We then report on our difficulties in eschewing the restrictive nature of frameworks and models in such research and the problem of dominant qualitative discourses seeping in around the edges of our theorizing in unexpected ways.

Our theorizing of the project in this way examines how we might work along-side teachers and how we might go about interpreting their experiences and narratives in respectful and ethical ways. Narrative inquiry focuses on the lived experiences of participants, and a philosophical approach invites consideration of ways to think, read, and analyze. Both narrative inquiry and philosophy are open to the possibility that both process and analysis emanate from the research concern itself. With this in mind, teachers will be invited to discuss and write about their lived experiences. Their narratives may intersect with the ideas that we unfold in our theorizing and conceptualization and may include influences on their pedagogy that we discuss in this chapter—influences such as curriculum ini-tiatives, leadership and management practices, research, and policy. Furthermore, because Auckland is a large urban city, their narratives may also reflect elements of globalization; internationalism; migration; and changing local, social, and cultural practices. However, what emerges will undoubtedly be more complex than this, and the theorizing we suggest here is simply a first engagement with understand-ing what it might be like to be a newly qualified early childhood teacher. We suspect that pedagogy for each of the teachers in this research will be unique and possibly problematic. It is imagined that this research will work at two levels: to extend participants' own thinking and engagement in collegial debate, and to contribute to critical scholarship about teachers' pedagogy in the early years of teaching. We anticipate working with 12 teachers who have already accepted our invitation to join the group discussions, and we hope that most will continue through the extended narrative work later in the project.

Context of Teachers' Work

This section briefly and critically outlines the wider context of the early child-hood education field in Aotearoa, including its national curriculum and the policy environment—a necessary foregrounding of context against which to read the development of the 'how' of this research. Preliminary discussions among the research team and conversations with colleagues suggest, initially at least, meth-odological and analytical strategies strongly related to the pedagogical aspirations inherent in the bicultural Aotearoa early childhood curriculum, *Te Whāriki* (Min-istry of Education, 1996), and to the social, cultural, and political contexts in which the teachers work.

In Aotearoa, the early childhood education (ECE) sector comprises children from birth through five years old. Generally children enter compulsory school-ing (Year One) soon after their fifth birthday. Free, universal, compulsory state schooling is provided for children aged 5–18 years. Early childhood education, however, is not free, nor is it provided for by the state, although the State has, over the last 20 years, recognized the place of ECE in the economy and has appeared favorably disposed to developing the sector through funding and regulation. Early childhood settings are subject to legislative requirements, and qualified teachers are subject to the same registration and ethical codes as their counterparts in the compulsory school sector. Although ECE is not compulsory, most children attend some form of ECE before entering school. Increasing participation rates in ECE has been a government priority for more than a decade, particularly for Māori and Pasifika populations (Ministry of Education, 2002). The sector comprises a range of services including all-day childcare, part-day kindergarten, parent-run Playcentre, language immersion Māori and Pacific Island early childhood settings, crèches, and home-based care.

In Aotearoa, as in other Western countries, the sector is regulated by specific legislation and regulatory requirements including: the Education (Early Childhood Services) Regulations (New Zealand Government, 2008); 'quality assurance' early childhood settings reviews conducted by the Education Review Office; and teacher registration for fully qualified teachers. Teachers are registered with the New Zealand Teachers Council (NZTC) and are obliged to fulfill commitments to the Treaty of Waitangi. This treaty is a bicultural agreement between Māori (the indigenous peoples of Aotearoa) and all other settlers represented by the British Crown and was signed around 1840. Registered teachers need to abide by the New Zealand Teachers Council Code of Ethics (NZTC, 2004). In brief, the sector is shaped by legislation, regulations, policy directives, and a national bicultural curriculum. It is also strongly influenced by standardized approaches to early childhood settings reviews, teaching qualifications, teacher registration, and Ministry-funded professional development programs for teachers.

A prominent feature of the landscape for early childhood teachers in Aotearoa is the curriculum. Aotearoa was one of the first countries in the world to develop a bicultural curriculum for early childhood: *Te Whāriki*. The name is a Māori term that literally translates as 'the mat,' metaphorically referring to the inter-relatedness or woven-ness of the curriculum: a weaving together of Western epistemology and Māori Kaupapa (protocols and practices). The curriculum is written in both Māori and English, and one of the sections comprises a dedicated curriculum for Māori immersion settings. It is conceptualized both in visual and textual form as woven threads representing weavings from the flax plant.[1] While the history and significance of its development has been written about extensively elsewhere (see, for example, Nuttall, 2013), what is important to outline for the purposes of this chapter is the framework of this curriculum.

Represented graphically in the document are the four principles and five strands that crisscross each other to provide the woven framework of *Te Whāriki*. These principles and strands are presented in both English and Māori languages: Empowerment/Whakamana, Holistic Development/Kotahitanga, Family and Community/Whānau Tangata, and Relationships/Ngā Hononga. The five strands are: Well-being/Mana Atua, Belonging/Mana Whenua, Contribution/Mana Tangata, Communication/Mana Reo, and Exploration/Mana Aotūroa. The messages within these principles and strands are not unlike other early childhood curricula with a holistic focus on empowering children to develop, learn, belong, and so on, and with a strong recognition of the social and cultural nature of child development. What is unique about *Te Whāriki* is its embeddedness in Māori ways of knowing (see, for example, Tesar, 2015), albeit not always borne out in practice.

The curriculum has become a standard text for teachers, so much so that student teachers can often recite the vision statement of *Te Whāriki* from memory; that is to say, the curriculum is part of the psyche of all ECE teachers. We developed our theorizing about the project with this in mind, knowing from experience that teachers in Aotearoa talk about their pedagogy with frequent reference to this document. Furthermore, participants in the study will undoubtedly be very familiar with this curriculum document having recently graduated from a program in which it was extensively used.

In Aotearoa, teachers are encouraged to engage in continuous pedagogical development through personal reflection, through dialogue within a collegial community, and through formal professional development sessions. For newly qualified teachers there are a number of challenges: establishing relationships (with children, teachers, parents, and the teaching communities); establishing personal support systems and networks; locating oneself in a workplace with a wide range of ethos; engaging in professional processes such as registration, induction, and mentoring programs; and becoming part of teaching teams.

We expect that legislative, regulatory, and curriculum constraints, alongside the social, cultural, and political environment in which teachers work, will strongly influence the way in which teachers talk about their personal experiences of pedagogy in their first year.

Thinking about and Theorizing the Project

We move now to the 'how' as in how to think about and theorize our research. Narrative and philosophy are avenues that we believe allow for a tentative but rigorous process, as well as critical and reflexive analysis of our own processes. We understand that we are engaging in an arena bounded by structures and frameworks, and we want to find ways to wrest open our own thinking—to explore our own discursive limits. This section outlines our two approaches—narrative inquiry and philosophy of education—and then provides a tentative description of our theorizing about the project.

Narrative Inquiry

Narrative inquiry provides an ideal way to begin: The idea of telling stories accords well with prior student experience and the reflective identity work that the teachers are exposed to in their final year of study. It also accords well with the discourses of professionalism in Aotearoa where understanding one's self is aligned with notions of teacher agency and autonomy. These ideas are embodied in the teachers' code of ethics, a code that also recognizes the importance of reflective practice and duty of care to act responsively and critically in their own practice (NZTC, 2004). There are many ways in which narrative inquiry work might proceed, and there is extensive literature behind the general view that narrative work is a comprehensive way in which to reveal the lived experience of both teachers and researchers (Connelly & Clandinin, 1990). Involving participants in "life writing" (Leggo, 2010) and reflective work, we see, provides continuity between the initial conversation groups with all of the teachers and the later personal conversations/interviews with us (Riessman, 2008). Furthermore, the set of relationships among narrative (in this instance the teachers' stories), time (teachers reflecting on and projecting from a unique point in time), and identity (an integral understanding of oneself as changing over time and place) (Ricoeur, 1991; Ollerenshaw & Creswell, 2002) seems a likely way to begin to theorize our project. It also provides ways to affirm, value, clarify, and inform teacher perspectives while recognizing and valuing the benefits of the participant/researcher partnership. This inquiry mode is usefully aligned to participants' recent studies at the Faculty of Education, where they had been involved in reflective practices throughout their teacher education program. In one of their final papers before graduating they reflected on, and explored in an inter-textual way, their anticipated transition from student to qualified teacher.

Philosophy as Method

Philosophy of education is vital to the project as a way of both uncovering knowledge and processing observations in new ways. The casting of philosophy of education as a form of research has been written about at length. As Moses (2002) points out, "Policy, methods, and practice in education presuppose philosophy and theory, though they often remain hidden" (p. 17). A recent special issue of the British *Journal of Philosophy of Education* was devoted to method in philosophy of education (Standish, 2009; Smith, 2009; Ruitenberg, 2009). In this issue, Ruitenberg explains the challenge for philosophers of education in talking about their research methods without submitting to the paradigms and expectations of the social sciences—especially the emphasis on 'data,' technique, and the tripartite breakdown of method into data gathering, data analysis, and data representation (Ruitenberg, 2009). She prefers to think of 'methods' as referring to "the various ways and modes in which philosophers of education think, read, write, speak and listen, that make their work systematic, purposeful and responsive to past and present philosophical and educational concerns and conversations" (Ruitenberg, 2009, p. 316). Standish goes on to argue that sometimes content and method are one, especially when we examine the words we use. Language, he suggests, is the "very stuff of the philosopher's work, messily entangled with, as it is, the conceptual clarity, perspicuity or theoretical alignments we seek to achieve, and inseparable from the practical purchase the enquiry yields" (Standish, 2009, p. i). In an earlier issue of the same journal, Smith (citing Sayer) sees as extraordinary the level of attention given in social science courses to 'methods' in the narrow sense of statistical techniques, interviewing and survey methods, and the like, with a blithe disregard for questions of how we conceptualize, theorize, and abstract (Smith, 2006, p. 160).

A special issue of the Australasian journal *Educational Philosophy and Theory* considers the relationship between philosophy and early childhood pedagogy. In their introduction to this special issue, Farquhar and White (2014) suggest that "philosophy and pedagogy keenly intersect" (p. 3) and argue for the work that philosophy can do to invigorate binding paradigms and "pedagogical certainty" (p. 6). They involve the idea that epistemologies of knowing and doing need to be broadened to take on discursive understandings of a myriad of practices and subjectivities. This is our aim in this project, where participants' conversations and documentation will guide the analysis (Gubrium & Holstein, 2008; Riessman, 2008).

Cognizant of our own discursive limits and open to multiple interpretations, we are developing a deconstructive research analysis of reading with/against each other—a form of checking each other's method and interpretation of data. In this process, we recognize that we each work in different/related disciplines and that our subjectivities will enable particular inclusions, absences, and constructions. We draw here on the deconstructive work of Lenz Taguchi (2010), which suggests that researchers' texts are acts of interpretation that can be reworked and that questions can be raised about each other's acts of interpretation and meaning-making. We have set to work a strategy of deconstruction within the collaborative processes of writing and talking. Rather than treating deconstruction as an object of philosophical study or applying theory to practice, we are working with the "turning, bending and twisting" of our own analysis, "questioning it and trying to displace the meanings of it" (p. 41).

It is likely that the analysis required in this philosophical and narrative approach may broadly involve a narrative analysis of identity (Ricoeur, 1991; Farquhar, 2010), a deconstructive turn (Lenz Taguchi, 2010), and a Foucauldian approach to power/knowledge and subjectivity (Foucault, 1980; Tesar, 2014a). We have begun a tentative theorizing that will provide an initial impetus to talking and thinking about what we may find. This theorizing is necessarily contingent—we are conscious of not developing a framework of analysis that may work against our intentions of being open to discursive possibilities that the teachers will bring to their work with us. Farquhar (2012) argues that teachers are unique and that their understandings are "not confined to the vocabulary of policy documents or statistical indicators" (p. 31). As teachers are in unique places to form various perspectives, so too are we as researchers in a unique place to put our theorizing to work and to challenge our own assumptions.

A Tentative Theorizing

Thinking about the complexities of this unique place, we played with *Te Whā riki*. *Te Whāriki* aspires to produce both an ideal child and a global child (Duhn, 2006), and as such it contributes to the government of childhoods that produces particular childhood subjectivities (Tesar, 2014b). We were struck with the question of what this might mean for early career teachers, how they might ponder the complexities of teaching in a place, as 'ideal' and 'global teacher,' as a 'good teacher,' governed by this curriculum framework? It is in this sense that we have woven the complexity of being and becoming a teacher and *Te Whāriki* together with our intention to develop a way of thinking about teachers' stories. The result is a tentative theorizing about the complex narratives that might arise from the teachers' engagement in this project—tentative in that it is only a preliminary step in our search for method and analysis. We hope for further clarity from the stories the teachers in the project tell.

The following paragraphs briefly outline the curriculum strands of *Te Whāriki*. The name of each is italicized, followed by a line of questioning elicited by the focus of the strand and some notes about our evolving discussion of some themes that might emerge in our treatment of each strand.

Belonging/Mana Whenua: What complex power relations are in place, and how are they recognized and harnessed as productive, rather than acting as damaging and repressive forces?

We recognize that a number of power issues impact on early childhood learning and teaching, including optimal teacher-child ratios; funding and retention of staff (Aitken & Kennedy, 2007); community versus private/corporate ownership (Mitchell, 2002; Farquhar, 2012; Duhn, 2010); teacher autonomy and issues of collaboration and community involvement; professional distance versus the need for intimacy (Dalli, 2006; 2008); differences between education and care; and the 'schoolification' of early childhood (Farquhar & Gibbons, 2010). This myriad of factors and forces will play out in particular ways for each of the teachers who bring their own subjectivities to their practice.

Contribution/Mana Tangata: How do newly qualified teachers negotiate professionalism in their everyday practice, and how do they construct their identity in the face of the complex and contradictory forces surrounding them? How are teachers protected, in the broadest sense, within these everyday negotiations, while they contribute to the professionalization of the sector?

Professionalism as a negotiated everyday practice calls for a broad understanding of what it means to be a professional in the sector. Woodrow (2007; 2008) suggests that the increasing control of the profession through curriculum, auditing, and the rise of commodified children's services works against the realization of a strong professional identity. In light of this, the teachers may reveal insight into the importance of engaging with professional issues and concerns that face emerging teachers.

Well-being/Mana Atua: What pedagogies of place/space/culture are present within rapidly shifting socio-political advancements, and how does this shape teachers' professional well-being?

Newly qualified early childhood teachers carry an 'imprint' of their own educational experiences, their practicum experiences, and their own narratives. The ideals and skepticisms about the field they are engaged in are encompassed in their narratives that construct their identity and in notions of being and becoming pedagogical in their professional careers (Sumsion, 2002). Notwithstanding these issues, early childhood education and care in Aotearoa New Zealand is regarded as a world leader, particularly on account of its bicultural curriculum *Te Whāriki* (Ministry of Education, 1996). Later curriculum and policy documents develop the sector further. These developments also need to be seen alongside other factors, such as advances in neuroscience emphasizing the importance of the early years in child development and the increasing numbers of mothers returning to work seeking care for their infants and pre-five children, which has increased the profile and/or perceived social need for formal early childhood education.

Communication/Mana Reo: How is professional identity currently understood, produced, and performed in Aotearoa New Zealand, and how do (or indeed, do) early years teachers participate in debates around professionalism?

The sector is regulated by specific legislation (New Zealand Government, 2008) and early childhood settings reviews (ERO), and registered teachers are obligated to fulfill commitments to the Treaty of Waitangi as well as abide by the New Zealand Teachers Council Code of Ethics (NZTC, 2004). A strong early childhood community, a national bicultural curriculum, and some Ministry-funded professional development programs for teachers set a framework for the development of professional leadership. Through participation and communication, teachers' narratives emerge from these regulatory environments, enriching discursive possibilities for professional identity. Throughout the literature, teachers' lives will be seen to be embedded within these regulatory environments and within a playing out of complex power relations between teachers and early childhood settings.

Exploration/Mana Aotūroa: In what ways can existing qualifications be improved to better contribute to the relevance and effectiveness of student learning experiences?

Early childhood education 'workers' were once among the lowest paid in the country (Mitchell, 2002), operating largely outside government regulation and funding. Increased government funding, regulation, support, advice, and guidance have established 'early childhood education' as a new profession in New Zealand and other Organisation for Economic Co-operation and Development (OECD) countries. Within this framework of an emerging and contested early childhood educational sector (Banfield, Gibbons, & Tesar, 2013), we hope that the teachers in this study will suggest ways in which to reconsider student-teacher experiences.

Problematizing Method

Alongside our tentative theorizing around the strands of *Te Whāriki*, we consider concepts of time, space, and movement—an adapted and problematized account of Ollerenshaw and Creswell's (2002) traditional analytic model. In problematizing and disrupting this model, we view teachers as moving through *time* engaging with past experiences, present successes, and constraints and having future dreams and hopes. Teachers operate and develop their emerging professional identities within particular *spaces/places*: of work, being 'on the floor,' in the office, having a break, driving back home from work. *Movement* refers to the emerging pedagogical identities as students change; to the flux in the process of becoming part of the team, community, and society; and to their own emerging professional identity. We recognize the potential of these concepts in considering how teachers negotiate their emerging identities, engaging with problems and challenges, and identifying what works and in what ways.

Of course, our current theorizing will be expanded, and dismantled, constructed, and deconstructed, as the project evolves. At the moment, we are being careful to ensure that participants' narratives are not prescribed by a particular framework, which might normalize or standardize their unique experiences as teachers. Our pre-figuration of the research is necessarily speculative and evolving. We hope the research will ultimately develop a range of unique narrative portrayals of the lives, identities, and pedagogies of teachers that emerge from their own narratives.

Our research design aims to disrupt and challenge the homogenizing effects of traditional research paradigms, methodologies, and methods, using philosophy as a method, as well as narrative enquiry, and adopting a tentative attitude toward both the process and the possible outcomes. The contribution of this chapter to our project is to document our early thinking and to problematize traditional thinking about conceptualizations of a research project. We have developed an alternative approach to research within a particular cultural and geopolitical setting and ways of contributing to the expansion of what counts as legitimate research in education. Our intention is to introduce different practices to early childhood education: in a mode not driven by empirical data sets or rigid theoretical frameworks and methodologies, but that is open to participant conversations and concerns, that engages with questions of how we as researchers, and teachers, conceptualize, theorize, and abstract in ways that are systematic and purposeful to the particular educational, societal, and political context. This chapter performs our argument that thinking about research process and design in relation to the philosophy as a method is as important as collected and interpreted research data and that in theorizing we do need to be "responsive to past and present philosophical and educational concerns and conversations" (Ruitenberg, 2009, p. 316).

Note

1 The flax plant is of cultural significance for Māori people and is used traditionally in the creation of clothes, food containers, and tools.

References

Aitken, H., & Kennedy, A. (2007). Critical issues for the early childhood profession. In L. Keesing-Styles & H. Hedges (Eds.), *Theorising early childhood practice. Emerging dialogues* (pp. 165–185). New South Wales, Australia: Pademelon.

Banfield, S., Gibbons, A., & Tesar, M. (2013). The quality of qualifications: Early childhood associate teacher views on policy, practicum and partnership. *A report to the Auckland University of Technology School of Education.* Auckland, New Zealand: AUT University.

Connelly, F., & Clandinin, D. (1990). Stories of experience and narrative inquiry. *Educational Researcher, 19*(5), 2–14.

Dalli, C. (2006). Re-visioning love and care in early childhood: Constructing the future of our profession. *The First Years. Ngā Tau Tuatahi. New Zealand Journal of Infant and Toddler Education, 8*(1), 5–11.

Dalli, C. (2008). Pedagogy, knowledge and collaboration: towards a ground-up perspective on professionalism. *European Early Childhood Education Research Journal, 16*(2), 175–185. doi: 10.1080/13502930802141600.

Duhn, I. (2006). The making of global citizens: traces of cosmopolitanism in the New Zealand early childhood curriculum, Te Whāriki. *Contemporary Issues in Early Childhood, 7*(3), 191–202.

Duhn, I. (2010). 'The centre is my business': neo-liberal politics, privatisation and discourses of professionalism in New Zealand. *Contemporary Issues in Early Childhood, 11*(1), 49–60.

Farquhar, S. (2010). *Ricoeur, identity and early childhood*. Lanham, MD: Rowman & Littlefield.

Farquhar, S. (2012). Well-being and narrative identity. *Early Childhood Folio, 16*(1), 27–32.

Farquhar, S., & Gibbons, A. (2010). Early childhood education. In M. Thrupp & R. Irwin (Eds.), *Another decade of educational policy: Where to now?* (pp. 83–98). Hamilton, New Zealand: Wilf Malcolm Institute of Research.

Farquhar, S., & White, E.J. (2014). Philosophy and pedagogy of early childhood. *Educational Philosophy and Theory, 46*(8), 821–832.

Foucault, M. (1980). *Power/knowledge: Selected Interviews and other writings (1972–1977)*. Brighton, UK: Harvester Press.

Gubrium, J., & Holstein, J. (2008). Narrative ethnography. In S.N. Hesse-Biber & P. Leavy (Eds.), *Handbook of emergent methods* (pp. 241–264). New York: Guilford Press.

Leggo, C. (2010). Writing a life: Representation in language and image. *Transnational Curriculum Inquiry, 7*(2), 47–61.

Lenz Taguchi, H. (2010). Doing collaborative deconstruction as an 'exorbitant' strategy in qualitative research. *Reconceptualizing Educational Research Methodology, 1*(1), 41–53.

Ministry of Education. (1996). *Te Whāriki: He Whāriki Matauranga Mō Ngā Mokopuna o Aotearoa, Early Childhood Curriculum*. Wellington, New Zealand: Learning Media.

Ministry of Education. (2002). *Strategic plan for early childhood education: Pathways to the future: Ngā Huarahi Arataki*. Wellington, New Zealand: Ministry of Education.

Mitchell, L. (2002). Differences between community owned and privately owned early childhood education and care centres: A review of evidence. *An Occasional Paper*. Wellington, New Zealand: NZCER.

Moses, M. (2002). The heart of the matter: Philosophy and educational research. *Review of Research in Education, 26*(1), 1–21.

New Zealand Government. (2008). *Education (Early Childhood Services) Regulations 2008*. Retrieved from http://www.legislation.govt.nz/regulation/public/2008/0204/latest/DLM1412501.html

New Zealand Teachers Council. (2004). *Code of ethics for registered teachers*. Retrieved from http://www.teacherscouncil.govt.nz/required/ethics/index.stm

New Zealand Teachers Council. (2011). *Knowing and working with the registered teacher criteria*. Retrieved from http://www.teacherscouncil.govt.nz/rtc

Nuttall, J. (2013). *Weaving Te Whāriki. Aotearoa New Zealand's early childhood curriculum document in theory and practice*. Wellington, New Zealand: NZCER Press.

Ollerenshaw, J., & Creswell, J. (2002). Narrative research: A comparison of two restorying data analysis approaches. *Qualitative Inquiry, 8*(3), 329–347.

Ricoeur, P. (1991). Narrative identity. *Philosophy Today, 35*(1), 73–81.

Riessman, C.K. (2008). *Narrative methods for the human sciences*. Los Angeles, CA: Sage.

Ruitenberg, C. (2009). Introduction: The question of method in philosophy of education. *Journal of Philosophy of Education, 43*(3), 315–323.

Smith, R. (2006). As if by machinery: The levelling of educational research. *Journal of Philosophy of Education, 40*(2), 157–168.

Smith, R. (2009). Between the lines: Philosophy, text and conversation. *Journal of Philosophy of Education, 43*(3), 437–449.

Standish, P. (2009). Preface. *Journal of Philosophy of Education, 43*(3), i–ii.

Sumsion, J. (2002). Becoming, being and unbecoming an early childhood educator: A phenomenological case study of teacher attrition. *Teaching and Teacher Education, 18*, 869–885.

Tesar, M. (2014a). My feelings: Power, politics and childhood subjectivities. *Educational Philosophy and Theory, 46*(8), 860–872. doi: 10.1080/00131857.2013.781496.

Tesar, M. (2014b). Reconceptualising the child: Power and resistance within early childhood settings. *Contemporary Issues in Early Childhood, 15*(4), 360–367. doi: 10.2304/ciec.2014.15.4.360.

Tesar, M. (2015). *Te Whāriki* in Aotearoa New Zealand: Witnessing and resisting neoliberal and neo-colonial discourses in early childhood education. In V. Pacini-Ketchabaw & A. Taylor, *Unsettling the colonial places and spaces of early childhood education* (pp. 145–170). New York: Routledge.

Woodrow, C. (2007). W(H)Ither the early childhood teacher: Tensions for early childhood professional identity between the policy landscape and the politics of teacher regulation. *Contemporary Issues in Early Childhood, 8*(3), 233–243.

Woodrow, C. (2008). Discourses of professional identity in early childhood: Movements in Australia. *European Early Childhood Education Research Journal, 16*(2), 269–280.

4

CRITIQUING TRADITIONAL COLONIAL PRACTICES IN TEACHER EDUCATION

Interpreting Normative Practices through Visual Culture Analyses

Richard T. Johnson

Of late I have been keenly aware of the importance of looking closely at popular images in schooling and borrowing from visual culture theory (Jameson, 1990; Jenks, 1995; Metz, 1982; Sekula, 1983). I am particularly interested in what images have been included in particular educational contexts and how we can further understand the meaning(s) of these images. In concert with Alan Sekula's work on images, I am intrigued and interested in understanding and using images/ photographs to assist in understanding the question, "How is historical and social memory preserved, transformed, restricted, and obliterated by photographs?" (Sekula, 1983, p. 193).

This chapter seeks to untangle some of the 'entangled events' that are a part of our field-based teacher preparation program, a part of our new master narrative in teacher education. Through the critical lenses (Lather, 1998) of visual culture I will consider issues of colonization, desire, tourism, and identity as these impact our so-called—as National Council for Accreditation of Teacher Education (NCATE) alignment would have us believe—high quality field-based teacher education programs.

(Re)Reading Landscapes

In her visual culture work on family pictures, included in the article "Masking the Subject: Practicing Theory" (1994), Hirsch suggests that family pictures "produce and reproduce dominant ideologies" and that typically we enter that viewing of the family picture expecting to "perceive what we are prepared to perceive" (p. 109). Hirsch's theoretical considerations reverberate strongly with this work here and my particular personal and professional concerns. This is readily apparent when I consider the view of the educational 'family picture' as one in which we also quite readily and without assumption "perceive what we are prepared to perceive"—fixed, stable and happy, static and monolithic ideas we best know and have come to believe and be comfortable with in their various representation(s). In sharp contrast to this stance, Hirsch (1994) suggests that, instead, we "consider how the camera and the image might, in the words of Jo Spence, be useful for its 'unfixing' rather than its 'fixing' qualities. . .' Here we must begin to question photographs, asking not what we think they show us . . . but what they don't (can't) show us." Hirsch (1994) suggests that this *unfixing*, this *questioning* and searching for what they don't/can't show us, is a "return to the etymological roots of theoria—defined as an act of viewing, contemplation, consideration, insight" (p. 110), theory defined in relation to visuality. As well, Bakhtin's (1990) historical work on the "cult of unified and exclusive reason" is beneficial here as he discussed the trap of limiting events into a particular, single consciousness. In this way if an event is only understood and critiqued within this single consciousness, then we run the risk of "impoverishment and domination rather than mutual enrichment" (p. 87).

Here I will explore, from several different angles, theories of visual culture as applied to teacher education research and practice (Orvell, 1995; Sturken & Cartwright, 2001). In this chapter I incorporate visual culture as a theoretical standpoint (MacDougall, 1997) to explore the complex realities of constructing, producing, and consuming media imagery in educational research and practice. The idea of visual culture has recently made tentative inroads into educational research (Fischman, 2001). However, the concern has largely been about how the media industry manipulates representation both inside and outside of schools. Little attention has been paid to how individuals in the educational setting produce media imagery or what role it can play in representing research or articulating educational practice. Consequently, there has been little discussion concerning the epistemological or practical value of imagery to educational research and practice (Pajaczkowska, 2001). This appears as a large gap in educational research and practice because in our modern media-saturated culture the media image dominates all forms of cultural representation (Jameson, 1990; Jenks, 1995). In this work I take a broad interpretation of visuality and visual culture that includes a visual orientation to a particular space and place, the deconstruction of disparate meanings embedded in an image, and visual culture as a metaphor for thinking in new ways about educational practice and research.

Several years ago Gustavo Fischman (2001) warned educators and educational researchers that they "ignore visual culture at their own peril" (p. 30) because, he argued, contemporary culture and its impact on human social and cultural life was becoming increasingly visual (Jacobs, 2004). Television, film, photography, and cyberspace constitute a growing and increasingly influential sphere of meaning making, action, and cultural production that is incessantly visual. As a society our experience(s) with the world and our ability to articulate cultural practices and representations are increasingly mediated through a cultural logic that owes its presence and its form to the modern mechanically and electronically reproducible image (Lewis & Fabos, 2005). The ubiquitous image and its many forms have become the central and most compelling artifact of modern, or postmodern, social life. This is especially evident when one views the ever-popular and present visual images in elementary school classrooms and school walls today (see examples in Figures 4.1–4.3).

In my recent work(s) I have begun to map the field(s) in an attempt to create various visual narratives or montages that illuminate the imperialism of traditional early childhood discourses and practices. This coincides with understandings that "subjectivity is formed by perpetual adjustment of images passing before the subject, who makes them into a whole that is comprehensible because it is continuous" (Bal, 2001, p. 5). In this mapping I have witnessed the elevation of particular expressions of knowledge, the adoption of specific classificatory taxonomies, and the reification of certain designated responses and actions that collectively have produced safe (at least for those who acquiesced to being colonized) but controlling and therefore limiting spaces. Through critical readings of specific images and artifacts in the proposed montage, I will build

FIGURE 4.1 Public school poster

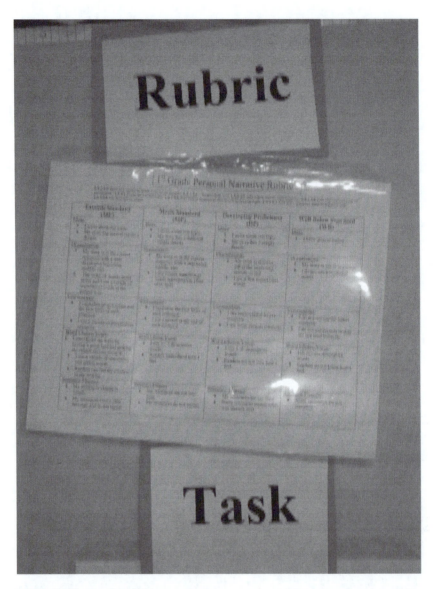

FIGURE 4.2 First grade rubric

from previous work (Johnson, 2013; 2011; 2010; 2009; 2004) to assist efforts to destabilize and dismantle this imperialist legacy and to create new spaces that value cultural and theoretical plurality and hybridity and possibilities for educational practitioners and researchers and to generate new possibilities for practitioners, researchers, and policy-makers.

FIGURE 4.3 Classroom writing standards board

Teacher Education in the Colony

Our undergraduate and graduate teacher education initial licensure programs mirror the abundance of so-called progressive teacher education programs state-wide, nationwide, and, more and more so, globally. Upon entry into our college, our pre-service students are placed into small cohort groups of about 25 students each, where they collectively stay for the two years it typically takes to reach matriculation. These cohort groups attend methods-based courses (e.g., math methods, science methods, social studies) together and work in Hawai'i Department of Education partnership schools within this same time frame. This program prides itself on the number of hours, 12–15 per week, that our third-year undergraduate students spend in the classroom (i.e., the field) each semester (three total) before they student teach—spending all day, every day over a 16-week semester teaching in an elementary classroom. The axiom 'more is better' certainly applies to our field-based internship practices and our zeal to get our future teacher candidates out of the university and into the 'real world' to see practicing 'expert' teachers, students, and pedagogical practices firsthand.

While most of the courses are taught along disciplinary lines (e.g., math, literacy, science) by related content-area methods specialists (e.g., math, science, arts), each instructor in each cohort works off an agreed-upon college-wide *Conceptual Framework* stating that our teachers are to be *knowledgeable, effective,* and *caring.* The college website (http://www.hawaii.edu/coe) professes that these three standards are a part of all learning experiences in our teacher education program. Here is a brief overview directly from that web page that supposedly assists in defining our students/teachers:

A. Knowledgeable

Teacher candidates are knowledgeable about content, pedagogy, and professionalism; human growth and development; and the physical, mental, emotional, and social needs of students with diverse backgrounds and learning needs.

E lawe i ke a'o malama, a e 'oi mau ka na'auao: He who takes his teachings and applies them increases his knowledge (Pukui, 1983).

'A'ohe pau ka 'ike i ka halau ho'okahi: All knowledge is not taught in the same school. One can learn from many sources (Pukui, 1983).

B. Effective

Teacher candidates have the professional experience and skills to teach so that all children can learn.

Ho a'e ka 'ike he'enalu i ka hokua o ka 'ale: Show [your] knowledge of surfing on the back of the wave. Talking about one's knowledge and skill is not enough; let it be proven (Pukui, 1983).

C. Caring

Teacher candidates care about students and their families and communities, teaching and learning, and their own professional development.

E kuahui like i ka hana: Let everybody pitch in and work together (Pukui, 1983) (http://www.hawaii.edu/coe/departments/ite/CourseSyllabi.html).

The professional dispositions shared in this course reflect the standards and expectations of the College of Education, the Institute for Teacher Education, and the Elementary and Early Childhood Education Program. Teacher candidates must demonstrate acceptable or target professional dispositions during all program-related activities (i.e., coursework, field experiences, meetings, and conferences). Any category marked with a "U" requires a conference, plan of assistance for improvement, or dismissal. Professional dispositions can be found on the EECE website at: http://www.hawaii.edu/coe/departments/ite/index.html

FIGURE 4.4 Professional dispositions statement

Each of these three standards have the respective Knowledge, Skills, and Dispositions aligned with their original intent that are uniformly strived for as the official faculty syllabi attest and as national accreditation structures (NCATE for our college) demand. For example, our college website expounds upon this uniformity when they profess:

Several syllabi mention that "during your teacher education program, you will find yourself immersed in standards-based education" and continue to inform and direct students to the following scripted items:

- The Hawai'i Teacher Standards Board (HTSB) sets standards for Hawai'i teachers. The *Hawai'i Teacher Performance Standards (HTPS)* can be found in the Elementary and Early Childhood Teacher Education Program Handbook.
- *The Hawai'i Content and Performance Standards (HCPS III)* for K–12 students are set by the Hawai'i Department of Education (DOE). These can be viewed on the DOE website at: http://standardstoolkit.k12.hi.us/index.html or http://www.hawaii.edu/coe/departments/ite/CourseSyllabi.html.

To further align themselves with other states throughout the United States, Hawai'i announced several years ago (June 18, 2010) in the media that "Hawaii Schools Join 'Common Core Standards Initiative'" (http://www.hawaiinewsnow.com/global/story.asp?s=12672057).

The Department of Education claims that the adoption of these Common Core Standards will assist in "defining the knowledge and skills students will need to graduate high school fully prepared for college and careers." The standards are:

- Aligned with college and work expectations;
- Clear, understandable and consistent;
- Built upon strengths and lessons of current state standards;
- Informed by other top performing countries, so that all students are prepared to succeed in our global economy and society; and
- Evidence- and research-based.

(http://hawaiidoereform.org/enews/2010–12/Update-Common-Core-State-Standards)

Nation Building: Teacher Education from the Empire

In their public mission statement, the National Council for Accreditation of Teacher Education refers to "accountability and improvement in teacher preparation [as] central to NCATE's mission" (2002, p. 1). Given that our teacher education program is NCATE approved, we (the college, that is) glowingly share among ourselves and with the public NCATE's assurance that our graduates "have acquired the knowledge, skills, and dispositions necessary to help all students learn" (p. 1). In close alignment with their partner professional teacher education member organizations (e.g., Association for Childhood Education International, National Association for the Education of Young Children, National Council of Teachers of Mathematics, National Council of Teachers of English), NCATE professes that new professional teachers should be able to, among other things: (1) teach to P–12 student standards set by specialized professional associations and the states; (2) explain instructional choices based on research-derived knowledge and best practice; (3) apply effective methods of teaching students who are at different developmental stages, have different learning styles, and come from diverse backgrounds; and (4) reflect on practice and act on feedback (2002, p. 4).

Adhering to these same principles and practices, our teacher education programs build coursework and field-based experiences that are closely aligned with these national 'best practices.' They must be aligned to reach *proficiency* and pass muster for initial and continued accreditation, from the NCATE document to the College of Education accreditation to the walls of elementary and secondary schools.

Undoing the Done

Because of my own individual and collective professional and personal interests in issues of globalization, imperialism, and colonization (Johnson, 2010; 2009; 2004), in my theoretical work here I am choosing to critically engage and critique discourses of teacher education through both local and global lenses. In my analyses I read teacher education in a particular traditional way and then seek to critically question the orderly, patterned, ritualistic ways in which it is structured, seemingly beyond dispute, especially if one seeks recognition as an accredited (i.e., NCATE) institution. This stance mirrors Beth Tobin's work (1999) in which she critically engages sets of particular eighteenth-century paintings as colonial discourse. Her research offers that "one way to recover subaltern subjectivity from an elite text is to read the imperial text symptomatically—that is, reading what is not there but is implied and called into existence by a series of oppositions" (1999, p. 12). Like Tobin, I am interested in a particular set of images, how they represent a field of study, and how they too speak to a dominant discourse in teacher education. Here

I recognize that as a poststructuralist reading, "Words and images do not merely reflect the world, but mediate, even create, what we believe to be reality" (Tobin, 1999, pp. 13–14). For instance, the following visual artifacts (Figures 4.5–4.8) from the walls of colleges of education represent the field of early childhood education's (ECE) reliance on the pedagogical subject as natural, innocent, normative child(ren) of the field of ECE.

FIGURE 4.5 College of Education's NCATE bulletin board

FIGURE 4.6 College of Education's NCATE tool

Image Analyses

This interdisciplinary focus (Davey, 1999) on the visual assisted in analyzing teacher education–related materials and their links to broader education discourse(s) (e.g., No Child Left Behind and Common Core). Initial baseline analyses of these images offers a way of exploring how the images present and construct particular ways of seeing the world. This particular type of discourse analysis critiques

Elementary and Early Childhood Education Program
Professional Dispositions Assessment

Teacher Candidate _____   Mentor Teacher _____
_____ UHM Supervisor _____
Person completing this form _____   Semester # _____
Cohort # _____   Date _____
Course (✔):   _____ ITE 317 (Semester __1 __2 __3)   _____ ITE 415L
_____ ITE 416L   _____ ITE 390

Assess each disposition overall with a check (✔):

Disposition	Needs Improvement—Does Not Yet Meet Expectations (circle bullets)	Meets Expectations for a Teacher Candidate This Semester	Target—Exceptional Performance for a Teacher Candidate This Semester
1. Professional and ethical conduct **Assessment:**	• Reluctantly accepts or ignores feedback • Does not make suggested changes • Becomes defensive, argues or makes excuses for behavior • Shows conduct that is unethical or disrespectful • Is unwilling or unable to meet program requirements • Shows poor professional judgment • Shows inattention to children's well-being or safety **Unacceptable ☐**	• Accepts feedback • Makes changes without being defensive • Accepts responsibility, and does not explain away behavior • Shows integrity and ethical conduct • Works within program requirements • Is responsive to needs of children • Creates a safe physical, social, and emotional learning environment **Acceptable ☐**	• Consistently welcomes feedback • Expresses understanding and responds to feedback by making suggested changes • Is solution-oriented • Models integrity and ethical conduct • Maximizes learning opportunities within program requirements • Helps children learn how to contribute to a safe physical, social, and emotional environment **Target ☐**
2. Individual and cultural sensitivity **Assessment:**	• Expresses apathy or disrespect for diversity • Is judgmental or inflexible in response to others' perspectives and feelings • Is culturally insensitive **Unacceptable ☐**	• Recognizes diversity • Listens and responds appropriately to others' perspectives and feelings • Demonstrates cultural awareness **Acceptable ☐**	• Consistently respects and values diversity • Capitalizes on the strengths of diverse populations • Seeks and responds appropriately to others' perspectives and feelings • Models cultural sensitivity and actively promotes it in the classroom **Target ☐**
3. Effective work habits **Assessment:**	• Is consistently unreliable or disorganized • Disregards time commitments • Fails to follow through on commitments and assignments • Provides work that is low or inconsistent quality • Is late or absent without notifying mentors or instructors • Dresses inappropriately for partner school setting **Unacceptable ☐**	• Work habits and follow-through are consistent, requiring only minimal support from mentor or supervisor • Exhibits organization and time management skills • Completes quality assignments • Is present and punctual • Dresses appropriately for partner school setting **Acceptable ☐**	• Is consistently and independently reliable and punctual • Demonstrates high level of commitment to the teaching profession • Consistently completes exemplary assignments (e.g., depth, thoughtfulness) • Exhibits exemplary organization and time management skills • Dresses appropriately for partner school setting **Target ☐**

FIGURE 4.7 College of Education's NCATE rubric

"how images construct accounts of the social world . . . paying careful attention to images, and to their social production and effect" (Rose, 2001, pp. 140–141), incorporating Cowling's (1989) methodologies of looking for commonalities, both textual and visual, to assist in understanding the many images presented here.

Geography has found a particular place in my personalized reading of the *field* of teacher education. Much like Groth's work, I too am intrigued by the ways "landscape denotes the interaction of people and place: a social group and its spaces, particularly the spaces to which the group belongs and from which its members derive some part of their shared identity and meaning" (Groth, 1997, p. 1). No matter our status, as historically located members in the field of teacher education we are implicated in how this particular field/landscape "reveals the effects of individuals and local subcultures as well as national, dominant cultural values" (Groth, 1997, p. 7). Noting some of the landscape of the teacher education field via these visual products replicates in many ways the images of travel photographers, which are "particularly suited to the naturalization of both the landscape idea and an imperial way of seeing" (Ryan, 1997, p. 46).

In this active, participatory movement my recent research has been attempting to more dynamically call to question things that once seemed stable, appeared to be readily fixed, and looked as if they were normal and typical but that, upon

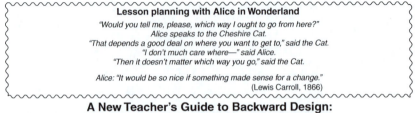

Lesson planning with Alice in Wonderland

"Would you tell me, please, which way I ought to go from here?"
Alice speaks to the Cheshire Cat.
"That depends a good deal on where you want to get to," said the Cat.
"I don't much care where—" said Alice.
"Then it doesn't matter which way you go," said the Cat.

Alice: "It would be so nice if something made sense for a change."
(Lewis Carroll, 1866)

A New Teacher's Guide to Backward Design: Four Big Steps for Unit and Lesson Planning

Adapted from *Integrating Differentiated Instruction + Understanding by Design*, Tomlinson and McTighe, ASCD, 2006

Step 1 Standards	**Desired results: What should your students know and be able to do?**
Do steps 1 and 2 match? Does it all make sense?	Standards for students • What's your **essential question** (big and important) for students to answer? • Hawaii General Learner Outcomes (focus on one) • Hawaii Content and Performance Standards and benchmarks (focus only on a few) • "I Can" statements for students (match these to the benchmarks, in "kid language") • IEP objectives for students with special learning needs • Other objectives, if you need them Standards for teachers • Hawaii Teacher Performance Standards (focus on one) • Council for Exceptional Children (CEC) Standards, where applicable
Step 2 Assessment	**Evidence: How will your students demonstrate what they know and can do?**
Do steps 1, 2 and 3 match? Does it all make sense?	Performance task (be specific) • What will students do to show what they've learned? (Where's the evidence?) Criteria • How good is good enough? (Include checklists, rubrics, guidelines, instructions, etc.) • Rubrics with three categories (does not meet standards, meets standards, target) usually make the most sense for unit and lesson plans. • You don't always need a rubric—a checklist (yes/no) often will suffice.
Step 3 Learning Plan	**Learning: What experiences and instruction will help students learn?**
Do all steps match? Does it all make sense?	There are many ways to write learning/lesson plans! For example: • Introduction, learning activities, closure + materials, time, resources, modifications • Attending cue, anticipatory set, purpose, modeling, guided practice, independent practice, evaluation (state in step 2), closure • Do—Say—Write (get students actively engaged, talk about it, represent it in writing) • WHERETO (see Tomlinson and McTighe, page 31)
Step 4 Reflection	**What happened? What did you and your students learn? How will you improve the unit or lessons?**
	Questions to guide you: • What happened? (What did your students say and do? Help others see and hear it.)

FIGURE 4.8 DOE lesson planning guide

further viewing/theorizing, were visualized as strangely unfixed and unfamiliar. In my pursuit of the unknown, visual culture theory has been highly assistive given our interest in countering these truth(s), theoretically recognizable "by an awareness of spectacle as an autonomous site of contestation" (Cohen, 1998, p. 7). In his work *In/different Spaces*, Victor Burgin (2000) illustrates that "visual culture—the combined product of 'the media' and a variety of other spheres of image production—can no longer be seen as simply 'reflecting' or 'communicating' the world in which we live: it contributes to the making of this world" (p. 21–22).

The particular images (i.e., Figures 4.1–4.4) shared and critiqued in this narrative were selected for their broad typicality as increasingly common pictures or images present in common popular teacher education structural positions, including university syllabi, professional journals, web-based education consumer catalogues, professional teacher education organizations, schools, and classroom settings. For instance, I studied consumer goods from the following teacher education materials:

> *Curriculum guides:* statewide curriculum mapping and other normative exercises; university teacher education curriculum (i.e., course syllabi).
> *Popular textbooks:* syllabi; bookstore offerings.
> *Accreditation scales and norms accompanying normative scales:* NCATE and Specialized Professional Associations (SPA) affiliations (as an example, all elementary education programs approved by NCATE, like our host institution, must follow the Association for Childhood Education (ACEI) standards).

These visual samples were chosen based on their relative familiarity and increasing tendency to represent the field of teacher education more specifically as teacher education cultural props. As was mentioned, these particular images were visually studied and theoretically critiqued over a brief period of time (Tonkiss, 1998) as a way of understanding how a particular discourse is structured and how that structuring re-enacts certain kinds of knowledge.

Looking at Images

As I view the presented images again and again, I am struck then with considering my body's newfound, altered status, that active placement in a particular subjugated position whereby it has been conquered, dominated under the control of another. This is reminiscent of the notion of the 'stranger'—the foreigner, outsider, or alien in a country and society not their own—as well as the notion of strangeness within the self—a person's deep sense of being, as distinct from outside appearance and his or her conscious idea of self (http://www.powells.com/book/strangers-to-ourselves-9780231071574). Here I am reminded of the historical work of Mary Douglas (1966), which helped me understand how certain control measures act to bring purification back to my subjugated body—me the scapegoat, so that I am effectively cleaned of "contamination and reinstated as clean in their [my] own eyes . . ." (p. 14). To me, when I look at the photographic evidence and place that alongside another body, that body of personal evidence-memories I have shared here and elsewhere, I am dumbfounded about my newfound foreign stature, stature reminiscent of Kristeva's (1994) notion of "that which does not fit" (pp. 76–77).

Guimond (1994) revealed that there can be a "creative, constitutive relationship between images and a person's identity in autobiographical works because 'visual' memory, the 'reading' of images . . . can often be integral to the construction of [an] identity" (p. 191). The reading and rereading of images assists in my understanding that the subjugation of my body, my subjectivity, began early in my education career. Those readings help to reveal, just as Carriker (1998) noted, "that there is only one subject position . . . Such a privileged spot is reserved for those who share the appearance of the graceful, beautiful, delicate, and perfectly formed" (p. 37). While not closely aligning myself with these terms of "graceful, beautiful, delicate, and perfectly formed," I do see how the effective practitioner at the time of induction practices in my undergraduate and graduate career, the same follower of best practices today, readily and steadily, without questioning, assumes the 'one subject position.'

Colonization and Objectification

As I mentioned earlier, all elementary education programs approved by NCATE, like our host institution, must follow the Association for Childhood Education (ACEI) standards (https://acei.org). The first of 19 standards for elementary education programs is stated as:

> Development, learning, and motivation—Candidates know, understand, and use the major concepts, principles, theories, and research related to development of children and young adolescents to construct learning opportunities that support individual students' development, acquisition of knowledge, and motivation.

Many critical theorists (Burman, 1994; Canella, 1997; Canella & Viruru, 2004; O'Loughlin, 2006) have questioned the structural, normative nature of the early childhood and elementary profession(s) to continuously resort to dated singular theoretical perspectives (e.g., developmental psychology). Yet, as witnessed earlier, "major concepts, principles, theories and research" continue to dominate early childhood practices and child developmental theoretical principles (Ryan & Grieshaber, 2005). Burbules and Torres (2000) illustrate that our continued reliance on these standardized practices "privileges, if not directly imposes, particular policies for evaluation, financing, assessment, standards, teacher training, curriculum, instruction, and testing" (p. 15).

In his critique of the way natives were colonized through classic colonial photographic depictions, Ryan (1997) noted, "the processes of objectification in which photography played an important role were a central means by which individuals and collective cultures framed their understanding of what it meant to be 'normal' against that which was different or 'other'" (p. 145). This objectification works quite well in early education as time and time again, throughout the history of the field—from the enchanted romantic era, through progressivism and on into today—that child is valued for his/her natural being, s/he who is one with nature, innocent, to be protected, loving, angelic, hopeful, the everlasting iconic "ray of sunshine" continuously cast "as an agent of Western enlightenment" (p. 166). This "process of objectification was a critical aspect of gaining global dominance—the ability to visualize without actually seeing a place, its people, its plants, and other resources, and this kind of visualization relies on accumulating traces—sketches, descriptive notes, specimens, measurements—from those places" (Tobin, 1999, p. 213). This systematic, cumulative construction of 'the child' "coincides with the apogee of English colonial imperialism: indeed, it was an idea of 'the child'—of the not yet fully evolved or consequentialist subject—which made thinkable a colonial apparatus officially dedicated to the improvement of a colonized people" (Wallace, 1994, p. 176).

When that improvement includes scientific knowledge, popularized early in the last century during the child study movement, later with Piaget and others, and now in the newly defined age of empiricism (i.e., the United States's No Child Left Behind and Common Core), then we can only be hopeful for our intervening in the life of 'the child.' We first witnessed this quite clearly with the initial popularity and continued reliance (reconceptualists might say over-reliance) on Piaget's "articulation of cumulative developmental stages as the place in which various knowledges of 'the child'—in formation since the Enlightenment—accumulate in a newly hegemonizing, because 'scientific', discourse" (Wallace, 1994, p. 180). And so again, this process of objectification further clarified what it meant to be 'normal' against that which was different or 'other.'

While reading the images presented from these popular historical and current textbooks and teacher education journals, journals that consistently (i.e., monthly for paid members) reach hundreds of thousands of educational practitioners worldwide, we see both the construction of the idealized child(ren), childhood, and the fields of early, elementary, and secondary education, but we can also read "critically into the missing 'Other' child(ren)—'uncivilized, non-white, lower class'" (p. 146). The constant, continuous looking at the normative, idealized depiction(s) of the child leaves us critically considering notions of "what it means to be 'normal' versus that which is different or 'other.'" As Pajaczkowska (2001) notes in her work on feminist visual culture, "the seen is considered evidence, truth and factual, as sight establishes a particular subject relation to reality in which the visual aspect of an object is considered to be a property of the object itself" (p. 1). Early childhood education historically made sure the 'seen' was what they wanted to be ever-seen, normative images that have therefore functioned quite steadily as they have assisted in the imperialist shaping of particular identities, values, and histories by producing and legitimating specific cultural narratives and resources, bringing to mind Foucault's 'docile body.'

(Re)Reading a Field, (Re)Reading a Landscape

If we envision our collective theoretician/practitioner selves and the greater field from a critical, action-oriented research perspective (Gruenwald, 2003), to progress we have to self-consciously and collectively incorporate resistant methods of studying (Mohanty, 1995), interpreting, and further understanding the various disciplines we encounter in our individual and collective work. These potentially emancipatory, rebellious (MacCannell, 1999) methods could assist us in moving past the simple replaying of typical ways of seeing teacher education practices and assist us in reworking (Loomba, 1998) and renegotiating the past and the present (Tompkins, 1995). Part of our emancipatory practices includes moving out of traditional standardized educational modes of perceiving and further understanding our research methods and findings from multiple perspectives. My interests are tightly aligned with Lather's plea for "a multiplicity of readings by demonstrating how we cannot exhaust the meaning of the text, how a text can participate in multiple meanings without being reduced to any one, and how our different positionalities affect our reading of it" (1998, p. 125).

My work considers alternative theoretical and methodological landscapes and the multitude of different ways of knowing and navigating these spaces and places. In our thinking here we are attempting to (re)establish particular cartographies that assist us in critically deliberating and reconsidering teacher education. I recognize that our cartographical skills, these rewritten maps—maybe like Kristeva's *recasting of borders* notion, might not be of benefit for all, but personally they temporarily guide me in/outside of places known and unknown, knowable and unknowable. Part of the exciting and unsettling nature of this work is anticipating that in the reconceptualizing cartographic work, many theoretical and practical aspects of our theorizing could change, including, as Lefebvre (1991) revealed, the "objects represented [in the maps and their codes], the lens through which they are viewed, and the scale used" (pp. 85–86).

Initial work in this piece mirrors Rogoff's (2000) theoretical framework whereby this project pursued alternative ways of looking at "knowledge in which a semblance of parity and reciprocity might take place between the constitutive components of the study and through which a form of cultural politics could emerge from rather than be imposed on its materials" (p. 8). For my work here these research methods actively assist me in progressing in my respective discipline(s) as I seek to "open [up], disinterring the repressed and troubling questions . . . that loosen the ties that bind" (Pajaczkowska, 2001, p. 124). Visual culture theory offers tremendous opportunities for rewriting culture.

The success of the imperialist teacher education theoretical field can be attributed, in part, to the seductiveness of the discourses of so-called innovative education ideas and their ability to resonate with and feed upon hopes and fears (Canella & Viruru, 2004). In an uncertain world, these discourses offer a degree of certainty and security. They afford "a way of seeing the world, an order of things that . . . [can] be learned as true and proper" (McLeod, 2000, p. 21). They promise a 'sameness' of values, practices, perceptions, and representations regardless of context and create sharply delineated borders that separate the sanctioned from the unsanctioned, the appropriate from the inappropriate — in other words, "the safe from the unsafe" and "us from them" (Anzaldu, 1987, cited by Canella & Viruru, 2004 p. 27). And in doing so, they create a sense of connectedness, belonging, unity, and, dare it be said, superiority and exclusivity. In these ways, by their very seductiveness, they colonize minds and imaginations.

This seductiveness draws attention from the controls and restrictions put in place to preserve and enhance the cultural capital of early childhood education. These controls govern who is allowed to speak and listen, what is allowed to be spoken and heard, and who and what are silenced. In this way, early childhood educators, like children, become colonized subjects, defined in terms of the narrowly defined cultural capital they are accorded and permitted.

Imperialism comes at a cost because it is only by continually critiquing our knowledge bases and practices and how these are perpetuated that we can move forward as a field. To borrow from Canella and Viruru (2004), "the imposition of any *one* form of interpreting the world" limits possibilities and options (p. 94). It does so by legitimizing only some versions of reality, usually simplified, sanitized, and one-dimensional versions that subsume complexity and ambiguity, creating dangerous dualisms and judgments concerning what is condoned as appropriate and normal and what is not and, in many cases, fostering habits of authority, superiority, and arrogance rather than those of generosity and receptiveness to other possibilities. Is this what we want for innovative teacher education?

To counter the practice and legacy of imperialism, I urge support for endeavors to decolonize the field. Like Smith and Katz (1993), cited in Gruenwald (2003), here I use decolonization to refer to processes of "recognizing and dislodging dominant ideas, assumptions and ideologies as externally imposed" (p. 9) not simply for the sake of rejecting these but to open up new possibilities, especially those that lead to the greater likelihood of agency. These processes involve nurturing dispositions and abilities that enable one to read early childhood texts, traditions, and discourses 'against the grain'; to identify and critique alternative knowledge(s) and possibilities; to think and act otherwise to the early childhood canon; and to find ways to resist controlling forces, agents, and institutions (McLeod, 2000). A post-imperialist early childhood education would involve dismantling and reaching beyond the discursive and cultural boundaries that have traditionally characterized the field (Young, 2003). It would be characterized by generative relations between multiple discourses, readings, and practices and a dynamic hybridity characterized by complexity, negotiation, and change (Young, 2003) that move well past our continuous nostalgic acts of saturation (Lowenthal, 1985), acts that do not necessarily serve all of us equally well. Unless teacher education programs can redefine their respective cultural capital in this way, I believe they run the risk of being rendered an irrelevant imperialist relic.

Bibliography

Banks, M. (1998). Visual anthropology: Image, object and interpretation. In J. Prosser (Ed.), *Image-based research: A sourcebook for qualitative researchers* (pp. 9–23). Philadelphia: Falmer.

Beckett, J., & Cherry, D. (1994). Clues to events. In M. Bal & I.E. Boer (Eds.), *The point of theory: Practices of cultural analysis* (pp. 48–55). New York: Continuum.

Bloom, L. (1999). Introducing with other eyes: Looking at race and gender in visual culture. In L. Bloom (Ed.), *With other eyes: Looking at race and gender in visual culture* (pp. 1–16). Minneapolis: University of Minnesota Press.

Chambers, E. (2000). *Native tours: The anthropology of travel and tourism*. Long Grove, IL: Waveland Press.

Clancy-Smith, J., & Gouda, F. (1999). *Domesticating the empire: Race, gender, and family life in French and Dutch colonialism*. Charlottesville: University Press of Virginia.

Crimshaw, C., & Urry, J. (1997). Tourism and the photographic eye. In C. Rojek & J. Urry (Eds.), *Touring cultures: Transformations of travel and theory* (pp. 176–195). New York: Routledge.

Jarvis, B. (1998). *Postmodern cartographies: The geographical imagination in contemporary American culture*. New York: St. Martin's Press.

Johnson, R. (2005, March). *The naturalization of the early childhood citizen in a global world*. Paper presented at the International Globalization, Diversity, and Education Conference, Pullman, WA.

Shaafsma, D. (1998). Performing the self: Constructing written and curricular fictions. In T. Popkewitz & M. Brennan (Eds.), *Foucault's challenge: Discourse, knowledge, and power in education* (pp. 255–277). New York: Teachers College Press.

Tripp, S. (2004). Haunting in the age of electronic post-literacy. In K.D. McBride (Ed.), *Visual media and the humanities: A pedagogy of representation* (pp. 27–45). Knoxville: University of Tennessee Press.

Trouillot, M.R. (2003). *Global transformations: Anthropology and the modern world*. London: Palgrave Macmillan.

Urry, J. (2002). *The tourist gaze*. Thousand Oaks, CA: Sage.

Young, R.J.C. (1995). *Colonial desire: Hybridity in theory, culture and race*. New York: Routledge.

Zurbrugg, N. (1997). Introduction: Just what is it that makes Baudrillard's ideas so different, so appealing. In N. Zurbrugg (Ed.), *Jean Baudrillard: Art and artefact* (pp. 1–6). Thousand Oaks, CA: Sage.

References

Bakhtin, M. (1990). *Art and answerability: Early philosophical essays* (M. Holquist and V. Liapunov, Eds., V. Liapunov, Trans.). Austin: University of Texas Press.

Bal, M. (2001). *Looking in: The art of viewing*. New York: Routledge.

Burbules, N.C., & Torres, C.A. (2000). *Globalization and education: Critical perspectives (Social Theory, Education and Cultural Change)*. New York: Routledge.

Burgin, V. (2000). *In/different spaces: Place and memory in visual culture*. Berkeley: University of California Press.

Burman, E. (1994). *Deconstructing developmental psychology*. New York: Routledge.

Canella, G. (1997). *Deconstructing early childhood education: Social justice and revolution*. New York: Peter Lang.

Canella, G., & Viruru, R. (2004). *Childhood and postcolonization*. New York: Taylor & Francis.

Carriker, K. (1998). *Created in our image: The miniature body of the doll as subject and object*. London: Associated University Presses.

Cohen, J. (1998). *Spectacular allegories: Postmodern American writing and the politics of seeing*. Sterling, VA: Pluto Press.

Cowling, M. (1989). *The artist as anthropologist: The representation of type and character in Victorian art*. Cambridge: Cambridge University Press.

Davey, N. (1999). The hermeneutics of seeing. In B. Sandywell & I. Heywood (Eds.), *Interpreting visual culture: Explorations in the hermeneutics of the visual* (pp. 3–29). New York: Routledge.

Douglas, M. (1966). *Purity and danger: An analysis of concepts of pollution and taboo.* London: Routledge & Kegan Paul.

Fischman, G.F. (2001). Reflections about images, visual culture and educational research. *Educational Researcher, 30*(8), 28–33.

Grieshaber, S., & Ryan, S. (2005). Transforming ideas and practices. In S. Ryan & S. Grieshaber, (Eds.), *Practical transformations and transformational practices: Globalization, postmodernism, and early childhood education* (pp. 3–17). San Diego, CA: Elsevier/JAI.

Groth, P. (1997). Frameworks for cultural landscape study. In P. Groth & T.W. Bressi (Eds.), *Understanding ordinary landscapes* (pp. 1–21). New Haven, CT: Yale University Press.

Gruenwald, D.E. (2003). The best of both worlds: A critical pedagogy of place. *Educational Researcher, 32*(4), 3–12.

Guimond, J. (1994). Auteurs as autobiographers: Images by Jo Spence and Cindy Sherman. *Modern Fiction Studies, 40*(3), 573–591.

Hirsch, M. (1994). Masking the subject: Practicing theory. In M. Bal & I.E. Boer (Eds.), *The point of theory: Practicing cultural analysis* (pp. 109–124). Amsterdam: University of Amsterdam Press.

Jacobs, K. (2004). Optic/Haptic/Abject: Revisioning indigenous media in Victor Masayesva, Jr. and Leslie Marmon Silko. *Journal of Visual Culture, 3*(3), 291–316.

Jameson, F. (1990). *Signatures of the visible.* New York: Routledge.

Jenks, C. (1995). *Visual culture.* London: Routledge.

Johnson, R. (2004, April). *(mis)Representations of identity in pretend play props: Critiquing pretend play from a visual cultural perspective.* Paper presented at the Annual Meeting of the American Educational Research Association, San Diego, CA.

Johnson, R. (2009). *Idealized portraits of (dis)embodied figures: A visual cultural-historiographic analysis of early childhood education.* Paper presented at the Annual Meeting of the American Educational Research Association, San Diego, CA.

Johnson, R. (2010). Putting myself in the picture: Oppositional looks as sites of resistance. In M. O'Loughlin & R. Johnson (Eds.), *Imagining children otherwise: Theoretical and critical perspectives on childhood subjectivity* (pp. 111–134). New York: Peter Lang Press.

Johnson, R. (2011, April). *Critiquing traditional colonial practices in teacher education: Interpreting normative practices through visual culture analyses.* Paper presented at the Annual Meeting of the American Educational Research Association, New Orleans, LA.

Johnson, R. (2013). Contesting contained bodily coaching experiences. *Sport, Education and Society, 18*(5), 630–647, doi: 10.1080/13573322.2012.761964.

Kristeva, J. (1994). *Strangers to ourselves* (Leon S. Roudiez, Trans.). New York: Columbia University Press.

Lather, P. (1998). Staying dumb? Feminist research and pedagogy within the postmodern. In H. Simons and M. Billig (Eds.), *After postmodernism: Reconstructing ideology critique* (pp. 101–132). Thousand Oaks, CA: Sage.

Lefebvre, H. (1991). *The production of space.* Malden, MA: Blackwell.

Lewis, C., & Fabos, B. (2005). Instant messaging, literacies, and social identities. *Reading Research Quarterly, 40*(4), 470–501.

Loomba, A. (1998). *Colonialism/postcolonialism.* New York: Routledge.

Lowenthal, D. (1985). *The past is a foreign country.* Cambridge: Cambridge University Press.

MacCannell, D. (1999). *The tourist: A new theory of the leisure class.* Los Angeles: University of California Press.

MacDougall, D. (1997). The visual in anthropology. In M. Banks & H. Morphy (Eds.), *Rethinking visual anthropology* (pp. 276–295). London: Yale University Press.

McLeod, J. (2000). *Beginning postcolonialism.* Manchester, UK: Manchester University Press.

Metz, C. (1982). *Psychoanalysis and cinema: The imaginary signifier*. London: Macmillan.

Mohanty, C.T. (1995). Feminist encounters: Locating the politics of experience. In L. Nicholson & S. Seldman (Eds.), *Social postmodernism: Beyond identity politics* (pp. 68–86). Cambridge: Cambridge University Press.

National Council for Accreditation of Teacher Education. (2002). *Professional standards for the accreditation of schools, colleges, and departments of education*. Washington, DC: NCATE.

O'Loughlin, M. (2006). On knowing and desiring children: The significance of the unthought known. In G. Boldt & P. Salvio (Eds.), *Love's return: Psychoanalytic essays on childhood teaching and learning* (pp. 185–201). New York: Routledge.

Orvell, M. (1995). *After the machine: Visual arts and the erasing of cultural boundaries*. Jackson: University Press of Mississippi.

Pajaczkowska, C. (2001). Issues in feminist visual culture. In F. Carson & C. Pajaczkowska (Eds.), *Feminist visual culture* (pp. 123–128). New York: Routledge.

Pukui, M. (1983). '*Olelo No 'eau* 203. Honolulu, HI: Bishop Museum Press.

Rogoff, I. (2000). *Terra infirma: Geography's visual culture*. New York: Routledge.

Rose, G. (2001). *Visual methodologies*. Thousand Oaks, CA: Sage.

Ryan, J.R. (1997). *Picturing empire: Photography and the visualization of the British empire*. Chicago: University of Chicago Press.

Ryan, S., & Grieshaber, S. (Eds.). (2005). *Practical transformations and transformational practices: Globalization, postmodernism, and early childhood education*. San Diego, CA: Elsevier/JAI.

Sekula, A. (1983). Photography between labour and capital. In B. Buchloh & R. Wilkie, (Eds.), *Mining photographs and other pictures: A selection from the negative archives of Shedden Studio, Glace Bay, Cape Breton, 1948–1968* (pp. 193–268). Halifax: Press of the Nova Scotia College of Art and Design.

Sturken, M., & Cartwright, L. (2001). *Practices of looking: An introduction to visual culture*. New York: Oxford University Press.

Tobin, B.F. (1999). *Picturing imperial power: Colonial subjects in eighteenth-century British painting*. Durham, NC: Duke University Press.

Tompkins, J. (1995). "Spectacular resistance": Metatheatre in post-colonial drama. *Modern Drama, 38*, 42–51.

Tonkiss, F. (1998). Analyzing discourse. In C. Seale (Ed.), *Researching society and culture* (pp. 245–260). London: Sage.

Wallace, J. (1994). De-Scribing the water babies. In C. Tiffin & A. Lawson (Eds). *De-Scribing empire* (p. 171–184). London: Routledge.

Young, R.J.C. (2003). *Post-colonialism: A very short introduction*. Oxford: Oxford University Press.

5

PARENTS AS PRODUCERS OF ENDURING KNOWLEDGE THROUGH INQUIRY

Paige M. Bray and Erin M. Kenney

Introduction—Context and Arc of the Work

This chapter will address the use of collaborative, community-based, participatory methodology as a means of not only delivering information to parents as consumers of information, but also, and more importantly, recognizing parent knowledge and fostering parent leadership. Parents are the producers of enduring knowledge for their own children as well as vital conduits of knowledge for their community. By attending to parent knowledge in systemic ways, early childhood education and community supports move beyond token parent contributions and marginalized parent influence. When engaged in authentic problem-solving, parents become leaders who can contribute in meaningful and productive ways.

Our scholarly work in dynamic inquiry draws from the rich legacy of practitioner-based inquiry, valuing local knowledge and belief in human capacity and agency writ large. Young children, early care educators, and parents are understood to be the stewards of their lives and operating in a context. Included within this area of scholarship has been our three years of research with parent leaders. Thus, our scholarly work in dynamic inquiry has not only been vested in community-specific contexts, but also serves as a form of capacity building. This scholarly effort has been formalized in the Parent Inquiry Initiative, known as Parentii (see http://www.hartford.edu/parentii for more information), as part of the Institute for Translational Research (ITR) at the University of Hartford as an outgrowth of Bray's original work in teacher inquiry. The ITR serves as a college-wide umbrella for collaborative research activities promoting academic excellence through relevant, community-engaging research and scholarship. This research reinforces the importance of early childhood education by linking research and programming, specifically research methods foregrounding parents and community. The establishment of Parentii furthers the understanding of parent leadership as a component of necessary infrastructure in early childhood success. Parentii is now contributing to decades of the interwoven efforts of community and state-level entities providing information, access, and education to Connecticut's parents and families.

The conceptualization of the child operating in the context of family, cultural, community, and societal norms as articulated by Bronfenbrenner (1979) undergirds the work that took place in partnership with the parent co-researchers. For the purposes of this work, learning community refers to the parent co-researchers and university-based researchers. Parent co-researcher refers to parents who were members of this learning community. The title co-researcher identifies and honors parents and university researchers as essential collaborators in the creation of enduring knowledge through our shared research process.

This work began with the Parent Information Action Research Project funded by the William Caspar Graustein Memorial Fund. This initial two-year project set out to engage parent co-researchers from five communities in inquiry and specific action research methods to identify issues in community-oriented parent leadership. These engaged parent co-researchers, in collaboration with each other and the parents in their home communities, identified their own inquiry questions and practical outcomes. During the first year of the project the parent co-researchers worked with us as the university co-researchers along with colleagues at both the Memorial Fund and Kettering Foundation to name an overarching question focused on the well-being of young children across the state: How should we nurture children to be healthy and make better choices?

At that point, a plan for learning what answers parents, residents young and old, business owners, educators, and community members would provide was developed with the parent co-researchers. Across the state, parent co-researchers enacted this plan and listened to over one hundred individual responses. In addition, a statewide forum was conducted. We ensured full participation over a period of months, consistently meeting with the parent co-researcher team to reflect on experiences observed. Furthermore, reflections included questioning if we had met our own expectations to connect to the diversity of residence in a given town or city and the state. The outcome of this first year of the project was the issue guide publication, *Looking for Answers Together* (http://discovery.wcgmf.org/lookingforanswers together). An issue guide is a "nonpartisan, unbiased resource to help you think through a difficult issue in alternative ways, weighing and evaluating values, priorities, pros, cons and trade-offs" (Public Agenda, 2015). This issue guide publication has been produced in English and Spanish to increase access and engagement throughout a given community. This issuing was particularly important in our specific communities where English-only materials privileged the institutional representatives and deterred authentic parent engagement. English and Spanish guides were distributed locally and nationally as a product of the project.

In the second year we continued the work with the parent co-researchers as a learning community, coming together at least monthly to observe actions, reflect on implications, challenge ideas, and support each other. During this year, the parent co-researchers now named their own specific inquiry question focusing on the well-being of young children in their specific community. Each parent co-researcher developed a community-specific project plan informed by what they heard during the first year of listening. While all parent co-researchers worked in the learning community, some worked solo and others worked in pairs on a community-specific project. Subsequently, the action step(s) were undertaken with focused intent, with the learning community offering compassionate listeners and solution-oriented feedback generated by Bray and Kenney's group facilitation in the face of obstacles. In addition to being a problem-solving resource, the learning community acted as a buoying source, celebrating each inroad and success. With the ongoing conversation among co-researchers and a shared vested interest in authentic outcomes, parents statewide cut across the isolation that comes with bringing new ideas and actions.

As co-researchers pushed forward in their geographic locations, the learning community functioned as an intellectual, conceptual, and strategic sounding board. The outcome of the second year of individual parent co-researchers applying the inquiry and action research cycle in their own communities appeared at the local level. Additionally, parent co-researchers presented their application of this inquiry and action research cycle at a statewide Connecticut conference (see presentation documentation at http://discovery.wcgmf.org/stone_soup_2012 and video documentation *Looking for Answers within Our Community* at http://parentii.word press.com/2013/10/18/looking-for-answers-within-our-community/).

The university-based researchers sought to further build on the parent co-researchers' experience by pursuing the desire to make public parent leadership work beyond typical scholarly venues (see Bray, Pedro, Kenney, & Gannotti, 2014 as an example). This resulted in securing additional funding for accessible dissemination from the William Caspar Graustein Memorial Fund. The expressed intent was for public and multi-media outcomes (Bray & Kenney, 2012; see also the YouTube video *Parent Information Action Research Project* at http://www. youtube.com/watch?v=25GEqHrPWYY). Such outcomes captured the parent co-researchers' experience of engaging in dynamic inquiry over a two-year period. This video is the first of three public access, mainstream, multi-media deliverables and brings the results of the research back to the parent leaders and communities in an accessible format.

Finally, the desire to support parent leaders' capacity to establish sustainable, self-perpetuating networks or learning communities has garnered the third dimension of this William Caspar Graustein Memorial Fund–supported research that dovetails with the Kettering Foundation learning agreement; this agreement is to follow the parent co-researcher lead in disseminating the *Looking for Answers Together* guide into communities.

This collective documentation of the parent co-researcher experience and the central role of parents as knowledge producers as opposed to consumers offers a bold and unique methodological significance and methodology very much in line with aspects of engaged scholarship. In the initial and subsequent phases of funded research focusing on parent information and leadership, the university-based researchers engaged the parent co-researchers, acting as facilitators and as resources, but not as the sole producer of knowledge. In this collaborative, participatory work is an inherent exchange of information, which cuts across the potential power dynamics of research where the university-based 'researcher' holds expertise and knowledge without the intent or obligation of sharing this information with the participant, or 'research subject,' from which data will be extracted. In this project, knowledge was exchanged among all people in the process with the express intent of knowledge production and capacity building across the community.

Theoretical Frame

The relational understanding of family and community (Bronfenbrenner, 1979) sets the theoretical frame for this project. Bronfenbrenner's (1979; 2005) ecological systems theory serves to ground work with parents, delineating the importance of the environment and socialization (frequently provided by parent(s)) on children's learning gains. Ecological systems theory notes the importance of family contexts as they hold the strongest influence on the young child. Bronfenbrenner (1979) further distinguishes the value of community environments and their potential lasting influence on both the young child and the family unit. Understanding that a child affects as well as is affected by the settings in which a child spends time, the quality of the child's connection to these settings (and person(s) within the same settings) also has important implications for his/her development.

Across the arc of this Parent Inquiry Initiative (Parentii) work, we have continually utilized a community-based (Greenwood & Levin, 2000; Horton, 1998; Stringer, 1999; 2008), participatory action research model (Freire, 1974; Kemmis & McTaggart, 2000; Maguire, 1987) with the parent co-researchers. It is important to note that the context of this work (as previously explained) serves as explicit framing of this work. We understand this work is located in an explicit set of social values and assumptions inherent to the context-specific methodology. These assumptions include the research process as: a) engaged 'with' people in a process, not 'for' or 'on' research subjects; b) a democratic, inclusive process that enables participation of all parent leaders while developing critical consciousness; c) an equitable process recognizing human capacity and an individual's ability to contribute; and d) a liberating and life-enhancing activity with the expressed commitment to practical outcomes that transform structures and relationships.

Methodology

The specific community-based, participatory action research methods utilized are a systematic cycle of question/problem identification that informs the process of inquiry and its practical aftereffects. The systematic cycle begins with the process of identifying, and articulating, inquiry questions. Literally, what will be the focus of the inquiry and action research methods? At first this inquiry can seem daunting, especially if individuals think the origin of the inquiry is outside themselves or their experience. Inquiry questions come from within and are located in our own sphere. Sometimes called a 'burning question,' inquiry questions are identified by paying attention to what one consistently wonders about. In thinking about the work, what comes up over and over again? Asking, "What topic is consistently on my mind that I must talk to my colleagues and family members about?" Such an inquiry is almost a puzzle or riddle one must work out. As noted, identifying an inquiry question is seldom accomplished in isolation. It is through talking and/or writing in a learning community that the nuances and dimension of the questions take shape. This initial act of identifying the question can be a new experience for parents. The undertaking serves as the initial capacity building experience in order to embrace one's own intellectual authority to determine the question and define the inquiry, which can be a new experience for parents.

Once the focus of the inquiry is identified, the action research cycle is engaged. This is an opportunity to build capacity in taking action. More typically through life experience, parents have a foothold on taking action via advocating for their own children, community organizing, and even parent leadership development opportunities. Yet this action research cycle builds capacity by honing that action in on desired effects. The cycle of: 1) plan, 2) take action, 3) observe what occurs as a result of that action, and 4) take the time to reflect on what has been observed is a cycle that is repeated. The intentionality of the cycle is what moves the inquiry toward authentic action outcomes.

Data Collection

During the initial two years of this research, data sources included: engaged collaborative team meetings and web-based interactions over time, focus groups, and a final individual, in-depth interview (Rossman & Rallis, 2003; Seidman, 2006) with the parent co-researchers to capture their lived experience (Collins, 2002), and their reflections on such experience, in their own words. Practical effects included: community-based action projects undertaken by each co-researcher as well as a nationally distributed issue guide, *Looking for Answers Together: How Should We Nurture Children to Be Healthy and Make Better Choices?* (Bray, 2013). The conceptualizing and ownership of this issue and the issue guide by the co-researchers are captured in other scholarly work (Bray et al., 2014).

Data—An Inquiry Example

Here, we present data from across the initial three years of our work, with parent co-researchers in the same systematic cycle of question/problem identification format that we have utilized throughout the project. Presented this way, this chapter is both a model of how one can address questions as well as a resource for how this specific question around communication was addressed in this research context. The trustworthiness (Merriam, 1998) of this research was ensured through multiple techniques: a) prolonged engagement, b) researcher journal, and c) inherent and extensive member checking. After we present the data, we address practical aftereffects of the study.

Initial Question

In what ways do communication structure(s) reflect the formal and informal power dynamics operating in this parent inquiry research work?

Plan for Intentional Action

The communication structure for this research work was forged from the early phases to ensure that parent co-researchers were at the center of the communication (see Figure 5.1). There were explicit and direct lines of communication established between the university-based researchers and parent co-researchers that set some of the more typical community and provider players outside the direct communication from the very beginning. The plan was enacted in order to keep the decision-making power located with the parent co-researchers rather than have there be any buffering or mitigating features to the communication flow. As well, this action plan was committed to during the first years of inquiry (see Figure 5.2) and has continued during the trajectory of this research (see Figure 5.3).

Action

The enactment of the communications structure over the course of the project proved to require a continual re-centering of the parent co-researchers by directing others to them for responses and answers. This was part of our visible efforts as facilitators and participatory researchers to keep communication flowing in order to further the parent-led work in contexts where 'professionals' or systems disregard or co-opt parent action. Like all plans, the actual enactment has many moving parts and complex interactions. The type of information—administrative, financial, reporting, outreach, securing of physical resources—mattered greatly. In the daily doing of the communicating, reflexive power structures were consistently revealed that sought to revert to dominant communication patterns and structures. For example, providers and coordinators who have streamlined the handling of fiscal matters or community outreach sought to use familiar channels rather than parent co-researchers implementing what made sense to meet their needs.

Participatory Observations

In our participatory observations, we used researcher journals, meeting notes, and multi-media documentation to capture what co-researchers meant by "information

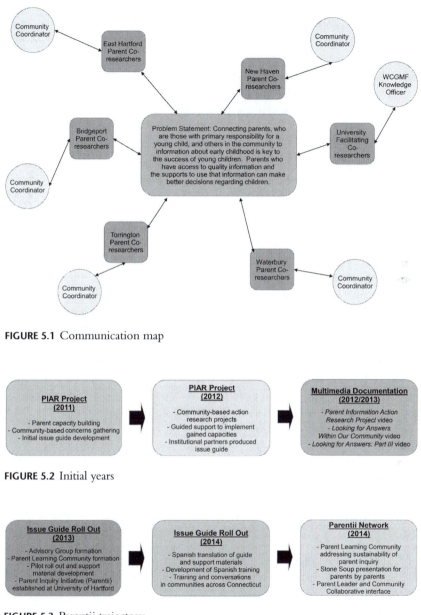

FIGURE 5.1 Communication map

FIGURE 5.2 Initial years

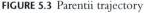

FIGURE 5.3 Parentii trajectory

is power" in the context of our shared work. An important aspect of forming a supportive learning community was establishing norms and expectations regarding communication both during and outside of meetings. Basic meeting norms were established including basic communication expectations and researchers' promises to provide food, childcare, and transportation assistance to all meetings.

University-based researchers made clear that the communication should flow directly between the parent researchers and the researchers. As a learning community, the team then agreed upon certain levels of communication and support beyond the team including support from parent co-researcher to parent co-researcher and from parent co-researcher to community liaisons and members.

When not in face-to-face group settings, we faced the challenge of communicating with parent co-researchers residing in locations across the state with varying levels of transportation access. Furthermore, parent co-researchers presented initially with a broad spectrum of technological capabilities and access. Transportation challenges were frequently resolved by us traveling to the parent researchers' towns for meetings with individual community research teams. This was a natural application of available resources. People with cars traveled as much as 45 minutes to those who relied on public transportation. Additionally, group meetings were scheduled in a central location easily accessible by public transportation.

Communication between physical meetings was addressed in several ways. In addition to the variety of modes already mentioned, a private website was created including such features as a discussion board, file storage, and individual community team pages. This website allowed parent co-researchers to have constant access to research materials, a schedule of events, and the opportunity to be in contact with other parent co-researchers between meetings. Creating communication modes that did not place us at the center and at least facilitated, if not fostered, direct parent co-researcher to parent co-researcher interactions was the intent. The discussion board particularly became a place the parent co-researchers utilized as a sounding board to brain-storm new ideas, offer feedback on materials, and generally support one another throughout the project. This website also served the additional, and transparent, purpose of archiving materials and parent researcher discussions for later use.

The following is a synthesis of our observations about effective and desirable communications:

- Accuracy: Communication content was required to be accurate and complete if parent co-researchers could effectively make use of it for their inquiry. Communications that were in anyway coded with professional jargon, assumed a level of background knowledge, or required one to 'be in the loop' to make meaning of the code only frustrated the co-researchers as is set them outside their own work.
- Applicability: Communication needed to be direct, focusing on the essential issue(s). Extraneous information or talking around the central point bogged down communication and at times could be seen as undermining efforts.
- Mode: Communication mode was paramount. Parent co-researchers had different levels of access and ability to be connected via email, voice, text, web-based forums, or postal service. In addition, transportation to physical meetings created yet another level of communication to coordinate. While

there was always steady whole-group communication, additional efforts were customized to make sure everyone received communications.

- Reliability and credibility: Communication was quickly assessed for reliability and credibility by the parent co-researchers. To be able to depend on communication coming with enough advance notice and consistency mattered greatly to the parent co-researchers with their multi-faceted, complex lives. The credibility of the source of communication determined whether response(s) were provided or not.

To further illuminate this section, we interject additional detailing of our data. Our co-researcher journal took the form of a shared electronic document. We also kept individual journals with reflections about our learning as we bring different life experience and were at distinctive career places. Our co-researcher document provided a common space for our facilitating researcher thinking and meaning making about the co-construction with parents as well as the layers of university and philanthropic demands. The content of the entries included noting shared and distinctive perspectives such as how parents noted their direct access to resources and the response to their requests for their work without need to align to institutional initiatives—their agenda became our primary agenda. This documentation was also where we captured the most effective mode of communication for each parent. Parents receive many general emails and fliers, but this work intentionally documented (see meeting notes) and crossed technological access and literacy issues by customizing our efforts to ensure effective communication.

Our meeting notes documented the discussion and interactions of our learning community. There was some structure provided to our meetings and the notes by our constructed timelines, which identified items needing attention; however, the bulk of the notes captured questions, ideas, required or requested resources, definitions, and decisions. A key example is the documenting of the initial discussions and meaning making of what we understood "parent" in the initial project title—Parent Information Action Research Project—to mean. Multiple iterations of a working definition over months were documented. And finally the agreed-upon definition that would be used in the guide was documented. During the meetings, notes were taken on chart paper or using a computer and projector so the note taking was visible to all in the moment and was being edited or under revision while in the process of being created. Another key example is documenting the introductory information presented about action research, connecting that to an individual's prior experience and points of reference, and identifying what we collectively understood as the next need or step. After a meeting, notes were transcribed and circulated back to all members of the learning community for correction, reference, and reflection. The notes, and particularly the agreed-upon next steps, informed subsequent meetings or web-based communication.

Multi-media documentation began as still photographs with artifacts used to make visible individual efforts to the full learning community. An early public presentation made clear the power of parents' voices spoken rather than quoted in print. Photo documentation continued throughout, and culminating documentation of the initial two years was done using video. This video, *Parent Information Action Inquiry Project* (Bray & Kenney, 2012), was intentionally produced for YouTube dissemination and linked to web-based outlets for visibility. These early multi-media documentations became the basis for a sustained commitment to accessible dissemination (Bray & Kenney, 2014).

What is pivotal about our data is the role it played in informing the co-construction. The diversity of personal experience, cultural norms, educational history, and skills among those of us in the learning community was rich and at times wild. Through our individual reflections, the transparent and co-constructed documentation, we were able to name the experiences with power differentials, desired individual trajectories, and community action. While we did not start with a common vocabulary of 'positivism' or 'neoliberal' or even shared understanding of 'parent' or 'information' or 'action research,' our data informed our understandings. What we shared was common experiences with inequities of power or the feeling one gets when someone is co-opting the agenda. Each of us could speak to the power and the reality of our lives and community. And like academics, practitioners, and the population at large, there remains a range of beliefs and conceptual alignments among us. Thus the role of the facilitators, not necessarily that of the university-based researchers, but as the facilitators, is moving the work forward through data. The facilitator then is not only the documenter but also the provisioner, creating a supportive environment including learning opportunities that do move an individual and the collective to another place.

Reflection

Parent inquiry and action research methods build upon human capacity in a systematic way. This work offers an authentic example of co-constructing knowledge, honoring parent co-researchers for the knowledge they possess as well as vital knowledge producers. The parent co-researchers' engagement with and through inquiry was an intellectual capacity building experience. The parent co-researchers' repeated enactment of the action research cycle was capacity building of applied skills.

We experienced, consistently and profoundly, genuine exchange of information. This information and feedback stretched our capacities as we sought to find effective modes of reciprocal sharing with the parent co-researchers and their communities. Our engagement in the learning community brought into questions norms of interactions as our involvement was seeking to cut across the potential power dynamic of research where the 'researcher' holds expertise and knowledge. The decoupling of university researcher expert authority from facilitator role assisted in our addressing the assumption that the facilitators would dictate norms rather than facilitate agreed-upon norms. An additional layer was the group ownership of norms and self-monitoring rather than positioning the facilitators as enforcers. This initial decoupling of expert authority from facilitator roles established co-researcher authority and responsibility. It was on these enacted decisions that initial, hard-won trust was established and norms internalized.

Conclusion

There are several enduring understandings across the arc of our work with parent co-researchers that we believe inform not only specific community-based, participatory action research methods, but also reveal nuances of engaging in co-constructing processes of inquiry. These practical understandings not only inform our specific trajectory, but also the focus of further research efforts.

- Information that is important to parents is that which is desired by, and therefore relevant to, parents.
- Inquiry is both a skill set and a set of procedures toward parents' dynamic understanding (both knowledge production and capacity building).
- Prioritizing listening, learning with application, and engagement is not only good protocol, but all three serve as forms of accountability.
- Systems tend to design 'answers' and desire them neatly packaged with shrink wrap for easy dissemination; however, as soon as ideas are sealed in shrink wrap they are without air, dead, no longer in the making, and thus no longer responsive to individual people or specific community contexts.
- There is power in the teaching and modeling of inquiry as when we co-created the *Looking for Answers Together* guide. There is also power in having supported opportunity to implement the cycle of inquiry independently, for example in pursuit of community-specific questions.

This methodology and the particular methods focused on parents being producers of vital knowledge as well as engaged stakeholders in participatory, community-based research. The intended value-added resultant for this initiative are:

- Parents *owning* the data;
- Parents listening for community needs that directly inform inquiry process;
- Parents making data-driven decisions;
- Parents taking action towards desired community-based outcomes.

These parent co-constructed insights call for revisiting of typical early childhood education and community systems in order to move beyond token parent contributions and marginalized parent influence. Our research learnings as documented by our meeting notes and accessible dissemination reinforce the need to listen to parents, the importance of spaces for parents to hear each other and engage in the complexities of inquiry. Our research learnings also call for more typical parent engagement to connect with parents in solution-oriented efforts around authentic community-based issues. As is the nature of all inquiry, from our research learnings also came more questions: How can we keep co-research authentic and meaningful? In what ways can we address the power-stratified norms we encounter in institutions as we engage in a learning community trying to cut across such norms? What is the place for direct information to develop skill sets that can be in tension with shared decision making as we engage in intentional actions?

Final Discussion

The seminal ecological model underscores the importance of understanding the environment and systems that affect a child's learning, especially in the early childhood years. Parents, arguably the child's first teachers and professionals (e.g., teachers, community-based caregivers), play a unique role in nurturing young children and ensuring positive child outcomes. This work brings parents together with early childhood professionals in a common research goal and offers an opportunity to garner understandings of each other. This information underscores an urgent need to engage in reflective dialogue (Stein & Gewivtzman, 2003) more broadly and dual-impact capacity building work, specifically.

The *Looking for Answers Together* guide provides a framework for having reflective dialogue around the subject of nurturing young children. The development of the tangible issue guide outcome honored existing parent knowledge and provided experiential learning designed to build up, and upon, the capacity of parent co-researchers. Effectively taking parent co-researchers from their starting place as adult learners and moving collectively forward in their capabilities meant balancing our commitment to a shared understanding of an inquiry and action research structure while also remaining flexible enough to respond to individual and contextual needs. Parent co-researchers' self-reported being prepared to lead in the video-captured final interviews. As participant observers witnessing parent co-researchers leading in community settings across the state and effectively furthering the dialogue surrounding nurturing young children, we are not only corroborating their self-reporting but also underscoring the actual impact of their efforts. Because of the parent co-researchers' efforts, conversations about nurturing young children have occurred in new contexts along with existing spaces. These efforts by parent co-researchers as leaders in their communities and across the state have the ability to influence how children are nurtured at multiple levels across the ecological systems model, including early care and education settings.

While the documentation of this work has been supported by higher education structures, state and national philanthropic entities, and the diverse human capacity of the individuals involved, engaging in inquiry and enacting community-based action research does not require much in the way of resources beyond knowledge and time. All of the actual work with parent co-researchers has occurred in community centers, schools, even the local house of worship, for these were the centrally located places. And while this work has had investment in documentation, there is no question that all resources have aimed toward authentic, systemic change, one parent at a time.

In closing, we want to underscore that it has been the visibility of the parent co-researchers themselves in a variety of typical and atypical settings that continues to inform what active parents can do for themselves, their children, and their community around nurturing all of our communities' young children. In this work, parent co-researchers literally created spaces for new conversations and co-created a tool to promote deliberative exchange. Not focusing on education exclusively, this work further informed consumers of all education and reinforced parents as producers of enduring knowledge about their children. Healthy parents can support their children, as a community can support parents in nurturing their children toward meaningful growth as engaged and contributing members of community.

References

Bray, P.M. (2013, May). *Looking for answers together: How should we nurture children to be healthy and make better choices?* Kettering Foundation Issue Guide, invited manuscript. Connecticut dissemination by William Caspar Graustein Memorial Fund; National dissemination by National Issues Forum. Retrieved from http://www.nifi.org/discussion_guides/detail.aspx?itemID=24236&catID=15

Bray, P.M., & Kenney, E.M. (2012, May). *Parent Information Action Inquiry Project.* Video documentary capturing parent experience during 22 months of the Parent Information Action Research Project. Running time 10 minutes. Funded by the William Caspar Graustein Memorial Fund, RFP: Parent Leadership Inquiry.

Bray, P.M., & Kenney, E.M. (2014). Parent leaders taking the lead: Community-based, participatory research and co-constructed relevance. *Journal of Public Scholarship in Higher Education, 4,* 93–109.

Bray, P.M., Pedro, J.Y., Kenney, E.M., & Gannotti, M. (2014). Collaborative action inquiry: A tool for, and result of, parent learning and leadership. *Journal of Community Engagement and Scholarship,* 7(1), 3–14.

Bronfenbrenner, U. (1979). *The ecology of human development.* Cambridge, MA: Harvard University Press.

Bronfenbrenner, U. (2005). *Making human beings human: Bioecological perspectives on human development.* Thousand Oaks, CA: Sage.

Collins, P.C. (2002). *Black feminist thought: Knowledge, consciousness, and the politics of empowerment.* New York: Routledge.

Freire, P. (1974). *Pedagogy of the oppressed.* New York: Seabury.

Greenwood, D.J., & Levin, M. (2000). In N.K. Denzin & Y.S. Lincoln (Eds.), *Handbook of qualitative research* (2nd ed., pp. 85–106). Thousand Oaks, CA: Sage.

Horton, M. (1998). *The long haul: An autobiography.* New York: Teachers College Press.

Kemmis, S., & McTaggart, R. (2000). In N.K. Denzin & Y.S. Lincoln (Eds.), *Handbook of qualitative research* (2nd ed., pp. 567–605). Thousand Oaks, CA: Sage.

Maguire, P. (1987). *Doing participatory research: A feminist approach.* Amherst, MA: The Center for International Education, School of Education, University of Massachusetts.

Merriam, S.B. (1998). *Qualitative research and case study applications in education*. San Francisco, CA: Jossey-Bass.

Public Agenda. (2015). Issue guides. Retrieved from http://www.publicagenda.org/pages/issue-guides

Rossman, G.B., & Rallis, S.F. (2003). *Learning in the field: An introduction to qualitative research*. Thousand Oaks, CA: Sage.

Seidman, I. (2006). *Interviewing as qualitative research: A guide for researchers in education and social sciences* (3rd ed). New York: Teachers College Press.

Stein, S.J., & Gewivtzman, L. (2003). *Principal training on the ground: Ensuring highly qualified leadership*. Portsmouth, NH: Heinemann.

Stringer, E.T. (1999). *Action research* (2nd ed.). Thousand Oaks, CA: Sage.

Stringer, E.T. (2008). *Action research in education* (2nd ed.). Upper Saddle River, NJ: Pearson.

SECTION 2

Democratizing the Research Process

6

(RE)IMAGINING PARTICIPANT OBSERVATION WITH PRESCHOOL CHILDREN

Allison Sterling Henward

This chapter illustrates unconventional and imaginative methods in participation observation with children in an attempt to break down structural hierarchies and barriers between adults and children. I reimagine possibilities for locating and amplifying children's voice in research by adopting a participant observer role that attempts to join in the social and cultural worlds of children. In order to position myself as participant observer, it is imperative that I adopt a role that enables me to be closer to children and as far from adults as possible.

Sociologist Thorne (1993) frames the challenges adult researchers face when researching the interworkings of children's culture. She writes, "I knew that if I were too associated with adult authority I would have difficulty gaining access to kids' more private worlds" (Thorne 1993, p. 16). In the following chapter I describe my attempt as participant observer to actively disengage with the adult world and instead adopt the behaviors and mannerisms of children, including the direct and implied rules expected of them.

Mapping the Landscape: Research with Children

In the United States, there is currently substantial attention paid to preschool-aged children as a result of state and federal educational policies extolling the importance of early childhood education and quality early experiences. Additionally, social science disciplines such as anthropology, sociology, and psychology have mapped children and childhoods in previously unprecedented ways with sociology and anthropologic-oriented research placing children as a focus beginning in the 1990s.

I argue that despite increased attention, a crucial and fundamental factor is routinely overlooked in research with children. Children are often not given the respect or consideration of other more dominant groups in research (Kehily, 2008). This marginalization is rooted in longstanding constructions of children as incomplete and the power differentials between adult and child in society. Enveloped in a discourse of "developing" the sociocultural construction of children and childhoods has a substantial impact on research designs and objectives in studying children. Categorized or observed, qualitatively or quantitatively, because of the assumed cognitive and developmental "advancement" of adults (which masks a discourse of superiority), rarely has the focus been on children interpreting their own experiences in research.

As Speier (1970) writes:

> What is classically problematic about studying children is . . . sociologists (and that probably goes for anthropologists and psychologists) commonly treat childhood as a stage of life that builds preparatory mechanisms into a child's behavior so that he is gradually equipped with the competence to participate in the everyday activities of his cultural partners and eventually as a bona fide adult member himself.
>
> *(p. 208, as quoted in James, Jenks, & Prout, 1998)*

Speier's (1970) assessment of the often-diminished voice of children in research exemplifies the common assessment of children as still forming, still developing. It reflects the implicit paradigmatic assumption that children will develop rational thought only as they mature (Piaget, 1959; Viruru & Cannella, 2001). This paradigm is taken for granted and rarely questioned; from a Foucauldian perspective it is the power that inserts itself into spaces until it becomes naturalized. Consequently, it is normalized and prevents researchers from considering children worthy of the role of informant. Yet, as I will argue, it is a fundamental right of children to speak on their own behalf in research (Reynaert, Bouverne-de-Bie, & Vandevelde, 2009). I suggest children's voices can be heard—located and amplified through careful ethnographic studies that place a central focus on children's voice, or their emic perspective.

Approaching children's perspectives from anthropological traditions suggests we must privilege the child as informant to his or her own culture rather than attempting to describe from the outside. Although in contemporary anthropologically oriented studies of adults, few researchers would attempt to speak on behalf of informants, the same consideration is not often extended to children. As sociologist Thorne (1993) reminds us:

> To learn from children, adults have to challenge the deep assumption that they already know what children are like both because as former children adults have been there and because as adults they regard children as less complete versions of themselves. When adults seek to learn about and from children, the challenge is to take the closely familiar and to render it strange.
>
> *(p. 12)*

Data collected when children are not considered central to the research process does little to enhance our understanding of children's lived experiences; children's experiences are spoken for, interpreted, and above all described through an adult lens with the pretense that adults are somehow better at explaining the lived experiences of another.

Borrowing from the traditions of critical decolonizing and feminist methodologies (Ramazanoglu & Holland, J, 2002; Smith,1999; Mutua & Swadener, 2004), I argue children's voices and experiences are conspicuously absent in research. Children have perspectives, understandings, and beliefs that are quite different from adults but still pervasively written about from adult perspectives (Jenks, 2005). In this understanding children are hegemonically silenced. I further argue that researchers concerned with the social and cultural worlds of children must adjust research methods, techniques, and approaches to more carefully understand the emic perspective of children. Yet in suggesting this it is easy to construct false separations between methods—adult and child (Prout, 2008). This is not my intention. In lieu of this, I am arguing that the full consideration and "rigorous application of general methodological principles" that are the norm with privileged members of our society also be extended to children (Prout, 2008, p. xv).

Next, I explore existing paradigms of participant observation with children. I then move to explorations of a multi-sited ethnographic study I conducted in which I attempted to access children's engagement with popular culture. I outline the tactics the children used in testing my belonging, beginning with questions of rule enforcement and authority. Finally, I move to discuss how the question of participant observer membership in a group needs to be considered in context; I include data from three preschools to discuss how these roles were contextualized and altered in each of the preschool programs reflective of their pedagogy and curriculum. I conclude with discussions of acceptance not being universal but occurring at separate times in the preschool and within preschools as socially and culturally dependent.

Membership Role

Every active researcher takes up membership roles and the various perspectives of those playing along in the project. Membership roles for fieldwork exist on a spectrum. Ranging from "detached observer to the fully-fledged participant" (Adler & Adler, 1987), researchers choose and adapt roles with informants. Adler and Adler (1987) suggest there are three possible categories which one falls into: 1) Peripheral, 2) Active, and 3) Complete membership roles. Adherence to these roles dictates "the type of information available to the researcher and the kind of ethnography written" (p. 13).

The *peripheral membership* role "is the most marginal and least committed to the social world studied. Researchers who adopt this role interact closely, significantly and frequently enough to be considered insiders within the culture studied. They however are not central members and most importantly, they refrain from participating in activities. They furthermore do not assume functional roles within the group" (Adler & Adler, 1987, p. 36). With children, a peripheral membership role would involve the researcher observing children's activities closely, but the researcher would have no interaction in and with the children's play. The perspective of a *peripheral membership* role is that children and adult cannot relate to each other on equal terms. Those attempting a more involved role criticize this perception. As Mandell (1988) conceptualizes, "our hierarchical structure of age roles and adult ethnocentrism preclude a complete involvement role . . . where children are conceptualized as socially incomplete, intellectually immature and culturally ignorant" (p. 434).

In an *active membership* role, the researcher does more than participate; he or she takes place in the core activities of the group. The researcher "assumes functional, not solely research or social, roles" (Adler & Adler, 1987, p. 50). In research with children, an active membership role assumes researchers attempt to play and interact with children but do not attempt to interact as a member of the interest group. In Mandell's (1988) writing this is "the semi participatory role," which recognizes some dimension of authority as separating children and adults in research. The goal, she writes, is "not to achieve equal status" but to become a "non-interfering helpful role of adult as friend" (p. 434).

Complete membership assumes that the researchers immerse themselves in the field as "natives." They and research informants relate to each other as status equals dedicated to sharing in a common set of experiences, feelings, and goals. It involves the researcher adopting the "*weltangshauung*, or worldview of the informants" (Mandell, 1988, p. 436). In research with children, this means actively working to dismantle the structural privileges afforded to adults and denied of children. It suggests that researchers should exist in the world as a child.

In ethnographic research with children, there is much debate about the possibility of adult researchers adopting a complete membership role. The essence of the debate centers on the ability of adults to gain complete membership into the culture because of their size and structural privilege. Notable sociologists studying children (such as Mandell and Corsaro) have recognized the importance of adopting childlike behaviors in research with preschool children. In this understanding, researchers mimic movements and behaviors of children while in preschool. However, there are variations and subtle differences in accounts. Corsaro's (1979) and Corsaro and Molinari's (2008) attempt falls more in line with a peripheral and sometimes active membership role whereas Mandell's (1988) approach is self-described as a complete membership role. Mandell's account addresses the systematic approaches one takes in attempting to dismantle innate and inherent power differentials of adult/child in research to privilege child voice and interpretation (Fine & Sandstrom, 1988). Mandell suggests that the adult-child dichotomy is ideological in nature and that by intentionally dismantling structural privileges one can access and better understand child culture. She describes the many tactics she used in fieldwork to gain membership. She went to great lengths in order to suspend adultlike behaviors to decrease structural privileges of adults studying children. She suggests that a complete involvement in children's culture "is accepted as a tenable possibility" (p. 434).

Mapping the Terrain

The ethnographic study from which this chapter is taken examines how three preschools engage with popular culture and how students, teachers, and parents at these three sites think and talk about popular culture and its place at school. Kline (1995) argues that popular culture artifacts (and preschools themselves) are social symbols that articulate social aspirations and convey complex social relations. The interpretations of these objects depend on a shared understanding of meaning and vary from setting to setting. Within preschool settings, the meanings of objects of popular culture can vary greatly between children and their parents and teachers. In other words, children in each setting are in a sense like a class or interest group. Children's culture function with their own beliefs and forms of cultural capital. These beliefs and forms reflect without reproducing those of the adults, peers, and media around them. It is possible in this understanding for children, parents, and teachers to have vastly different opinions of popular culture.

What is heavily desired by one culture (such as children) may lie in opposition to teachers and parents. Children often enjoy popular culture that is less than valuable to parents and teachers. Many researchers over the years have documented that children pass on tales, songs, beliefs, parodies, and an appreciation for objects such as games, candy, television songs, and trading cards that are often not understood and rarely appreciated by the adults around them (Opie & Opie, 1969; James et al., 1998). Furthermore, ethnographic studies have documented that children are aware that their media and popular culture interests are not valued and sometimes not permitted in schools (Hodge & Tripp, 1986; Henward, 2015).

Because this prohibition can invite clandestine behavior and resistance on the part of children to sneak their interest into schools, I attempted a role that positioned me as separate from the teachers in the school. Drawing on Mandell (1988) and aspects of Corsaro (1979), Thorne (1993), and Corsaro and Molinari (2008), I attempted a full membership role of participant observation. As I will describe, in fieldwork, I endeavored to "suspend all adult like behaviors" (Mandell, 1988) and to only engage in "childlike" behaviors when in the presence of children. Yet accessing children's culture can prove difficult, particularly in schools where adult cultural norms, beliefs, and procedures reign. Significant problems can arise for adult researchers who look, behave, and identify more like the teachers in the class than the children, their principal informants. In describing my approach, I argue ethnographic research with young children needs to start with a careful analysis of adult behaviors and the implications these behaviors can have in research.

The Study

The data in this chapter comes from a larger comparative ethnographic study located in the greater metropolitan area of Phoenix, Arizona. This study examined how three diverse preschools treat children's interests in popular culture and focused on how children reacted to school rules related to popular culture, which is often discouraged in schools (Hodge & Tripp, 1986; Seiter, 1999). The preschools varied significantly in social class, program philosophy, ethnic composition, class size, and program length (see Table 6.1). In each preschool I observed for a period of approximately eight months, although the bulk of the observations took place in a truncated two- to three-month period. I visited the classrooms three to four times a week, with observations typically lasting three to four hours. Although my observation times at each school varied by day, the majority of the observations took place in the morning as the children in two of the three preschools napped for two hours in the afternoon. The following table describes the social class dynamics and the philosophy of each school.

While my participatory role attempted to incorporate attributes described by Mandell (1988), Thorne (1993), and Corsaro (1979), upon entering the field and in review of my field notes, I noticed there were significant differences in my approach. The central difference was in how I conceptualized my membership role.

In comparison to Mandell's (1988) account, I modified my approach by placing the child informant central in my role conceptualization; my guiding principle

TABLE 6.1 Preschool descriptors and philosophies

Preschool	Class Descriptors	Preschool Type/Philosophy
Hermosa Preschool	• Poor and working class • All children qualified for free or reduced lunch and tuition waivers • Majority of students Latino/a although population diverse	• Public pre-K • "Readiness" preschool • NAEYC (National Association for the Education of Young Children) accredited
Biltmore Montessori	• Upper-middle class • Tuition 1,200 USD per month • Majority white	• AMI (Association Montessori International) • Private
Faith Christian	• Lower-middle class • Tuition 400 USD per month with additional charges for after-school care • Vast majority white	• Private • Religious, evangelical, conservative Christian

was to center my attention on children's capabilities and the rules to which they found themselves subject. This consisted of two central principles:

1. If the majority of children could not accomplish a task, then neither could I.
2. I followed the same classroom rules as the children.

I illustrate the first with an example of tying shoes. In "The Least-Adult Role," Mandell (1988) gives the example of a child asking Mandell to tie her shoes. In response, Mandell wrote that she told the child that she was not a teacher and suggested the child should find a teacher. In my fieldwork I found myself in the same situation—the vast majority of preschool children had not yet learned to tie shoes. While Mandell's deflection centered on her unwillingness to pick up the role of a capable teacher or adult, my deflection centered on the capability of children (and by extension myself) to perform the role. When I was asked to tie the child's shoe, I responded that I did not know how. Using children's capability as a barometer, if the children had not learned to tie shoes, than neither had I learned to tie shoes.

When teachers, parents, or any adults in the classroom button pants, tie shoes, pat backs to sleep, wipe noses, or push swings, they are engaging in pedagogies of care (Rockel, 2009); these actions build relationships between adults and children and answer the daily needs of children. In these everyday encounters, while adults help children, they also work to separate adult and child roles in the classroom and reinforce the expertise, mastery, competence, and, above all, sense of authority of adults. Because of the reinforcement of roles, I argue pedagogies of care, while crucial for preschool teachers, must be avoided in field research with preschool children. While the "inability" of an adult to complete tasks such as tying shoes can seem odd at best and duplicitous at worst, by refusing to engage in behaviors reserved for adults, this example illustrates my attempt to minimize adult behaviors and disassociate from authority.

The second principle is based on the concept that adults in the classroom often regulate and dictate children's actions. While this primarily consists of overt rules, it also applies to the tacit procedures of the classroom and how teachers typically regulate children. In comparison to other ethnographic accounts that take place in schools wherein researchers can and do adopt a somewhat looser role of authority (Lewis, 2003; Lubeck, 1984; Ferguson, 2001), my role was to follow the rules and requirements to which children found themselves subject.

Children's bodies are often regulated in schools; in some preschools children have little autonomy over their actions and are assigned to activities while in others they have considerable choice. School philosophy determines this to a substantial degree, and as a result my role in each classroom was considerably different. The programs' considerable variation demanded that I vary my approaches for working with children, and these approaches complicated my role with the children. For example, Hermosa Preschool, a public preschool accredited by NAEYC, placed an emphasis on the children working in centers. For the majority of the day children were able and expected to move between and from certain centers. Their exploration and free play was encouraged. In following these classroom rules I was able to let the children's behaviors and whims dictate how I interacted with them. Because children would move often between activities, I would often follow children from one activity to the next.

In Hermosa Preschool I was able to engage in parallel play with the children and allow them to approach me through interesting activities. In initial observations in each setting, I noticed there were certain "high draw" areas where children congregated. In Hermosa Preschool it was the kitchen. Each morning I would strategically position myself close to this area and attempt to interact with the materials in a parallel fashion. This was marginally successful; most of the time children would comment on my activity, but very rarely was I invited to play with the children. However, my tenacity eventually proved successful as children, in order to play with the materials, would approach me or talk to me while I was close to interesting materials. In comparison, in Faith Christian preschool (private, religious, evangelical, conservative Christian) teachers assigned centers, and children were expected to remain in assigned centers until told otherwise by the teacher. As there was little autonomy, I joined the centers and began joining in on the assigned tasks. Finally in Biltmore Montessori, a private preschool consistent with Montessori philosophy, children were able to choose their activities for much of the day. While autonomous, the expectation was for children work individually, and often silently, on "works"—the Montessori term for a purposeful activity (this did vary, depending on the activity).

These expectations for children within the classroom had a substantial impact on my participant observation role. Abiding by the child-as-barometer principle, whatever rules children were subject to then so was I. As my focus was children's interpretation and use of media, it was essential I be able to spend considerable amounts of time with the children and have access to their play. The Biltmore Montessori philosophy, with its focus on individual work, did not always allow this. In comparison, Faith Christian preschool spent much time in teacher-directed, whole-group activities, allowing me to join in the group, and Hermosa Preschool's great degree of autonomy allowed for me to spend a great deal of time interacting and playing with the children.

While familiar with the Montessori philosophy, I was unprepared for the adverse effect it would have on data collection. By following the expectations for the children, I would be working independently with little access to the children's actions and thoughts. Additionally, the teachers did not look kindly on another "child" in the class. The head teacher seemed to see it as a bit strange and an annoyance to have me using Montessori materials (often in an incorrect fashion). Consequently, in Biltmore Montessori I altered my role. When children were in "work time," I would often deviate from the role of child to be able to sit next to the children and play and talk with them. My role would then resume childlike behaviors when the children were in all other activities.

I staggered my entry into the three preschools (August, September, and October). In entering the Hermosa Preschool (in August), I intentionally delayed my "start date" until two weeks after the school year began. Drawing on my background as a former early childhood classroom teacher, I was aware that the first week or two are when routines and procedures are typically set. As a researcher, I actively avoided this time, as I wanted to not be associated with the routines and avoid picking up a peripheral or pseudo-authority role. More importantly, I also wanted to learn about school from the perspectives of the kids. By asking the children to guide me in my acclimation to the classroom, I was able to ask them questions about the rules in general but also rules pertaining to popular culture. Positioning children as experts in school routines and procedures allowed me to adopt a subordinate role in an attempt to combat power differentials. Following suite, I surmised that if I had little understanding of the school, and the routines and expectations, I would be able to "learn the rituals, practices and habits of preschool children" from my informants, the children (Mandell, 1988). In conceptualizing this, I drew on Corsaro and Molinari's (2008) account in Reggio Emilia, Italy, in which Corsaro attempted to insert himself into children's culture. Corsaro writes that as a monolingual English speaker not knowing Italian, the children relegated him to a somewhat subordinate role in their relationship. He was taught by the Italian children, who would often correct him in violations of routines and mistakes in language. I wished to emulate the same position in preschool and allow children to teach me.

As the children became more comfortable with my presence, they initially regarded me as an adult. This was their initial interpretation, most likely because of my size. In preschoolers' worlds, adults are people who offer assistance. Despite my attempts to dissuade them, children assumed I was an authority-wielding adult. They demonstrated this belief by asking for assistance, which fell into two categories, rule regulation and physical assistance with tasks (such as shoe tying or pushing swings).

Rule Violations

Once the novelty of my presence had worn off, children appealed to me as they would to a teacher to report an infraction or violation. Common transgressions took the form of hitting, name calling, and toy stealing. My response typically was to shrug and say, "What can I do?"

One morning at Hermosa Preschool I was sitting on the ground, playing with two young girls. After five minutes of playing, a four-year-old boy named Matthew sat down next to us. He began telling us that his dad lets him use expletive language; he then gave us several examples. Although I noticed the infraction (it was not permitted to use this type of language in the preschool), I did not react; I simply continued playing Barbies. Elisa, one of the preschool girls, noticed the rule violation and made an "ooooooohhh" tattling type of noise in response.

While she did this, she appeared to be looking over at me, as if she wanted or expected me to intervene. Instead I looked over at the wall and pretended not to have heard. Not satisfied by my reaction, she repeated "oooooooohhhhh," slightly louder, and then directly asked me if I had heard Matthew. I ignored her question. She then repeated her objection to the group (but directed at me). I continued to not wish to intervene; instead I shrugged my shoulders. After this interchange she sighed loudly and then begrudgingly walked over to the assistant teacher, where she reported the infraction. The assistant teacher called Matthew over to her and spoke to him about using "bad" language in the classroom.

This encounter had the effect that I intended. To ignore and then refuse to intervene was in direct opposition to a rule in the classroom to not to use "bad words." Rarely would children be requested to intervene when another child was using language that violated rules. That role was relegated to adults. In comparison to Thorne's (1993), Mandell's (1988), and Corsaro's (1979) likeminded understandings of a participant observer, I felt that even by acknowledging that a child should "tell a teacher," I would be siding with authority or passing judgment on a particular action. I would still be playing the role of a reporter or at the least a redirector. Oftentimes I had witnessed this to be a behavior of paraprofessionals or parents, when they did not have or did not want to have authority but still felt some type of responsibility to "do something." This was not a behavior frequently displayed by children. Using this logic, it was essential I not react or attempt to impose any type of sanction.

This incident also showed that Matthew did not consider me an authority figure, but that Elisa still did. This was supported by the fact that she made repeated appeals for me to intervene and deliver some form of reprimand. When I continued to act indifferent, she became frustrated and appealed to someone she knew would intervene. Interestingly, Elisa after this incident routinely engaged in surreptitious behavior around me, even showing me popular culture makeup and asking me not to tell the teacher about it. While I have no way of knowing if this incident contributed to her cavalier behavior, I can surmise it did not detract from it.

Physical Assistance

One of my conscious decisions before entering fieldwork was to not engage in any act reserved for adults, specifically actions and behaviors in which children could not complete the task to the degree or with the ease of an adult. Examples included dressing children, reaching for objects, tying shoes, turning on water, and reaching paper towels. In response to the children's requests for assistance, I would shrug and answer, "I'm not sure how "or "I don't know how." I was careful to use this "inability" as a rationale; to answer, "Go ask someone else" conveys a different message and more importantly was a behavior that children did not engage in. For example, one of the children, upon entering the classroom, walked over to me and pointed to her jacket zipper. "I need help . . . my zipper." I responded "I'm not sure . . . I don't know how."

Contextualized Approaches

While I cannot suggest my role was entirely successful, I was able to dismantle structural privileges to such a degree that most children had little problem revealing secrets and surreptitious behavior to which teachers were not always privy. In each of the three preschools the children would whisper or show me activities that violated school rules surrounding popular culture (Henward, 2015). In many of the examples children would acknowledge they were breaking a rule and then talk about why the teacher did not like them playing with or talking about popular culture. By doing so they showed knowledge of authority and that I was not included in that category.

As evidenced by the children revealing and inviting me to engage in surreptitious behavior, children in each preschool eventually accepted me as a confidant and one who had no interest in changing or altering their behavior. As they freely shared transgressions and acknowledged their actions to be in direct violation of the rules, I can assume by the end of fieldwork I was considered a member.

In describing my account of membership, I do not wish to suggest there was a uniform acceptance by the children. In each preschool there were children who were quick to accept me as a complete member and children who were more reticent. There was a substantial difference between how children approached me in each preschool. While children in Hermosa Preschool engaged in the most requests for assistance and tested my positionality, children at Biltmore Montessori were much quicker to display subversive behaviors around me. While children at Hermosa Preschool were slow and methodical in determining who I was, children at Biltmore Montessori were much more direct.

Additionally, children at Hermosa and Faith Christian preschools appealed to me to assist them in a much greater manner than did children at Biltmore Montessori. There are several possible explanations. Because Biltmore Montessori had been in school a full two months before I began fieldwork, it is possible the children had already identified authority figures (and by extension excluded me from that category). In the other two preschools (Hermosa and Faith Christian) my entrance was closer to the beginning of the school year. However, I suggest an alternate explanation, that social class and program philosophy contributed to this variation. Children in the lower middle-class conservative Faith Christian preschool were expected to defer to authority in a greater degree than the upper-middle-class children attending the Biltmore Montessori program. Children in Biltmore Montessori often showed greater self-assurance in comparison to other children from working-class and lower-middle-class backgrounds. Lareau's (2011) understanding of class distinctions and class specific socialization outlines how children of varied social classes are taught to interact with adults in distinctly different manners. This contextualization helps in understanding why this high degree of self-assurance, coupled with elaborated rules limiting popular culture, led to frequent rule violations. But there are other possible explanations specific to this environment.

Additionally, the Montessori philosophy typically stresses a more egalitarian model that expects self-sufficiency and independence from children. I suggest these factors could have contributed to children being less reticent to question adults and be more comfortable accepting me as a complete member.

As evidenced in this chapter, research with children is dynamic and affected by many factors. A multi-sited ethnographic study identifies that acceptance by children is not uniform, but dependent on children's existing relationships with adults. For children who are typically encouraged to have a greater degree of self-assurance with more egalitarian roles, the idea of a researcher breaking down hierarchical structures does not conflict to the same degree that it might for children who are taught deference to adults and a strong separation between adult and child roles.

Children's voices and opinions have much to contribute, yet in many aspects the methods in which adult researchers can and should work with children resemble traditional paradigms. I suggest that in order to avoid speaking for children, we must employ more imaginative methods in order to break down traditional hierarchies that polarize researcher and child informant. This involves constant, reflective researchers operating with ever-changing and ever-evolving methods. While these methods do not operate in traditional paradigms, traditional paradigms do not operate to listen to children as experts who are more knowledgeable than researchers. In order to change the paradigms, we must change the methods.

References

Adler, P.A., & Adler, P. (1987). *Membership roles in field research* (Vol. 6). Newbury Park, CA: Sage.

Christensen, P., & James, A. (Eds.). *Research with children: Perspectives and practices*. New York: Routledge.

Corsaro, W.A. (1979). 'We're friends, right?': Children's use of access rituals in a nursery school. *Language in Society, 8*(2–3), 315–336.

Corsaro, W.A., & Molinari, L. (2008). Entering and observing in children's worlds. In P. Christensen & A. James (Eds.), *Research with children: Perspectives and practices* (p. 239–259). New York: Routledge.

Ferguson, A.A. (2001). *Bad boys: Public schools in the making of black masculinity*. Ann Arbor: University of Michigan Press.

Fine, G.A., & Sandstrom, K.L. (1988). *Knowing children: Participant observation with minors* (Vol. 15). Newbury Park, CA: Sage.

Henward, A.S. (2015) "She don't know I got it. You ain't gonna tell her are you?" Popular culture as resistance in American preschools. *Anthropology and Education Quarterly, 46*(3), 208–223.

Hodge, R., & Tripp, D. (1986) *Children and television: A semiotic approach*. Stanford, CA: Stanford University Press.

James, A., Jenks, C., & Prout, A. (1998). *Theorizing childhood*. New York: Teachers College Press.

Jenks, C. (Ed.). (2005). *Childhood* (Vol. 2). New York: Psychology Press.

Kehily, M.J. (2008). *An introduction to childhood studies*. New York: McGraw-Hill International.

Kline, S. (1995). *Out of the garden: Toys, TV, and children's culture in the age of marketing*. New York: Verso.

Lareau, A. (2011). *Unequal childhoods: Class, race, and family life*. Berkeley: University of California Press.

Lewis, A. (2003). *Race in the schoolyard: Negotiating the color line in classrooms and communities*. New Brunswick, NJ: Rutgers University Press.

Lubeck, S. (1984). Kinship and classrooms: An ethnographic perspective on education as cultural transmission. *Sociology of Education, 57*(4), 219–232.

Mandell, N. (1988). The least-adult role in studying children. *Journal of Contemporary Ethnography, 16*(4), 433–467.

Mutua, K., & Swadener, B.B. (Eds.). (2004). *Decolonizing research in cross-cultural contexts: Critical personal narratives*. New York: SUNY Press.

Opie, I.A., & Opie, P. (1969). *Children's games*. Oxford and New York: Oxford University Press.

Piaget, J. (1959). *The language and thought of the child* (Vol. 5). New York: Psychology Press.

Prout, A. (2008) Foreword in P. Christensen & A. James (Eds.), *Research with children: Perspectives and practices*. New York: Routledge.

Ramazanoglu, C., & Holland, J. (2002). *Feminist methodology: Challenges and choices*. Thousand Oaks, CA: Sage.

Reynaert, D., Bouverne-de-Bie, M., & Vandevelde, S. (2009). A review of children's rights literature since the adoption of the United Nations Convention on the Rights of the Child. *Childhood, 16*(4), 518–534.

Rockel, J. (2009). A pedagogy of care: Moving beyond the margins of managing work and minding babies. *Australasian Journal of Early Childhood, 34*(3), 1–8.

Seiter, E. (1999). Power Rangers at preschool: Negotiating media in child care settings. In M. Kinder (Ed.), *Kids' media culture* (pp. 239–262). Durham, NC: Duke University Press.

Smith, L.T. (1999). *Decolonizing methodologies: Research and indigenous peoples*. London: Zed Books.

Speier, M. (1970). The everyday world of the child. In J.D. Douglas (Ed.), *Understanding everyday life: Toward the reconstruction of sociological knowledge* (pp. 188–217). Chicago: Aldine.

Thorne, B. (1993). *Gender play: Girls and boys in school*. New Brunswick, NJ: Rutgers University Press.

Viruru, R., & Cannella, G.S. (2001). Postcolonial ethnography, young children, and voice. In S. Grieshaber & G.S. Cannella (Eds.), *Embracing identities in early childhood education: Diversity and possibilities* (pp. 158–172). New York: Teachers College Press.

7

WORDS AND BODIES

Reimagining Narrative Data in a Toddler Classroom

Emmanuelle N. Fincham

With a little coaxing from the teachers, Jake joins the other toddlers at the table for lunch. After walking around to see what was on the other plates, he looks at his food and rejects the idea that that is his plate—"oh, no . . . at's no my." He walks away from the table, head down, and goes to sit on the bench in the middle of the classroom. The act of sitting is elaborate, plopping down hard on his bottom, releasing a big, loud sigh, dropping his arms and shoulders down in front of his body as his torso angles forward, and finally, when the last bit of breath is released, his head drops and he looks at his feet. Out of the corner of his eye, he looks back at the table and everyone sitting there for lunch; he turns his body, swinging his legs over to the other side of the bench and repeats the long sighing, body dropping performance.

The influence of Vygotsky's (1978) theories in Western early childhood education (Bodrova & Leong, 2007; Copple & Bredekamp, 2009) have promoted a positioning of the teacher as scaffolder, always looking for that next step in development to support the child in reaching. During the toddler years, ages one to three, language is one of the most obvious developmental tasks that the child is undertaking, giving the teacher many opportunities to scaffold a child's use of spoken words. The adults in a toddler's world get excited during this time. With the development of verbal language, it seems we can finally understand them, and they can tell us what they want (or so we have come to believe). In the vignette, Jake begins by using language but then changes to a more physical response to communicate that he is not interested in his lunch at this particular time. It would not be surprising for a teacher in this situation to follow up with the oft-used and under-thought "use your words" approach (de Haan & Singer, 2003), assuming a verbal response from Jake would be more trustworthy in regards to what he was feeling and thinking. However, if I, the adult teacher, let go of this verbal push, a lens opens up to see how the bodily performance here provides another, quite powerful, site of understanding and meaning making, calling attention to the skill with which very young children communicate nonverbally.

As a toddler teacher, teaching one- to three-year-olds in the United States, I struggle daily in practice and research with my own inclinations toward the spoken and written word and the ease with which I ignore the language of the body. Somewhere along the way it seems we, teachers of young children, have all picked up the discourse of "use your words" and use it impetuously in our work with children. With so much focus on the word in our adult world and the pervasiveness in Western education, positioning *rational* thought of the mind as separate, distinct, and of a higher order than the *irrational* body, most of us have come to let the power of the mind's uttered word obscure the declarations of the body. This distinction has resulted in what Tobin (2004) describes as the disembodiment of early childhood education where the order of "use your words" thus implies to not use the body. When we encourage a move away from the body, we limit the possibilities of engagement with each other, the possibilities in telling our stories, and the possibilities in understanding.

In my work as a toddler teacher and teacher researcher, I align myself epistemologically alongside other reconceptualist scholars (e.g., Blaise, 2010; Bloch, Swadener, & Cannella, 2014; Ryan & Grieshaber, 2005) in my attempts at creating "new spaces of possibility" in research and practice (Soto & Swadener, 2005, p. 2). Provoked by the writings of Deleuze and Guattari (1987) and Butler (2006), I am intrigued by what happens when we take notice of how language signifies our own and others' subjectivities, consider the multiplicities inherent in interpretation and meaning making, and position the subject in a process of becoming. Rather than limiting the possibilities in engagement and research with young children by relying on the *word*, we can amplify our understandings of children's worlds by raising awareness of the *body* and examining the many and varied ways we interpret experiences within the verbal and nonverbal world.

Over the last several years, I have been working within the realms of teacher research (Cochran-Smith & Lytle, 1993; Gallas, 1994; Hankins, 2003) and narrative inquiry (Chase 2005; 2011; Riessman, 2008) and, over time, have found it challenging to situate my research with toddlers within these frameworks. To a large extent, narrative methods used in the social sciences have developed out of life story and oral history traditions where the main data source is the story as told by the narrator/subject. Consequently, "narrative research has relied on spoken and written discourse" (Riessman, 2008, p. 141).

Much knowledge can be produced through the telling of stories, but what if these stories cannot be heard by gleaning them through traditional approaches to methodology such as interviews. At first glance, narrative research seems simple—producing knowledge by telling stories—but how do we, as researchers, address the complexities involved in our attempts to know others' stories? What are the possibilities in the ways stories are told and heard? Who determines the meaning? These questions and more guide my inquiry in the classroom.

This chapter will serve as a space for me to interrogate my own understandings of narrative research and consider possibilities for narrative methods in teacher research in a toddler classroom. First, I will share my own continual becoming of a teacher researcher and describe how my gaze has turned toward a focus on subjectivities in conjunction with the "texts" of narrative data. Then, in the following sections, I will share some examples of the types of narrative data I have been working with, including rethinking interviews, reproducing the spoken "word" of toddlers, writing "impressionist tales" (Van Maanen, 2011), and looking at classroom artifacts as visual narrative "texts." With each of these examples, I will consider the possibilities for producing and interpreting these types of data in research with young children and then conclude the chapter with a discussion of the potential as well as the challenges for doing this kind of research.

Researching with Toddlers

When I first began thinking about teacher research, I was adamant that I would be doing a classroom ethnography since I was interested in looking at my classroom through a cultural lens. At that point, my meager vision was of collecting mountains of "rich" data in my classroom over the course of a year, which would tell the "real" story of my classroom. I was easily seduced by the humanist "mythic" qualities of classical ethnography that Britzman (1995, p. 229) describes, such as ethnography's ability to take the reader into the "actual world" of the inhabitants of a particular culture. Later, when I became aware of how some scholars (e.g., Cannella & Viruru, 2004) applied postcolonial theory to early childhood, I made even more connections to classical ethnography. The children could be characterized as the other—the native, the primitive, the less privileged—oppressed by the adult world. To me, this meant that classical anthropology had a lot to teach me about research, which I could translate into my own classroom. It took me quite some time to come to a place of questioning the traditions and articulating the problems of singular reality claims and the subjectivities at play in the researcher/other relationship as I encounter multiple meanings, realities, and "truths."

Conducting teacher research in my own classroom, I have moved from an ethnographic to an autoethnographic approach, *inhabiting the space between* as I acknowledge my own positioning within, yet also outside, the classroom culture. Cochran-Smith and Lytle (1993) claim that teacher research produces insider knowledge. As a teacher, I am part of the classroom culture, an "insider," if you will. However, as an adult, I am still on the outside of the child culture, not having an inside perspective on their experience. This insider-outsider position is an uncomfortable space when I think about my teaching and my research and the ethical dilemmas I struggle with in each. It is living within and beyond this space that has led me to continually question and explore possibilities for data and "capturing" the stories of the young children I spend my days with in the classroom. In the midst of letting go of the "real" story and accepting the impossibility of observing reality, I turn toward poststructural ethnography/autoethnography as a way to "bother the writer's and perhaps the reader's confidence in truth, in the visible, and in the real" (Britzman, 1995, p. 231).

The true, the visible, and the real are continuing concerns of much of the research in early childhood, particularly in the United States, and particularly in the research that "counts" in terms of educational policy and practice. Because of this preoccupation, as well as the influence of the UN Convention on the Rights of the Child in 1989, debate around the voice of children in qualitative research has been going on for over two decades (James, 2007). How do researchers "accurately" and "authentically" represent the voices of children in research? How do we respect the child as we make their voices heard? These questions, while important to attend to, stem from a modernist mindset, assuming there is a true "voice" to be heard. Turning to the postmodern, the notion of "voice" itself becomes a site for interrogation, especially when engaging in research with very young children requires a crossing of the distance between the voices of adults and children.

As I turn my attention to the *distant voices*, I am challenging myself (and others) to see the possibilities for narrative methods in my work when the method is so adult centric and verbal centric. In traditional qualitative research, the goal is finding meaning in the data that can be agreed upon, to some extent, by the researcher and the reader—meaning that is valid, trustworthy, and reliable (Bogdan & Biklen, 2007). Narrative research with adults seems more readily accepted than research with children because, as adults, we are closer to the ways of speaking and understanding language that we share with our adult subjects. In other words, we are more likely to trust the voice of another adult than the voice of a child, especially a child who is still coming into a fluency of spoken language. Research with toddlers relies heavily on observation of action and behavior as most children of this age are transitioning from a nonverbal to verbal way of life during this period. White (2011) speaks to this distance between our adult ways of communicating and understanding and those of the toddler, a distance that seems to engender some distrust in our understanding and interpretations:

> How much more challenging is such seeing when the subject of our gaze is an infant or toddler who speaks a distinct corporeal language that has long been forgotten by the adult, and who draws from a sociocultural domain that is only partially glimpsed by the early childhood teacher or researcher?
>
> *(p. 63)*

In considering a toddler's "voice," it is extremely limiting to focus on the word and neglect the body; thus narrative research that relies on the story being told through conventional speech inhibits our understandings of these young children and their experiences in classrooms. This then begs the question, how do we attend also to the corporeal voice in narrative research?

Taking influence from feminist poststructural thought and research (e.g., Blaise, 2005; Butler, 2006; Davies, 2003), the corporeal voice, which I see as a performance of the body, is a site of inscription and also a site for interpretation and understanding. Positioning these bodily performances as part of a dialogic social exchange, "'voice' can include any sound, gesture, movement, or word that has potential to be recognized by [an] other" (White, 2011, p. 64). When we as teachers and researchers turn our attention toward the body, the potential for multiple meanings and new knowledge abounds. Developmental knowledge could easily write off the distance between the nonverbal world of the young child and the verbal world of the adult as a developmental gap that is impossible to cross, leaving the zero-to-three age range in the dark when it comes to having their "voices" heard. However, looking at it through a feminist poststructural lens, this distance is constructed through the interplay of subjectivities and discourses, situated within particular socio-cultural-historical contexts, and is worthy of investigation. It is not my intention to try and close the gap but to shift my perspective in a way that regards this distance as an integral part of my research as I attempt to read the body as well as the word.

As I seek to make meaning of the children's stories and my own, I am not aiming to find the one, "real" story that they are living, but to attend to the multiplicity of meaning and the various ways stories can be told and understood. As with any research venture, my subjectivity as a researcher is in relation to the subjectivity of my subjects. Doing narrative teacher research, I conceptualize my work as autoethnography, so in many ways, I am my own subject; yet, as I research myself as a teacher, I am also studying how I read/hear the stories of the children and how those stories might be acknowledged, perceived, and understood, given the discursive contexts in which they are performed. I have recently been doing a lot of "messing about" (Hawkins, 1974) in my classroom as I am producing a variety of narrative data and trying to push the boundaries of traditional narrative representation. Next, I describe some of these "experiments" in narrative and imagine the possibilities for using this type of narrative data in teacher research with toddlers.

Toddler Narratives: Attempts at Locating, Representing, and Interpreting Their Stories

Narrative inquiry offers seemingly unlimited possibilities for producing data as narrative researchers generate and interpret a variety of texts. Narratives can take many forms as researchers engage in "meaning making through the shaping and ordering of experience" (Chase, 2005; 2011, p. 421). Here, I present four examples of how I have been reimagining the ways I portray and interpret narrative data in my research through rethinking interviews in the classroom, considering the poetics inherent in speech, composing tales of children's play, and discerning the aesthetic in the use of materials.

Rethinking Interviews

In so much of narrative research, interviews play a major role and are often the sole source of data, especially in oral narrative and life history work. Reading methodological texts on interviewing (e.g., Fontana & Frey, 2005; Rapley, 2004; Scheurich, 1997) led me to consider the place, if any, for interviews in my work. Several years ago, as an exercise for an introductory course on qualitative research, I had to conduct an interview. I immediately considered only other adults to interview, but after doing the exercise, I began to wonder if you could interview a toddler. Being stuck in a modernist web at the time, I came up with many reasons why you could not, based on traditional ways of conducting and using interviews. Then, I considered ethnographic approaches to interviewing and realized that the interview can be taken out of the context of two people, sitting across a table from each other, responding to a series of questions. I began to think about how interviews could happen in the course of daily conversations in the classroom.

Rapley (2004) and Scheurich (1997) both take up this notion of "interview as conversation" in different ways. Rapley gives a broad definition of interviews as "social encounters where speakers collaborate in producing retrospective (and prospective) *accounts* or *versions* of their past (or future) actions, experiences, feelings, and thoughts" (p. 16). He also comments that interviews draw on the everyday experience of asking and answering questions. In this sense, I can see interviews happening in the classroom with very young children as they engage in conversation with each other or adults, as they continually respond to experiences with their incessant "why's" and "what's" and furrowed brows, and as I, a teacher, prompt them to provide information about what they are thinking and doing. However, Rapley insists that interviews are never "just a conversation" (p. 26) due to the control the researcher has over the situation. Not as concerned with labeling the experience, Scheurich turns the focus toward the process and construction of meanings that happen during an interview: "Whether we call the interview interaction 'interviewing', 'conversation', 'storytelling', or simply, 'an interaction' is of much less importance than what we think occurs in this interaction" (p. 73). An important aspect of this interaction in my work with toddlers is to consider the conversation beyond words, as words "are only one form of communication; other forms (gesture, body movement, sound, images) precede words in human development and continue to communicate meaning through the life course" (Riessman, 2008, p. 141).

In considering classroom conversations as data, I am also influenced by Iorio's (2008) conceptualization of classroom conversations as aesthetic experience. Her work takes into account the role of each participant in the conversation and puts an emphasis on responses based on lived experience, leading to conversations that can contribute to a deeper sense of self for both the child and adult. In this sense, and connecting to the theoretical underpinnings of my work, seeing classroom conversations as a type of postmodern interview provides opportunities to attend to subjectivities in the classroom. In the following example, I recall a conversation I had with Joel where I purposefully considered notions of discourse and subjectivity as I made choices in my response. This purposefulness is important to consider as it signifies that certain types of conversations fit this construction and that not all classroom conversation would be considered "interviews" in the sense I am taking them up in my data.

Joel's Temporality of Gender

I was near the laundry with Joel, a just-turned three-year-old, in order to help him change back into the clothes he had worn to school. After spending an hour outside splashing in a puddle, his clothes and shoes went in the dryer and he wore his extra set. When given the option, he wanted to change back into his race car shirt rather than keep on his extra clothes. He also chose to change his underwear after remembering that he had been wearing a Batman pair earlier. I helped him balance as he took off his underwear, then held the Batman pair out so he could step in.

As he stepped the first leg through, he casually mentioned, "I have a penis today."

Unsure what he meant, I repeated, maybe asking for clarification, "Today, you have a penis?"

"Yup," Joel said while looking down at the item in question.

Not sure where to go with this, I pursued, "What about tomorrow?"

Joel looked off to the corner of the room in thought for a moment, then replied matter-of-factly, "If I didn't have a penis, I'd be a girl."

I left it at that.

This brief moment with Joel left me with many questions about his performativity of gender (Butler, 2006) and the way he was reading his body to define himself in gendered terms. His anatomy was key in telling him what he was not. However, I wondered if there was some temporality in how he identified himself in this moment by adding the constraining detail of "today." His body was inscribed with the logic of the gendered discourse surrounding his life: I have a penis, therefore I am boy. Yet it seemed that he was not fully buying into it and was creating a space for a performative subversion, considering the "what if," or what other possibilities, perhaps on another day, existed for his subjectivity. As the adult in this conversation, I could have easily responded with agreement, "Yes, you have a penis, you are a boy." But I was more inclined to wonder what the possibilities for resignification were when it becomes acceptable to bring reality into question. Reality, as Butler (2006) states, is changeable and revisable. Conversations like the one I had with Joel are moments where teachers and researchers have the opportunity to create openings for multiple subjectivities and allow for realities that are fluid and dynamic, considering theories of existence that may have been previously obscured. These types of classroom conversations can open up a space for the child, the teacher, and the researcher to question social constructs and consider different ways of seeing into the world. By utilizing these conversations as data in teacher research, attention is brought to the thoughts and interchanges beyond the questioning of a child by an adult, situating the conversation in a web of discourses.

The Poetics Inherent in Speech

Working with toddlers, I often make the argument that we push spoken language so much that the communicative abilities of very young children become neglected and devalued—the "dark side to language" (Stern, 1998, p. 114). This falls in line with my argument for a move toward the body in narrative research. Gallas (1994) provides a framework for understanding children's narratives in which "language is defined expansively to include a complex of signs" (p. xv). She argues that children do not limit their narratives to the spoken or written word but also express themselves through play and artistic activities. In an attempt to prove this point that we need to look beyond spoken language with toddlers, I set out to see just how limiting a narrative was that relied on the spoken word of toddlers at play. Utilizing a video recording of two two-year-old girls' play in the kitchen area, I transcribed their verbal language, and only that, in order to illustrate what I assumed would be missed by solely attending to the children's spoken word. Richardson (1997; 2000) suggests presenting spoken data as a poem, considering that speech may be closer to poetry than the typical prose of research writing, so I tried that with the words of these two-year-olds at play.

One morning in the kitchen

> oooo, lemonade, I yuv lemonade . . . can I have it? oh thank you.
> I gonna cut your melonade.
> okay, okay . . . thank you-hooo-hooo . . . I yuv lemonade . . . mmm, my fay-britt . . . I take it?
> ehhh I cut it for you . . . in pieces . . . ehhh, ahhh, uhhh . . . I make it warm for you.
> What is it?
> I can make it nice and warm for you.
> huh? Shekanasoman? Cook it? Is it ready? is ready? is ready? is read-EEEE?
> Is not ready. It's a cookin in there.
> okay, is cookin . . . just one minute.
> Where's your mommy day?
> my mom, that's my mom.
> your mommy?

yeah, that's my mommy . . . 8, 9, 10, 11 . . . hello mommy . . . I love you . . . That's my mommy.

I wan talk my mommy . . . MY mommy.

huh, my mommy. HEYYO MOMMY! call mine. call my mommy. call my mommy.

hee, hee, hee.

my mommy?

is my mommy.

thas mine.

My mommy.

Wait! I just saw the baby.

My original argument suggests that when a narrative is presented as only a person's words, it can be limiting, excluding elements that live outside of words—actions, gestures, body language, objects, setting, silence, and so on. In analyzing the poem, I first considered everything that was missing. However, by experimenting with telling the narrative in this way, I find that it is not limited but, instead, is just one version of the experience. There is still meaning to be made from this data. We might consider the gendered and heteronormative discourses at play amid the food preparation and the "whose mommy" argument or wonder about the ways the girls are enacting power through ordering the play and finding ways to subvert the subject positions being made available to them. For example, the polite collaboration around the lemonade counters the dominant narratives of egocentrism and the social incompetency of toddlers. Or the shift away from the "mommy" talk at the end could be interpreted as a resistance to an expected maternal attachment at a young age. Contrary to my initial assumptions, it now seems that presenting the not-yet-adult speech of toddlers in my classroom could be one compelling and worthwhile way of recounting and interpreting their stories.

Composing Tales of Children's Play

When thinking about the life story of toddlers, I would not expect them to tell us about their experiences of birth, learning to walk, growing, and so forth, rather I consider what may be most meaningful to them, how they perceive their life, and how they express their thoughts and ideas. For most children of this age, much of their life is happening in play. A toddler's life story is situated in a world of pretend-reality, as they move in and out of roles, characters, storylines, and relationships with others and objects. A toddler's way of seeing the world has not yet been confined by the adult binary of fantasy/reality. Working from this perspective, I have been experimenting with representing episodes of pretend play as impressionist tales that read more like fictional prose than observational data. Van Maanen (2011) labeled this type of tale based on impressionist painting where the artist's goal is for the viewer to see what the artist sees, from a highly personalized position in time and space. This type of tale goes beyond retelling an observation of play but aims for the reader to have a more sensory experience, able to feel and see what the narrator feels and sees in the story. It also allows for interpretation as data and a space to attend to the body as the author/researcher describes the narrator's readings of others' actions along with dialogue.

The following excerpts from one such tale illustrate this impressionist take on reproducing play episodes as textual data. These stories go beyond traditional observation and allow me, as the teacher and researcher, to position myself within the data as I engage in these episodes with the children in the classroom. Embedded in the telling of these stories are my own experience and moments of reflection as I make choices in how I participate in the play. Using these tales as data allows for an examination of the performances of knowledge within the play and the discourses that inscribe the roles and actions of the players.

The Day the Dragons Came, Excerpts

The campfire burns hot and bright as we rotate our marshmallows on sticks, careful not to let them burn. I sit near the fire, close but not too close, watching how the others take to this new concept of "camping." While enjoying the glow and warmth of the fire, we leisurely talk about what we are to do while camping. Out of nowhere, a firefighter appears! His face, shadowed by a red helmet, is serious. A hose is tucked tight under his arm, nozzle in hand. He runs toward us with much urgency. He must have heard about our fire or smelled the smoke and was ready to save us from certain death. I had to stop him.

"Wait, wait, wait!" I shout. "We are using this fire for camping. We need it, please don't put it out."

The firefighter freezes, terribly confused. He looks at all of us for a moment, then without a word, walks off in search of another need for rescue. Our attention is back on the fire, marshmallows are toasted, and we wonder what to do next.

. . .

"A dragon!" Peter shouts as he jumps out from the woods, entering our campsite with a roar, adding to the campfire story being told. To my surprise, a few of the campers transform into dragons and stand in line with Peter, gnashing their teeth, showing their claws, and growling a low, terrible growl. No doubt, the remaining campers were frightened. The story accelerates through the actions of the dragons, claws scratching at the remaining campers while they roar in our faces.

"But," I pose, "in this story, are these scary dragons or nice dragons?" The dragons stop roaring for a moment to think. "I'm a baby dragon," Peter says.

"Yeah, we are baby dragons," the others agree. Their behavior changes accordingly. Their roars turn into whimpers, and their scratching claws turn into playful paws. The story continues as the campers begin to care for these baby dragons, petting their scaly heads and offering them food and bottles of milk. Soon enough, the baby dragons want to play. I find some sticks lying around, and the baby dragons seem eager to take on a game of fetch.

Depicting an episode of play as I have here, I find myself inclined toward different lines of inquiry than I would be with traditional anecdotal data. In producing impressionist tales, I am not preoccupied with objectivity but instead forefront my subjectivity as the teacher and researcher in these moments. The positioning of myself as narrator allows me to interweave my own thinking and reactions amid the retelling of these stories that are acted out in the classroom, although I also wonder about the potential to write tales from another narrator's point of view, namely one of the children. Approaching data in this way takes me out of the observer role and forces me to see myself as a participant, describing and interpreting my own choices and actions in relation to the children and the discourses that surround us.

Discerning the Aesthetic in the Use of Materials

As I work to merge narrative inquiry with teacher research, I am not only reimagining narrative methods in researching with toddlers but also calling into question the traditions of teacher research and how my work with very young children fits into that methodology, which has been predominantly conceptualized within the K–12 classroom. In teacher research focused on school-age children, one of the most common sources of data is classroom "artifacts," in other words, samples of children's work. Many teacher research guidebooks prioritize the collection of student work and most often focus on inquiry related to academic curriculum. Hubbard and Power (2003) state, "an important data source for any teacher-researcher is student work" as they encourage teachers to "save everything" (p. 59) that students produce. Similarly, Dana and Yendol-Hoppey (2009) comment on how classrooms "naturally generate a tremendous paper trail that captures much of the daily classroom activity" (p. 81). This data that is produced by children in classrooms privileges the written word and shapes teacher inquiry that is concentrated on student progress in academic work.

As I think about the role of classroom artifacts and student work in my own teaching and research practices, I have to look beyond words on paper. I continually wonder: What artifacts are the young children in my classroom producing? How can those artifacts be documented? Along with physical, tangible artifacts, are there also artifacts that are immaterial? What is "student work" in a toddler classroom? In order to even consider these ideas, I have had to decouple the notions of artifacts and student work from spoken and written words. Doing so reveals many more ways children convey their knowledge and experiences, since "words, however, are only one form of communication; other forms (gestures, body movement, sound, images) precede words in human development and continue to communicate meaning through the life course" (Riessman, 2008, p. 141).

In my classroom, I am coming to define some of these "artifacts" as the remnants of children's play and engagement with materials, in other words, what they leave behind. In order to gather this data I have been taking photographs of objects after a child has arranged them in play. These photographs of the scene become a type of visual "text" (Riessman, 2008) that can be read and interpreted just as a written text might be. As with written data, the act of interpreting images is not a search for the "truth" of the image but an opportunity to engage in multiple readings (p. 179). As I work with these images and encounter these artifacts in the classroom, I am struck by the aesthetic quality of children's arrangements of materials and my own aesthetic response. There are different levels of creating and interpreting images occurring here as the child creates an arrangement, I perceive it and decide to photograph it, and then I make choices regarding how I position the camera to capture an image. These layers of aesthetic representation are ongoing and unstable but temporarily and deceptively fixed in the moment of the photograph.

Engaging with these photographs, Deleuze and Guattari's (1987) concept of *assemblage*—bringing together disparate pieces to make a whole—helps frame the way I read these images and also allows the decentering of the dominant subject. Each photograph represents a composition of time, place, subject, object, action, discourse, and so on. Considering an assemblage as a "composition of desire," MacRae (2012) explores the relationships among children and objects from an artist's stance, as she collected photographic images of children's engagements with her collected objects in an early childhood classroom. She saw the objects becoming animated through the children's desire but also saw how the objects became active themselves as they roused desire in the children. Thinking about this flow of desire in the assemblage, the emphasis is on the "*collective* in the composition of the shared moment" and "attention is spread more evenly across the people and the things that are singularly brought together for a brief moment" (MacRae, 2012, p. 120). Inspired by MacRae's study, I am now looking at my collected images in regards to how the child acts on the objects and vice versa. These images appeal to multiple readings beyond the assumed teacher viewpoint of child development. I chose two images to share and briefly comment on and I encourage the reader to encounter these images and engage in his or her own readings of these "texts."

In Figure 7.1, a child has meticulously arranged a set of orange objects that she collected from various corners of the classroom. An orange wooden ring sits inside an orange nesting block surrounded by four arrangements of orange cubes. My first reading of this image brings me to consider the aesthetic pleasure this child is experiencing having arranged these objects by color. I am also struck by how the light from the camera flash bounces off the plastic surfaces and realize that my perception of these objects is very different than what she may have intended as she arranged these items in the dimly lit classroom. When I look beyond the orange objects, which I have focused on in taking the photograph, my reading of the image expands to include the nearby features and positioning in the classroom. While she chose to set this up in a highly traversed area, she situated the pieces up against larger items, possibly creating a sort of boundary for her arrangement.

FIGURE 7.1 Aesthetic color experience

Figure 7.2 depicts the organization of a scene during a pretend play episode in the classroom kitchen area. The table is set, food is served, and the guest, Captain America, has arrived. This scene was created by a boy who spent a lot of time reenacting active superhero stories and wrestling with pillows that served as the "bad guys." Several things strike me about this image in terms of the child's subjectivity and ways of positioning himself in this play. He had Captain America cross a boundary here into the kitchen play as superheroes do not usually inhabit the domestic realm. This child also took on a subservient role to the superhero, and I read the scene as him showing respect to the character. He made sure to set things for Captain America before he set them for himself, and Captain America got the bigger chair, often a sign of power and age in the classroom.

Considering how we might move away from the spoken and written word to engage in narrative teacher research with very young children, visual narrative analysis offers yet another avenue for positioning the language of the toddler body in such a way that the voices of young children in classrooms can be heard. Susan Bell, as quoted by Riessman (2008), states that "visual images are so thoroughly embedded in our worlds that not to take them seriously, and not to work at making them part of analysis, is to reduce our understandings of subjects' worlds" (p. 182). By decentering the subject and concentrating on the elements of shared

FIGURE 7.2 Superhero play experience

moments, visual images are a powerful tool to utilize in narrative analysis, regardless of the subject's verbal abilities.

Conclusion

Looking across these examples of reimagined approaches to narrative data, I am reminded of St. Pierre's (1997) call for "transgressive data" in considering the concern researchers have for "pieces of data, words, to support the knowledge we make" and possibilities beyond conventional "language, which regularly falls apart" (p. 179). Toddlers' stories do not fit in the boxes constructed by traditional teacher research and narrative inquiry. In order to widen our understandings of the experiences of young children and teachers in classrooms, we must transgress the reliance on the written and spoken word of research and practice and turn our attention to the body and the stories told through the corporeal voice as well as the word. Challenges to these ideas persist, though, as I position my work within the domain of educational research, which is so tightly tethered to the written word and the obligation to represent meaning through text.

Nevertheless, possibilities for this type of work abound. Challenging the adult-centric narrative by opening spaces for toddlers' multi-faceted voices to come through provides opportunity for expanded understanding and a drive to cultivate multiple meanings around classroom experiences. As I continue to craft my methodology as a teacher researcher in a toddler classroom, I am inspired by Richardson's (1997) call for "a poststructuralist methodology—crystallization—a methodology that generates alternate theories and perspectives for writing and for living, deconstructing traditional notions of validity, glancingly touching some projects, lighting others" (p. 136), always expanding on the possibilities and potential of doing research with young children in classrooms. As a teacher researcher, this consideration of new possibility drives my practice as well. Expanding and imagining new spaces for narrative research and methods in the classroom also supports a shift in teaching practice. Early childhood teachers can utilize narrative methods like those I have described in this chapter to see beyond the developmental discourse that so prevails in our field and contemplate multiple readings of the ways children communicate with their words and bodies.

References

Blaise, M. (2005). A feminist poststructuralist study of children "doing" gender in an urban kindergarten classroom. *Early Childhood Research Quarterly, 20*, 85–108.

Blaise, M. (2010). Kiss and tell: Gendered narratives and childhood sexuality. *Australasian Journal of Early Childhood, 35*, 1–9.

Bloch, M.N., Swadener, B.B., & Cannella, G.S. (Eds.). (2014). *Reconceptualizing early care and education: A reader.* New York: Peter Lang.

Bodrova, E., & Leong, D.J. (2007). *Tools of the mind: The Vygotskyian approach to early childhood education.* Upper Saddle River, NJ: Pearson Merrill/Prentice Hall.

Bogdan, R.C., & Biklen, S.K. (2007). *Qualitative research for education: An introduction to theories and methods* (5th ed.). Boston: Pearson.

Britzman, D.P. (1995). "The question of belief": Writing poststructural ethnography. *Qualitative Studies in Education, 8*(3), 229–238.

Butler, J. (2006). *Gender trouble.* New York: Routledge.

Cannella, G.S., & Viruru, R. (2004). *Childhood and post-colonization: Power, education, and contemporary practice.* New York: Routledge.

Chase, S.E. (2005). Narrative inquiry: Multiple lenses, approaches, voices. In N.K. Denzin & Y.S. Lincoln (Eds.), *The Sage handbook of qualitative research* (3rd ed., pp. 651–679). Los Angeles, CA: Sage.

Chase, S.E. (2011). Narrative inquiry: Still a field in the making. In N.K. Denzin & Y.S. Lincoln (Eds.), *The Sage handbook of qualitative research* (4th ed., pp. 421–434). Los Angeles, CA: Sage.

Cochran-Smith, M., & Lytle, S.L. (1993). *Inside/Outside: Teacher research and knowledge.* New York: Teachers College Press.

Copple, C., & Bredekamp, S. (Eds.). (2009). *Developmentally appropriate practice in early childhood programs serving children from birth through age 8* (3rd ed.). Washington, DC: NAEYC.

Dana, N.F., & Yendol-Hoppey, D. (2009). *The reflective educator's guide to classroom research: Learning to teach and teaching to learn through practitioner inquiry* (2nd ed.). Thousand Oaks, CA: Corwin Press.

Davies, B. (2003). *Frogs and snails and feminist tales: Preschool children and gender.* Cresskill, NJ: Hampton Press.

de Haan, D., & Singer, E. (2003). Use your words: A sociocultural approach to the teacher's role in the transition from physical to verbal strategies of resolving peer conflicts. *Journal of Early Childhood Research, 1*, 95–109.

Deleuze, G., & Guattari, F. (1987). *A thousand plateaus: Capitalism and schizophrenia*. Minneapolis: University of Minnesota Press.

Fontana, A., & Frey, J.H. (2005). The interview: From neutral stance to political involvement. In N.K. Denzin & Y.S. Lincoln (Eds.), *The Sage handbook of qualitative research* (3rd ed., pp. 695–727). Thousand Oaks, CA: Sage.

Gallas, K. (1994). *The languages of learning: How children talk, write, dance, draw, and sing their understanding of the world*. New York: Teachers College Press.

Hankins, K.H. (2003). *Teaching through the storm: A journal of hope*. New York: Teachers College Press.

Hawkins, D. (1974). *The informed vision: Essays on learning and human nature*. New York: Agathorn Press.

Hubbard, R.S., & Power, B.M. (2003). *The art of classroom inquiry: A handbook for teacher-researchers* (Rev. ed.). Portsmouth, NH: Heinemann.

Iorio, J.M. (2008). Conversation as a work of art: Will it hang in a museum? *Contemporary Issues in Early Childhood, 9*(4), 297–305.

James, A. (2007). Giving voice to children's voices: Practices and problems, pitfalls and potentials. *American Anthropologist, 109*(2), 261–272.

MacRae, C. (2012). Encounters with a life(less) baby doll: Rethinking relations of agency through a collectively lived moment. *Contemporary Issues in Early Childhood, 13*(2), 120–131.

Rapley, T. (2004). Interviews. In C. Seale, G. Gobo, J.F. Gubrium, & D. Silverman (Eds.), *Qualitative research practice* (pp. 15–33). Thousand Oaks, CA: Sage.

Richardson, L. (1997). Louisa May's story of her life. In L. Richardson, *Fields of play: Constructing an academic life* (pp. 131–137). New Brunswick, NJ: Rutgers University Press.

Richardson, L. (2000). Writing: A method of inquiry. In N.K. Denzin & Y.S. Lincoln (Eds.), *Handbook of qualitative research* (2nd ed., pp. 923–948). Thousand Oaks, CA: Sage.

Riessman, C.K. (2008). *Narrative methods for the human sciences*. Los Angeles, CA: Sage.

Ryan, S., & Grieshaber, S. (2005). Shifting from developmental to postmodern practices in early childhood teacher education. *Journal of Teacher Education, 56*, 34–45.

Scheurich, J.J. (1997). A postmodern critique of research interviewing. In J.J. Scheurich, *Research method in the postmodern* (pp. 61–79). Philadelphia, PA: Routledge Falmer.

Soto, L.D., & Swadener, B.B. (Eds.). (2005). *Power and voice in research with children*. New York: Peter Lang.

Stern, D. (1998). *The diary of a baby*. New York: BasicBooks.

St. Pierre, E.A. (1997). Methodology in the fold and the irruption of transgressive data. *Journal of Qualitative Studies in Education, 10*(2), 175–189.

Tobin, J. (2004). The disappearance of the body in early childhood education. In L. Bresler (Ed.), *Knowing bodies, knowing minds* (pp. 111–125). Dordrecht, Netherlands: Kluwer.

Van Maanen, J. (2011). *Tales of the field: On writing ethnography* (2nd ed.). Chicago: University of Chicago Press.

Vygotsky, L. (1978). *Mind in society: The development of higher psychological processes*. Cambridge, MA: Harvard University Press.

White, E.J. (2011). 'Seeing' the toddler: Voices or voiceless? In E. Johansson & E.J. White (Eds.), *Educational research with our youngest* (pp. 63–82). New York: Springer.

8

"I AM WRITING NOTES TOO"

Rethinking Children's Roles in Ethnographic Research

Ysaaca D. Axelrod

I am sitting next to the family area of the classroom where a group of girls is sitting pretending to be at a beauty salon, doing each other's hair and makeup. I am taking notes in my field notebook as I usually do during play time.

Soraya comes over and plays with the corner of my notebook.

Soraya:	Are you writing everything down?
Me:	Yeah.
Soraya:	Did you do your hair? You are White. (playing with my hair)
	I continue to write.
Soraya:	What are you writing? You writing what I said? Read me your notes.

With this small incident I begin an unexpected story in my study, and, as often happens with ethnographic research, the most interesting stories are often surprising. Emergent bilingual children are habitually viewed as needing to be taught English, with little regard for their existing language(s), the development of these language(s), and the ways in which they use language in their homes and communities (Crawford, 2004; García, 2009). The voices of young emergent bilingual children are often disregarded in research and policy because of their age and language, rendering them silent on their experiences and uninvolved in the process of telling their stories. In this chapter I offer examples of young children who reflect on their language practices, offering a counter narrative to the idea that children are "too young" to be able to talk about their language experiences. At the same time, I reflect on my methodology and highlight the ways in which the child participants in my study challenged my research by inserting themselves into the data collection process, leading me to rethink my views on research with young children.

Data Collection: Design and Evolution

This chapter draws from data of a year-long ethnographic case study (Dyson & Genishi, 2005) examining the language practices of emergent bilingual four-year-olds in a bilingual (English/Spanish) Head Start classroom. The chapter explores the ways the children negotiated between/among their languages and their emerging languages, their language development over the course of a school year, and the possible ways in which these language practices were influenced by their families' and teachers' language ideologies.

Data were collected throughout the 10-month school year (September through July) by visiting the classroom two to three times per week. Observations during these visits focused on the children's language practices during their play time, whole and small group instruction, mealtimes, and outdoor play. In addition, I observed parent-teacher conferences and other classroom and school-wide activities with the families. The data include: field notes of classroom observations; artifacts of children's work, either photographs or scanned images; and transcriptions of interviews with teachers, families, and administrators. I conducted formal semi-structured individual interviews with the teachers, administrators, and families of the children, as well as had many informal conversations with the teachers and families. The purpose of these interviews was to learn about their language ideologies and practices in order to situate and understand the contexts within which the children were developing and learning language.

Reconceptualist scholars urge educators and researchers "to rethink relationships with those who are younger in ways that recognize agency, voice, and complex identities" (Grieshaber & Cannella, 2001, p. 3). I entered the research site with the notion that I was 'listening' (Cook-Sather, 2006; Rinaldi, 2006) to the children both literally and metaphorically. Literally, I was recording the ways in which children were learning and developing language within a classroom setting. I observed how they negotiated language differences within a classroom setting and the ways in which these language practices were situated within the language ideologies of the adults who supported their development. Metaphorically, my goal was to not only listen to the words the children were speaking but to situate these words within relevant contexts (physical and social) in order to learn more about how these emergent bilingual children were learning and developing language and how these processes were located, affected by, and had an effect on the social worlds in which the children lived.

The site for the study was a bilingual (Spanish/English) Head Start classroom for four-year-olds. There were 13 children in the class, three teachers, and myself the researcher. The families of most of the children were immigrants from the Dominican Republic and Mexico, and one child's family was Black with Jamaican heritage. All the families from the Dominican Republic spoke both English and Spanish in their homes. Among the families from Mexico, over half identified as being Mixtec (indigenous people from a region of Mexico around the states of Guerrero, Oaxaca, and Puebla) and spoke both Mixteco and Spanish in their homes. The families who identified as being Mexican spoke only Spanish in their homes. Two of the classroom teachers were from the Dominican Republic, and one was from Argentina. All of the adults in the classroom (myself included) were native Spanish speakers. All of the teachers felt comfortable speaking in English in the classroom, including giving classroom instruction in both English and Spanish.

My data collection methods centered on the children, with a particular emphasis on my observations and field notes. I engaged in participant observation in the classroom, whereby my role as participant and observer varied along a continuum depending on the activity, children, and stage of research (Bogdan & Biklen, 2007). At the beginning of the year I was less involved in the children's play and activities; however, as they got to know me better, they invited me into their stories and conversations, and I interacted with them more as a participant than as an observer. Initially I used "reactive entry strategy" (Corsaro, 1981, p. 131), where I only entered into conversations with children if invited in by a child and would leave the conversation as soon as the child no longer engaged with me. As the children and I developed relationships, I would join a child who was sitting alone or invite children to the art table to explore the materials and together create artifacts. I used these opportunities to engage the children in conversations about their language practices at home. When the children were engaged in conversations about language, I would join them and ask questions to further my understanding of their knowledge about language. In addition, the teachers would occasionally ask me to sit with a group of children during small group instruction or meals. On these occasions I would slip into a more 'teacher-like' role, where I would guide a lesson, help with management of materials, and support the teachers in their instruction.

Field Notes

I relied primarily on field notes to capture the language practices of the children in the classroom. My field notes were two layered, both descriptive and reflective (Bogdan & Biklen, 2007). I took notes in both English and Spanish, taking the notes in the language that was being used. For the most part I took notes as events were happening so that I could write down with the greatest detail and accuracy the words and actions of the children. When I was interacting with the children I would attempt to write or would take notes as soon as possible after a conversation or exchange in order to be as detailed as possible. These notes were transcribed after every observation in order to be able to include any details I might remember, but did not include in my notes.

I transcribed the notes into three columns. In the first, I typed the actual notes that were in the field notebook. The second column included any other details I remembered and wished to add, as well as any additional information that was relevant to the observations. These additions were not necessarily observations, but also might include an informal conversation with a teacher, child, or family member; additional information about an activity or lesson; or an event that occurred on a day I was not present that was relevant to events in the observation. The goal was to have the first two columns be what Geertz called "thick description" (as cited in Heath & Street, 2008), which is rich and provides as complete a picture as possible of the context in order for me to be able to later analyze the data. The last column was for any comments or reflections I had about any of the notes and was used for my initial thoughts about analyzing the data as the research study unfolded. Through the process of writing my initial reflections, some initial themes started to emerge, so I started to think about categories for my data analysis as I was collecting data. I continued to add notes and comments in the third column throughout the data analysis process, using a color-coded system to keep track of when the comments were added.

I took notes in a distinctive red notebook; the color was chosen so that it would stand out in the classroom in case I misplaced it. The children became familiar with the field notebook and would quickly return it to me if they found it around the classroom. One child, Javier, would on occasion find my notebook, open it, and pretend to write in it, telling the other children that he was "pretending to be Ysaaca." This story line always seemed to get the children excited, as they would come over and tell me what Javier was doing in a tone of "he is misbehaving" and would follow me as I would go over to recover my notebook. Javier would quickly assure me that he was "just pretending" and did not write in my notebook. The children seemed to understand that whatever was happening in the notebook was serious, although I did not initially share with them the contents, and I never gave the children any warnings not to touch or play with the notebook. It seemed there was an unwritten rule that the notebook was important, perhaps because I always carried it and was always writing in it.

Several months into the research study, the children in this classroom developed an interest in the content of my field notebooks and note taking. They asked questions about what I was doing in their classroom and what I was writing. The children's responses and desire to engage with my field notes, their choices about what events and stories they wanted me to record, and their responses to my rereading of notes made me wonder about ways to include children more explicitly in the process of collecting ethnographic data and how to include them in conversations around data analysis. The children's responses to my field notes of their language practices gave insight into their ideas about language, their views on their own bilingualism, and their understandings of print and text and its relationship to oral language. The children in my study pushed my original goal of "listening" to include the data collection process, where I not only was listening to their voices as they used and negotiated language with their peers, but also included their voices as we made choices about which data to highlight, record, and use as part of conversations about language(s) and language practices in the classroom.

In the following sections I share a few examples of the ways in which the children contributed to the research design and methodology and extended my understanding of having children as participants in my study.

Give Me Back My Letter (by Javier, Four Years Old)

My data collection for this study started in the classroom during the parent orientation and children's initial visits to the classroom prior to school starting. I had been collecting data in this classroom for two years prior to this study, so while many of the children were new to me (some of the children had older siblings in prior years), I was familiar with the teachers and curriculum. I was comfortable with the process of taking field notes in an early childhood classroom, and I was used to children coming over and inquiring about my role in the classroom. My usual response was that I was interested in learning about how they talked with their friends and that I was writing their words down. For the most part, the children would nod and walk away, leaving me to my task. For this group of children, I was a constant presence in their classroom, and they (together with their teachers and families) accepted me as part of the classroom community. I expected my role to be similar to prior years, with brief explanations of my role, but otherwise ignored. A few months into the school year, the following incident occurred:

> I am sitting in the classroom where I am collecting data for my dissertation, sitting on a child-sized chair, taking notes about the children in my notebook. Javier walks over, looks at my notes, points to a letter "j" and says, "Hey, that's my letter, give it back." I look at him, and respond completely confused, "How can I do that?" Javier, "Just give it back to me, all of them [pointing to them on the page], it's mine." I protest, "But I can't, I need them. The letter 'j' is in other words too, not just your name." At this point, another child zooms by and Javier joins him zooming around the room.

As a former kindergarten teacher, I was familiar with the possessiveness young children have with the letters in their name, in particular with the first letter in their name. As children learn that their name contains particular symbols, letters, they start to look for these letters in print and often assume that all instances of a particular letter refer to them or belong to them. This is also accurate of letters in their friends' and family member's names; they are learning to associate a symbol with meaning, building relationships between text and the people and things that are meaningful in their lives (Ballenger, 1999). Javier did return later to my notebook, and I explained that sometimes the letter "j" he saw referred to him and sometimes it was part of another word. He seemed satisfied with this explanation; however, a few months later, he was one of the children who became an integral part of shifting my data collection process.

I Am Writing Notes Too (by Soraya, Four Years Old)

Soraya was one of the first children who showed an interest in what I was doing. She would often point to my notebook and ask me what I was doing. I told the students that I was taking notes about what they were doing and saying, and for the most part this answer seemed to be satisfactory. Soraya wanted to know more, so I read her parts of my field notes. As she pointed to words on the page, she would say, "What you writing here?" During these readings, other children who heard their names would come and listen to me reread my notes, which recounted what they had played/said/done during the day. They would laugh and comment and point to each other, saying, "That's you" as I would read their names. This would happen quite often, to the point where I had to set aside time each day to reread my notes to the children so I could actually have time to take notes during classroom activities.

One day, Soraya sat next to me with her notebook and said, "Look, I am writing like you. You know I'm writing notes too, when I get home I am going to have my daddy buy me a notebook." A few days later she skipped by, saying, "I have my notebook, my notebook, my notebook" in a sing-songy voice, and she sat down and filled a page with notes. Figure 8.1 shows the notes she took while sitting next to me. She was learning her letters at the time, but it would appear that her "notes" mimic my cursive writing.

Me:	Can you read your notes to me?
Soraya:	You read them.
Me:	You have to read your own notes. I read my notes and you need to read your notes. (I did this because, as can be seen from the notes, I would not have been able to accurately read what she wrote, and I wanted to avoid misreading her writing.)
Soraya:	Okay, you read them to me.
	I read a few pages of notes. Several children come closer and listen, smiling when they hear their name.
Me:	Okay, now it's your turn.
	Soraya takes her notebook: I am shy.
Me:	Okay.

Playing with their notebooks became a popular activity for the children in the class, and they would go to different parts of the room, sit down, look around, and write in their notebooks, "playing at researcher." They never used that language, instead saying, "I am pretending to be Ysaaca." The act of taking notes became part of the classroom play, and we would often sit and share our notes with each other. Through their play, the children were being and becoming researchers of their language practices: their own, their classmates', and their community's. Their research became a part of mine, and their data gave me insight into their ideas about their language practices, bilingualism, and language ideologies.

FIGURE 8.1 Soraya's notes

My notebook also became a place to clarify ideas, for the children to write/draw and expand their thinking. Soto (2005) calls this process "the notion of 'visualizing voice'" (p. 9), whereby one shares and examines children's drawings in order to help understand and describe their ideas and theories about a concept. Estrella created the word "ganchulina" to describe a fancy dress. Her definition of the dress evolved over the year, and the word "ganchulina" became part of the classroom vocabulary (Axelrod, 2014). Toward the end of the school year, Estrella sat next to me. I was

"ganchulina"

June-21-2011

FIGURE 8.2 Estrella's "ganchulinas" drawn in the field notebook

trying to understand the newest, or updated, version of a "ganchulina," when she turned to me and said "*dame, yo lo dibujo*" (give me [your notebook], I will draw it).

Her drawing (see Figure 8.2) helped clarify what she meant by a ganchulina, and she was able to use multiple modalities, drawing and oral language, to describe the dress. Her drawing shows blue dresses with short orange sleeves and dots. The field notebook became a place to share ideas with each other, and, as the children developed an understanding between oral language and text, they were able to understand and recognize the power of having their words, experiences, and stories preserved in print.

¿Lo vas a Escribir? (by Javier, Four Years Old)

Javier is pushing truck around "*voy a llevar la basura*" (I am going to take the trash). Others pushing around trucks too "vroom, vroom," then words in Spanish, but I cannot understand what they are saying

Javier to Ysaaca: Did you hear me?
Me: Huh?

Javier:	*¿Me escuchaste?* (Did you hear me?)
Me:	*Si.* (Yes.)
Javier:	*Voy a llevar basura.* (I am taking the trash.)
Me:	*¿Si?* (Yes?)
Javier:	*¿Lo vas a escribir?* (Are you going to write it [pointing to my notebook]?)
Me:	*Si.* (Yes. [and I continue writing])

Javier would often play close to me, talking loudly, and then ask if I was writing down what he was saying and doing. He realized I recorded events that were happening close to me and would purposefully move around the room in order to be part of my field notes. At the same time, he also was careful not be close to me when whispering secrets to his friends and at times would move away from me if I attempted to sit close by during one of his whispering conversations.

Sharing stories with me would often guarantee they would be written down. One morning Soraya arrived to the classroom looking quite sad. She sat next to me and told me how her little brother had pinched her that morning. She then pointed to my notebook and said, "Are you going to write that down?" I asked her, "Do you want me to?" She nodded yes, and I start writing. She then asked, "Are you writing that? That he pinched me and it hurt?" I nodded as I was writing. She gave a big smile and walked away, as if she knowing that her brother's misbehavior had now been permanently recorded. As the children's understanding of the relationship between oral and written language developed, so did their interest in my notebook and the possibilities of what might be written in it.

I Want to Know What You Wrote

As the year progressed, the children became increasingly interested in my field notes, and we would often sit together and read my notebook. These conversations about my notes became a critical piece of my data. I would write my recollections of the conversations as soon as I was able to, and these notes became both "new" data, as well as elaborations on existing data, which I would add to the second column of my transcribed notes. The children's commentary about my written recordings of the events in their classroom gave insight into their thoughts of the experiences in the classroom and their language usage. In the following anecdote, Soraya and Jasmin are listening to me read an exchange between Javier and myself earlier in the day. I had read pieces of this exchange earlier with Soraya and Javier, so Soraya was familiar with part of the anecdote.

Jasmin:	What does it say?
Soraya:	Javier has a puppy.
	Jasmin (looks at me and points to the notebook): But what does it say?
Me:	Javier said *viste mi perrito en mi cubby?* (Did you see my dog in my cubby?)

Soraya:	And you said no.
Me:	No, I didn't say that, I asked if it would bite me.
Soraya:	That's silly, why would you ask that? It's a stuffed dog, they don't bite for real.

This anecdote raised two problems I had to negotiate with the children as we talked about the field notes. One was the fact that the notes were, for the most part, accurate, as I was writing what occurred, and in this case because I was the speaker I remembered what I had said. At times the children would want me to change what they had said or would claim not to have said something, in particular if it had resulted in a discussion among friends or if it was unfair (such as they had taken a toy from someone else). While I wrote down their new words, as part of data collection on the conversations, I usually did not alter the existing notes, unless I had marked in my notes that I was unsure of what they said, somebody's name, or if they were retelling an event that had occurred elsewhere. While this raised a dilemma for me in terms of honoring what they were saying, I also wanted to make sure I had some accuracy in my notes with regard to events that occurred in the classroom that I had observed. I was also interested in their take and interpretation of events and how they saw and recognized (or in some cases did not recognize) their actions and language in my notes. For the most part, the children did not request that text be removed or altered in drastic ways. For example, the children would declare, "I was playing with her too" or "I did too shared with him," details that did not alter the data for my study.

The children's analysis and commentary about what had occurred in the classroom, shifted my role in the classroom and as a participant observer. While, in this particular case, Soraya is pointing out the absurdity of my comment, for the most part the children's reactions and commentary to the retelling of classroom events were filled with compliments and compassion toward each other. When a child fell ill during class, and I wrote about it, during the retelling the children would talk about how to be nice to him the next day and how the medicine and doctors were going to help. The children complimented each other's creations (artwork, building structures, texts) and each other during episodes when I wrote about them creating particular pieces, and together we would take photographs of the work to save it.

My research questions revolved around their language practices; therefore, the most interesting conversations for me were around language, who was speaking in what language, what words they were using, and the children's interest in the language and text on the pages. My research and interest in language brought language practices to the forefront of the classroom. The teachers and I focused on and talked about the children's language practices. My recording of oral language signaled to the children a valuing of language, all of their languages. In addition to highlighting oral language, I modeled a literacy practice of writing, taking notes, and shared with the children my notes, both visually (they enjoyed looking at them, finding letters, looking at the small sketches I did of their classroom) and through my rereading of classroom anecdotes. We can see through the children's responses to the field notes the ways in which their literacy skills developed throughout the year, from finding and demanding the return of a letter, to playing at writing notes, to actually writing notes. My data collection of their language practices created opportunities for them to be apprentices of written language (Lindfors, 2008). The children played at and developed their own sense of how to use and manipulate symbols in order to express themselves through writing.

My role as a participant observer evolved throughout the year, and while at times I questioned my increased role as a participant, it seemed that my sharing of data with the children created an authentic opportunity for us to learn from each other. While books on the participant/observer continuum suggest that we attempt to achieve a balance between the two (Bogdan & Biklen, 2007), in this particular study, becoming more of a participant created opportunities for a shared experience among the participants and me that led to richer and more complex data.

Final Thoughts

In this research study, the adult researcher, myself, ultimately retained the greatest power over how the research was collected, disseminated, and presented, as is suggested in the research of Graue and Hawkins (2005). I continue to make choices about where to send off manuscripts, and the children in my study are perhaps not yet ready to read the academic manuscripts that describe their language practices and development. However, if my goal is to authentically listen to children, learn from them, and use their stories to advocate for their education, then I must continue to find ways to engage them as co-researchers in the process of telling their story.

The methodological implications of this study can contribute to the ways in which we engage in research with young children. However, it is an examination of the setting where this research took place that I believe has implications for the education of young emergent bilingual children, which ultimately was the purpose and significance of this research study: How can we learn from the language practices of young emergent bilinguals in order to better support their multilingual development? The children's ability and desire to interact with the data and engage in conversations about their language development highlight the flexible curriculum in the classroom that allowed the children the time and space to engage with me, the researcher, and with each other. The neoliberal agenda of narrowing curricular practices and reducing opportunities for children to interact with each other has made it even more difficult to hear their voices and the voices of their families within schools (Genishi & Dyson, 2009). However, in this classroom, children were given the time and space to play and learn in ways that allowed them to draw from their full linguistic repertoire and build upon their existing language skills. The flexible curriculum gave the children opportunities to interact with each other and learn from each other, highlighting the role and importance of peer (and adult) interactions in development. This flexibility also created opportunities for the children to interact with me, as the researcher. The teachers in the classroom recognized the language and literacy opportunities that were created and joined in the conversations.

As I reflect on this research study and think about some ways I could have planned for the children's engagement and involvement, I go back to the notion of the importance of authentic and meaningful experiences for children (Genishi & Dyson, 2009; Lindfors, 2008). If I had entered with ideas of how the children should engage with me and the data, would I be able to tell this story? Was it the openness and unexpectedness of the children's engagement that made this possible? In their work with children Hong and Genishi (2005) reflect on shifting identities during their work with young emergent bilinguals: "When we show children the purposes of research, they may feel empowered to follow our lead and voice what they have learned" (p. 173). As researchers, we need to be open about the work we do with young children, not assume that their age and language practices might not allow them to participate or, more accurately, participate in ways we have planned. We need to be open to possibility that the children in our studies might shift our studies and questions so that they are relevant to their lives, so that they can, in the words of Flor to me, as she knew I was not going to be there the next day: *"Escribir todo lo que dicen mis compañeros mañana para que tu oiga"* ("I am going to write everything my classmates say tomorrow so that you can hear it").

References

Axelrod, Y. (2014). "Ganchulinas" and "rainbowli" colors: Young multilingual children play with language in Head Start classroom. *Early Childhood Education Journal*. doi: 10.1007/s10643–014–0631-z.

Ballenger, C. (1999). *Teaching other people's children: Literacy and learning in a bilingual classroom*. New York: Teachers College Press.

Bogdan, R., & Biklen, S. (2007). *Qualitative research in education: An introduction to theory and practice* (5th ed.). Boston: Ally and Bacon.

Cook-Sather, A. (2006). Sound, presence, and power: "Student voice" in educational research and reform. *Curriculum Inquiry, 36*(4), 359–390.

Corsaro, W.A. (1981). Entering the child's world—Research strategies for field entry and data collection in a preschool setting. In J. Green & C. Wallat (Eds.), *Ethnography and language in education settings* (pp. 117–146). Norwood, NJ: Ablex.

Crawford, J. (2004). *Educating English learners: Language diversity in the classroom* (5th ed., formerly *Bilingual education: History, politics, theory and practice*). Los Angeles, CA: Bilingual Educational Services.

Dyson, A.H., & Genishi, C. (2005). *On the case: Approaches to language and literacy research*. New York: Teachers College Press.

García, O. (2009). *Bilingual education in the 21st century: A global perspective*. Malden, MA: Wiley-Blackwell.

Genishi, C., & Dyson, A.H. (2009). *Children language and literacy: Diverse learners in diverse times.* New York: Teachers College Press, and Washington D.C.: National Association for the Education of Young Children.

Graue, E., & Hawkins, M. (2005). Relations, refractions, and reflections in research with children. In L. Diaz Soto & B. Blue Swadener (Eds.), *Power and voice in research with children* (pp. 45–54). New York: Peter Lang Press.

Grieshaber, S., & Cannella, G.S. (2001). From identity to identities: Increasing possibilities in early childhood education. In S. Grieshaber & G.S. Cannella (Eds.), *Embracing identities in early childhood education: Diversity and possibilities* (pp. 3–22). New York: Teachers College Press.

Heath, S.B., & Street, B.V. (2008). *On ethnography: Approaches to language and literacy research.* New York: Teachers College Press.

Hong, M., & Genishi, C. (2005). Voices of English language learners. In L. Diaz Soto & B. Blue Swadener (Eds.), *Power and voice in research with children* (pp. 165–175). New York: Peter Lang Press.

Lindfors, J.W. (2008). *Children's language: Connecting reading, writing and talk.* New York: Teachers College Press.

Rinaldi, C. (2006). *In dialogue with Reggio Emilia: Listening, researching and learning.* New York: Routledge.

Soto, L.D. (2005). Children make the best theorists. In L. Diaz Soto & B. Blue Swadener (Eds.), *Power and voice in research with children* (pp. 9–20). New York: Peter Lang Press.

SECTION 3

Critical Issues in Early Childhood Research from New Perspectives

9

CURRENT PLAYWORLD RESEARCH IN SWEDEN

Rethinking the Role of Young Children and Their Teachers in the Design and Execution of Early Childhood Research

Beth Ferholt, Monica Nilsson, Anders Jansson, and Karin Alnervik

Introduction

If we consider research to be "re-searching," or searching again (Paley, 1992), then early childhood research is happening all the time in early childhood education, not only during academic research studies. This research is being carried out not only by researchers but also by teachers and young children as they form community and make meaning in their classrooms. How such re-searching takes place in one early childhood research project is the topic of this chapter.

Traditional early childhood research underestimates the capability of children and thus assumes that the objects of adult and child research must be different from each other and that young children are incapable of designing and executing research methods. Young children may obviously study, for instance, water or light, but they do not appear to most adults to study, for instance, meaning making, play, teaching, or learning. Young children cannot complete a statistical analysis or write a field note that would be considered valid in any current social scientific field. Therefore, within traditional early childhood research, children are not thought to be contributing to research as researchers, but are rather considered to be making all of their contributions to research from their position as objects of study.

Teachers, too, are often excluded from the position of researcher in traditional early childhood research, or at least excluded from this position unless they replace some of their language and accompanying perspective with the foreign language of a social scientific field. It is a rare teacher-researcher who persistently refuses to adopt a language that is foreign to her classroom and still finds some level of acceptance for her work in the early childhood research community.

Famed teacher-researcher Vivian Paley is one of the very few whose work is well known within this community. She is the exception that proves the rule.

In traditional early childhood research, researchers who study teacher and child as participants are rarely a subject in the study themselves. And such researchers do not need to modify their professional language and perspective to accommodate participants' language and perspective in order to perform re-searching that is accepted within the academy.

In this chapter we will describe a current research project in Swedish preschools that has used a recently emerging form of play, called playworlds (Lindqvist, 1995), to challenge the exclusion of young children's voices and their teacher's voices from early childhood research. As Conquergood (2002) might say, this project allowed us to bring into early childhood research the excluded knowledge, knowers, and means of knowing in early childhood. In doing so, this project required that participating researchers be challenged by new perspectives. We had to try out perspectives of teachers and children, and this changed both our research methods and our research questions in this study. As well, this project allowed teacher participants to rethink and perform anew their listening to children and their documentation of children's exploration and learning. Of note, with the exception of the researchers, all participant names have been changed to pseudonyms in our research study.

In functioning preschools, since adults and children are anything but impartial or detached, researchers being challenged by the perspectives of teachers and children constitutes a critique of conventional social science, in which the explicit goal is to see that which one studies objectively "without being influenced by personal feelings or opinions; in an impartial or detached manner" (Objectively, n.d.). Having our research methods and the objects of our research study changed by our trying out perspectives of teachers and children, and teacher participants rethinking and performing anew their listening to children and their documentation of children's exploration and learning, contributes toward the larger methodological project of challenging the divide between method and object in conventional social science. As children's play challenges the divide between form and content (play can be defined as having fun playing), we consider this larger methodological project itself to be, in this case, a result of bringing children's perspectives into early childhood research.

In this chapter we will describe first the playworld as subject, then the method of the succession of playworld studies that led to the design and execution of this current playworld research project in Swedish preschools, and then the project itself. We will then present conclusions from this project. We will end the chapter with further discussion of the ramifications of these conclusions.

Playworlds: Subject of Study

Lindqvist-inspired playworlds are uniquely situated to challenge the exclusion of young children's voices and their teacher's 'teacherly' voices from early childhood research. This is because of their place in the historical trajectory of play theory and practice, because of their theoretical base in Lindqvist's reading of Vygotksian play theory, and because of the ways they can be characterized by adult–child shared responsibility for directing adult–child joint play. As we discuss playworlds as methods in the following section, we pay particular attention to playwords' methodological roots and the intermediate concepts or solutions they generate.

Contextualization of Playworlds within a History of Play Practice and Theory

We begin our description of playworlds by presenting a broad history of play practice and theory. International playworlds are inspired by the work of Vygotsky (1971; 1978; 1987; 2004), and there is significant overlap across international playworld practices. Playworlds are currently being studied in Finland, Japan, Serbia, and the United States, as well as in Sweden (Baumer et al., 2005; Ferholt, 2009; 2010; 2012; 2014; Hakkarainen & Ferholt, 2013; Ferholt & Lecusay, 2010; Hakkarainen, 1999; 2004; Hofmann & Rainio, 2007; Lindqvist, 1995; Rainio & Marjanovic-Shane, 2013; Marjanovic-Shane et al., 2011; Miyazaki, 2008; 2009; Nilsson, 2010; Rainio 2005; 2007; 2008a; 2008b; 2009; 2010). However, the project that we describe in this chapter evolved from a Swedish playworlds tradition that is rooted in the work of Lindqvist (1995), so we will be placing playworlds based in Lindqvist's theory within this historical context and will be primarily discussing Lindqvist-inspired playworlds throughout the chapter.

In brief, the ideal of modern Western childhood, with its emphasis on the innocence and malleability of children (Aries, 1962; Fass, 2007), has combined with various social conditions to promote adults' direction of children's play toward adult-determined developmental goals and adults' protection of children's play from adults. Playworlds can be considered a new form of play because in playworlds adults actively enter into the fantasy play of young children as a means of promoting the development and quality of life of both adults and children. Such claims are of course based on an understanding of models of play as socially and historically determined, and as operating conceptually in ideas of childhood and empirically in the classroom, and in an understanding that certain of these models of play have dominated our thinking of play at certain places and at certain times.

We can describe a stereotypical modern condition in which children's play is isolated from adult activities and then either directed toward adult-determined developmental goals or protected from adult interference. The play of modern Western children often takes place in settings that isolate children and childhood activities from adults and adult activities: in preschools, schools, and after-school programs; in play rooms and on playgrounds and playing fields; on television and computer monitors; and in the offices of child therapists. These settings are carefully designed and supervised by adults whose goal is, usually, to shelter or direct this play so that children further their social, cognitive, or psychological development toward adulthood. These children do find time and space to play outside of these settings, on their own and away from adult protection and supervision, and also with adults (sometimes parents, more often grandparents or babysitters) for mutual benefits. However, these occurrences are haphazard; often rare; usually not consciously considered valuable and so not respected (they are the first activity to be interrupted or ended prematurely); sometimes considered suspect (as adult-child joint activities); and not institutionally or theoretically supported, protected, or cultivated. In contrast, playworld settings are systematically constructed to promote a form of play in which adults and children enter and exit a common fantasy, together. Adult and child participants do this through a combination of adult forms of creative imagining, which require extensive experience (disciplines of art and science), and children's forms of creative imagining, which require embodiment of ideas in the material world (play).

Along with this shift in play practice, we can describe a parallel shift in psychological theories of play. In contemporary Western European and American biological, psychoanalytic, cognitive-developmental theories of play (for example Groos, 1901; Freud, 1964; Klein, 1986; Piaget, 1951) we find the assertions that children's play is in no way fundamentally similar to adult activities and that adult knowledge, experience, or developmental stage is a teleology for children's play. However, Lindqvist (1995; 2001b; 2003) reinterprets Vygotsky's theory of play (1978; 1987; 2004) to argue that children's play is an early form of the artistic and scientific endeavors of adulthood and, therefore, produces new and intrinsically valuable insights—insights that can be of value to adults and children alike. Lindqvist's theory of play (1995; 2001b; 2003) does not share with Western European and American theories of play (for example Groos, 1901; Freud, 1964; Klein, 1986; Piaget, 1951) the inclination to describe adult knowledge, experience, or developmental stage as a teleology for children's play.

Theoretical Support for Playworlds

Lindqvist (1995; 2001a; 2003) reinterprets Vygotsky's theory of play through Vygotsky's *Psychology of Art* (1971) and through a modified reading of "Imagination and Creativity in Childhood" (2004). She agrees with D.B. Elkonin (2005) concerning the importance of Vygotsky's (1987; 2004) claim that imagination and realistic thinking act as a unity in the processes of invention and creativity. But she argues that Elkonin did not sufficiently focus on Vygotsky's assertion that children's play is a creative cultural manifestation in humans.

In "Imagination and Creativity in Childhood" (2004) Vygotsky begins by defining the creative act as "(a)ny activity that gives rise to something new" (p. 8). To hone this definition he makes a distinction between "reproductive" activity, in which "nothing new is created," but, instead, there is "a repetition of something that already exists" (2004, p. 8), and a "combinatorial or creative activity" in which one is "not merely recovering the traces of stimulation that reached my brain in the past" (2004, p. 9). In creative activity, Vygotsky writes, "I never actually saw this remote past, or this future; however, I still have my own idea, image, or picture of what they were or will be like" (2004, p. 10).

This basic distinction is what allows anyone who is engaged in creative activity, including children, to produce something novel. Vygotsky (2004) continues:

> If human activity were limited to reproduction of the old, then the human being would be a creature oriented only to the past and would only be able to adapt to the future to the extent that it reproduced the past. It is precisely human creative activity that makes the human being a creature oriented toward the future, creating the future and thus altering his own present.
>
> *(p. 9)*

The creative activity that Vygotsky is discussing is imagination. Vygotsky is arguing that imagination is an essential aspect of all thought. And Vygotsky (2004) explicitly argues that all humans, including children, are creative:

> There is a widespread opinion that creativity is the province of a select few . . . This is not true. If we understand creativity in its true psychological sense as the creation of something new, then this implies that creation is the province of everyone to one degree or another; that it is a normal and constant companion in childhood.
>
> *(p. 33)*

It is not only those at the height of their creative abilities who can produce something of worth to many others of all ages, meaning that even a child in play might inspire an adult. Vygotsky concludes, "If we understand creativity in this way, it is easy to see that the creative processes are already fully manifest in earliest childhood" (2004, p. 11). He goes on to tell us, "We can identify creative processes in children at the very earliest ages, especially in their play . . . all these children at play represent examples of the most authentic, truest creativity" (2004, p. 11). If children are creative producers of culture then traditional relationships between children and adults in the creative activity of play, and in adult creative activities, must be rethought.

Lindqvist's Playworlds and Playworlds in the United States

Lindqvist's playworlds were developed as a component of her creative pedagogy of play (1995), which in turn was designed to investigate how aesthetic activities can influence children's play and the nature of the connections between play and the aesthetic forms of drama and literature. She was trying with her pedagogy to find a "common denominator" of play and aesthetic forms, a denominator she called "the aesthetics of play" (Lindqvist, 1995). Lindqvist considered one of the most important conclusions of her investigations to be that the development of adult-child joint play is made possible through the creation of a common fiction, and it is this fiction that she calls a "playword" (1995).

In Lindqvist's playworlds the interaction between adults and children is structured around a piece of literature or another work of art. The adults and children work together to "bring the literature to life" (1995, p. 72) through drama (or, in some cases, dance—although we will discuss here dramatic playworlds). They assume roles, characters from the literary piece, and "make use of the intrinsic dynamism between world, action and character in drama and play" (1995, p. 72). Concretely, through joint scripted and improvisational acting and set design, the children and adults transform their classroom into a world inspired by a book (and, in the process, the book they are working from into a world inspired by their activity). Lindqvist gives rich and concrete examples in her publications of playworlds (1989; 1992; 1995; 1996; 2000; 2001a; 2001b; 2002).

While Lindqvist's students continued to create and study playworlds in Sweden, the influence of her work on Swedish preschools diminished through the 1990s and into the twenty-first century. However, during this time playworlds began to proliferate in Finland (Hakkarainen & Bredikyte, 2008) and in 2003–2004 a first US playworld was staged through collaboration and exchange between a Finish play laboratory, Silmu at the University of Oulu, and the Laboratory of Comparative Human Cognition of the University of California, San Diego. This first US playworld took place in a preschool, and several other US playworlds were subsequently staged in early childhood and childhood classrooms at public elementary schools on a military base.

Although the basic structure of the US playworlds were the same as Lindqvist's playworlds and most Finnish playworlds, the contrast between implementation of playworlds in Sweden, Finland, and the United States allows us to isolate three conditions we believe are essential in the creation of the shared responsibility for directing the adult-child joint play that is at the heart of playworlds (Ferholt & Lecusay, 2010). First, adults in a playworld enter fully into children's play by taking on play roles, putting on costumes, and entering character. In doing so they are required to partially step outside of their role as teacher and join the children in the role of fellow actor. Lindqvist (1995) writes of playworlds, "The more colorful the character which is being dramatized, the more scope for action. Consequently, dressing up to play the role is not enough—on the contrary. Giving life to the personality of the character and to the action is crucial to develop a play" (p. 210). And she writes of a specific playworld:

> Having played a role such as Fear or Groke, remaining neutral is no longer possible. Moreover, dramatizing and playing roles per se involve an aspect of duality. The "actor" is both teacher and character at the same time, which means that the contours of the individual become distinct in relation to the role which is being played. "Imagine, Groke is really Majlis (the teacher)!
>
> *(p. 210)*

Second, children as well as the adults co-construct the environment in which play takes place. The children do not play in an environment that has been designed for them by adults alone. Third, Lindqvist's pedagogy grounds play in works of children's literature that address epistemological and ethical dilemmas that are of great interest to people in a variety of life stages. Because of this grounding the teacher is personally invested in the topics, and therefore the process and conclusions, of a playworld. The teacher is at least as interested in play as a means for furthering the children's and his or her own understanding of a topic, such as 'fear,' as he or she is interested in furthering the students' learning. Furthermore, these dilemmas are such that it is the combination of different perspectives, rather than skills or experience that come with age, which produces solutions (e.g., What is real? What do you do if someone you love is doing something harmful to themselves and others? What does one do in the face of conflicting options?) (Ferholt & Lecusay, 2010).

As playworlds are in some ways both subject and method of this research, such shared responsibility between adults and children for directing playworlds necessitates children taking responsibility for playworld research itself. This point will be discussed further in the following section on playworlds as method.

The Current Playworld Research Project in Sweden

The current playworld project in Sweden was designed to bring the playworld activity to three Reggio Emilia–inspired Swedish preschools in order to bring a current approach to playworlds into interaction with the *pedagogy of exploratory learning* that was being practiced in these preschools. In *exploratory learning and pedagogy* of *listening* (see Wehner-Godée, 2011; Åberg & Lenz Taguchi, 2005) children's exploration of the world based on their own interests and questions is emphasized. The pedagogy of exploratory learning holds that children have and develop theories and hypotheses about the world that should be considered to be equally possible to those of adults (Lenz Taguchi, 2010).

In exploratory learning children's theories and hypotheses can be developed and investigated through aesthetic creations and the 'hundred languages,' as well as through discussions, problem solving, and reflection. In this way children learn and develop their understanding of and knowledge about the world. This learning process is described as rhizomatic, meaning creative and circular rather than linear, pre-determined, and goal related (Olsson, 2009).

In exploratory learning children are regarded as cultural and knowledge creators (Dahlberg & Lenz Taguchi, 1994). The teachers' task is to create environments that encourage and challenge children to explore. This is done, for example, by actively listening to children's thoughts and theories but also through carefully formulated problems and projects, chosen materials, and aesthetic activities.

Although an appreciation of children's creativity, and of the ability to support adults' listening to children, are clearly elements of significant similarity between playworlds and exploratory learning, play is not emphasized in exploratory learning. In exploratory learning play is often seen as an expression of a traditional Fröbel-inspired preschool didactics based on a view of the child as "nature" (Dahlberg & Lenz Taguchi, 1994). Play is also sometimes spoken of as "playful learning," which is a resource in the exploration (personal communications with Gunilla Dahlberg).

The research project's stated point of departure was a playworld perspective, which holds that in children's exploration of the world and themselves play is crucial. Our research team of three (Karin Alnervik was not formally on the initial research team) believed that this view of play would be compatible enough with exploratory learning for the project to take place because we held the view of play that Gadamer (1997) presents: that play ontology is linked to experiencing, understanding, and "Bildung" (culture) and that play thus has a value in itself. This did not mean we believed that, from a preschool didactics perspective, we were not interested in the function of play in the children's (and educators') development. However, because our interest in what play does for children's cognitive, emotional, social, and so forth development did not necessarily mean that we followed an instrumental approach, or that we viewed play as a means to achieve goals in the curriculum or other predefined goals determined by adults, we did believe the project could take place across the differences in practical and theoretical approaches to play of playworlds and exploratory learning.

It was the combination of these differences and similarities between playworlds and exploratory learning that was the inspiration for the research project. The project was designed to 'play with' the contradiction that arises when one appreciates both the value of children's creativity—their ability to produce new insights, which may be of value to people of all ages—and the need to enculturate children if our species is to continue. The project was also designed to contribute to a preschool didactics that takes inspiration from both 'modern' and 'postmodern' theory and practice while bridging the duality between the two. The research team hypothesized that playworlds might form a bridge between exploratory learning and (free) play. We also wanted to see what would happen with Lindqvist's playworlds, modified as they were in the United States, if they were to be staged in a very different institutional setting than a US public school on a military base.

As we will be making an argument that it was playworlds as subject of study and as method *within this particular exploratory learning context* that supported our bringing into early childhood research the excluded knowledge, knowers, and means of knowing of teachers and children, this project description will conclude with a brief description of the research setting—the three preschools. We will also briefly describe some non-traditional-researcher connections our research team had to the preschools. The choice of setting based on the characteristics we will discuss, and the non-traditional-researcher connections to the setting, were both part of the conscious design of the research project.

Some of these aspects of the project design had research-based justifications. For instance, we knew from past playworld projects that a certain level of trust between teachers and between teachers and administrators is needed if teachers are to consider putting on costumes and going into role. Some of these aspects of the project design had logistics-based justifications. For instance, Beth Ferholt could not join the research team full time for a year if she was not given a space for her child in a preschool she could trust. However, the distinction between these two categories of justifications deserves to be challenged. We argue that it was precisely through watching the development of Beth's child at close range that Monica and Beth were able to better understand various teachers' claims concerning the concept of development. This argument is the focus of a forthcoming paper, where we also explore the ramifications this claim has for understanding the proleptic nature of the development of the research project itself.

The three preschools of the study quite impressively fulfill their explicit goal of having their teachers and the children, as well as the preschool director, pedagogista (who is responsible for the pedagogical work), and atelieristas (who are responsible for the various aesthetic forms of expression that are important in an approach that is based on exploratory learning), feel that they are listened to as participants. This is our impression from both observations and interviews, and we believe that these expectations on the part of the community of the three preschools influenced our receptiveness to teacher input. We researchers were invited to join a community in which the explicit and often-achieved goal was to listen to everyone whenever it was possible to do so.

Furthermore, two members of our research team were closely connected to these preschools in roles aside from that of researcher, and thus were influenced by this community in several different but powerful ways that must have shaped the research practice. Karin is co-owner of the three preschools, with her husband, and is also the preschools' pedagogista. She is a full member of the research team but did not initially design the research project—although she did approve the initial research design. To have the three preschools be places where, as she says, 'everyone is listened to' is in good part her vision, her mission, and her doing.

As mentioned earlier, Beth is the parent of a two-year-old child who was attending one of the preschools during our data collection year. Beth was considered by the teachers to be both a researcher and a parent, although our research team did not engage in person with playworlds in her child's group. Beth was also, as parents often are, strongly emotionally engaged with the preschools and was also emotionally engaged in different ways than she might have been if she had not been a parent. For instance, as her child thrived at the preschools Beth came to believe that these preschools were, in many ways, the very best preschools in the world. It is beyond the scope of this paper to explore the possible implications of these two project design elements in relation to our argument that perspectives of teachers and children that changed our research methods and subjects of study were incorporated into this research project.

We began this research project with some research questions and a list of data sources, but the design is intentionally open to change in method and subject. We currently are in the data analysis phase of the project and are able to place our findings in several different clusters. The findings we address in the following are from just one of these clusters.

It is important to note that the research project was influenced by US play-world research projects. For instance, one US playworld produced data that supported the claim that Vygotsky's concept of the zone of proximal development should be expanded so we see not only the unidirectional development of a child toward an adult stage of development in this zone, but also the simultaneous development experienced by adults participating in the zone with the child (Ferholt & Lecusay, 2010). We began our research project with expectations that playworlds would create zones of proximal development in which both teachers and researchers would develop and, thus, that many of our most interesting findings would most likely be unexpected and could most likely be found in those moments when teachers and researchers were in these zones with children.

There were also significant initial findings by Lindqvist that shaped this current playworld project in related ways. Of adults' creative approach to children's play in playworlds, Lindqvist writes the following (italics added):

> During the course of the theme, *I have seen the teachers become someone in the eyes of the children. They have turned into interesting and exciting people.* I have often had the feeling that staff members at a day-care center are perceived as rather anonymous grown-ups. Sometimes, the children will not even notice if a teacher is ill and has been replaced. In a way, *assuming roles has liberated the adults*—it has enabled them to step out of their 'teacher roles' and leave behind the institutional language which is part of the teacher role in pre-schools and schools. By virtue of the fictitious role, the teachers have dared to try new attitudes and ways of acting.
>
> *(1995, pp. 210–211)*

> The children like playing with the adults. *When adults act out roles, the children know they are playing and do not have to worry about 'adult conventions.'* The adults show the children that they know how to play—that is to say, that they are aware of the rules of play.
>
> *(2001b, p. 12)*

> The children have often been longing to meet the different dramatized characters or personalities. The play settings which have been established have inspired them to play, but *the playworld would not have come alive if it had not been for the physical presence of the living, breathing characters* (played by the adults).
>
> *(1995, p. 211)*

When we designed this current playworld project we expected that "living, breathing characters" who were also the teachers and researchers would "liberate" adults from their traditional teaching and research roles, thus allowing these adults to rethink both early childhood teaching and early childhood research. However, as we will discuss, we thought we would have more control than we did over when adult teachers and researchers stepped into and out of role. (See the two photographs of adults in role in a current, Swedish playworld of this study. These photographs were taken by Rachel Kahn.)

Playworlds: Method of Study

Although Lindqvist did not use this term, this current Swedish playworld research project, US playworld research, and Lindqvist's playworld research can all be described as "formative interventions" (Engeström, 2008). Y. Engeström argues (2008) that Vytgotsky's methodological principle of double stimulation leads to a concept of formative interventions. He describes formative interventions by contrasting formative interventions with "the linear interventions advocated . . . by the literature on design experiments" (p. 15) (Engeström refers to the work of Cobb et al. [2003] and Collins, Joseph, & Bielaczyc [2004] when discussing design experiments. Brown [1992] describes design experiments as "engineering innovative . . . environments and simultaneously conducting experimental studies of those innovations" [p. 141].)

Engeström (2008) states that the crucial differences between formative interventions and linear interventions are as follows. In linear interventions:

1. The contents and goals of the intervention are known ahead of time by the researchers. In formative interventions, the subjects (whether children or adult practitioners) construct a novel solution or novel concept with contents not known ahead of time to the researchers.
2. The subjects are expected to receive and implement the intervention without argument; difficulties of reception are interpreted as weaknesses in the design that are to be corrected. In formative interventions, the contents and course of the intervention are subject to negotiation and the shape of the intervention is eventually up to the subjects.
3. The aim is to control all the variables and to achieve a standardized intervention module that will reliably generate the same desired outcomes when transferred and implemented in new settings. In formative interventions, the aim is to generate *intermediate concepts* and solutions that can be used in other settings as tools in the design on locally appropriate new solutions.

(pp. 15–16)

One "intermediate concept" or solution that was generated in a US playworld and then used in the current Swedish playworld research project of this chapter is the method of "film-play" (Ferholt, 2010).

FIGURE 9.1 Adult in role in a current, Swedish playworld of this study (photograph by Rachel Kahn)

FIGURE 9.2 Adult in role in a current, Swedish playworld of this study (photograph by Rachel Kahn)

Named in reference to Jean Rouch's (1978) *ciné-trance*, film–play is a synthetic-analytic means of analysis in which researchers play with their video data by creating short ethnographic films of playworlds that allow for the re-experiencing of emotional responses to playworld events (Ferholt, 2009; 2010). With these ethnographic films, researchers enhance emotional re-engagement in the playworld, thus strengthening their roles as participating observers, by using a specific technique derived from their joint-play with children. In children's play the imaginary is often intertwined with the real through investing inanimate objects with an emotional life and with the ability to act on their own. Researchers using the method of film–play invest their video footage with an emotional life and agency by freeing this footage from the category of 'data' and by pushing it to become 'film,' thus imparting to this footage that quality of film Vivian Sobchack calls "lived momentum" (1992; 2004).

The current playworld project was designed to support film–play, in part through the inclusion of an artist, a photographer, in data collection and preliminary data analysis. More traditional ethnographic methods were also used. However, our argument here, as mentioned, is that playworlds were a method as well as a subject of this project.

Perspectives of Teachers That Changed Our Research Methods and Subjects of Study

There were two points in the year-long data collection phase of this project when the perspectives of teachers changed our research methods and/or subjects of study. The first point came when the visual atelierista, Isabel, called for a meeting with Monica and Beth. She sought to convince them that Vygotsky's argument about one-year-old children not engaging in sophisticated pretend play was incorrect. She showed us, for example, how these children took part in play, pretending that a grass straw was a key to open up a pretend door and imagining characters eating and sleeping behind that door. She claimed the children could do all of this at the age of one year because of the extensive use of "the hundred languages" (multimodal education as described by Malaguzzi in his poem, *A Child Has a Hundred Languages*) in their preschool and because their teachers were curious and attentive to the children's "worlds." Monica and Beth were at first skeptical of Isabel's claim, then gradually convinced they were missing something if they did not attend to Isabel's claim on its own terms, and later in the project the evidence Isabel presented in this meeting became a central piece of evidence for analysis in the research project.

The second point during the year when the perspectives of teachers changed our research method is not a story we can write about directly. We will explain this dilemma of our non-traditional methodology before we proceed. To stifle misplaced curiosity we can say that no one aside from the participants would find the event starling or even noticeable. We have found that in playworlds research the key events needed to support our conclusions are sometimes ethically impossible to publish and are sometimes even practically impossible for us to write about in field notes that are or may be open to some participants. To do so would hinder the project continuing as some degree of trust is required to put on a costume and go into role in a playworld.

We believe this conflict occurs with increased frequency in playworld research in which researchers have a commitment first to the teachers and children with whom we are playing and only second to our research. An example of this shifting of commitment is found in one US playworld project. A pivotal moment in the play and research narratives occurred when a researcher told the teacher, sincerely, that she would give up her dissertation thesis if this would make the teacher comfortable. This might of course be perceived as an idealistic position for this researcher to take, but we understand it to be an ontological and perhaps existential position that challenges identity: first researcher and then human being, or the opposite?

Interestingly, this shift is similar to something that happens in play. Play cannot happen unless we suspend disbelief (refuse to break frame). Instead of making this point through play theory we will refer to a literary reference. There is an event in the play *Peter Pan* that illustrates this point well. Tinkerbell, the fairy, is dying, and she can only be revived if the audience believes in fairies, and the play goes on as the audience claps loudly to show that they believe in fairies. The trick to pulling this off in the theater is to make sure everyone claps loudly enough that they become immersed in the collective experience of clapping loudly with many other people and also make their commitment to their belief in fairies heard (and so that much more true). The overt content of this moment in *Peter Pan* also explains our methodological point: In play, and in our playworlds research, as in *Peter Pan*, what you trying to pull off is made possible by the fact that you believe in its existence at the expense of other concerns (i.e. your embarrassment at wearing a wig, your interest in a scientific finding, or your annoyance at being coerced into clapping). Once you have clapped to save Tinkerbell's life, you have made fairies come alive, actually, at least this one in this play and also more broadly the idea of fairies through the play. So your proclaimed belief in fairies is supported through its result.

What occurred in this research project is that Monica and Beth had a walk back to their offices from the preschools after they saw something that disturbed them. (We cannot discuss this event, but all was resolved with a positive outcome very quickly.) They have both worked as teachers for a decade or more of their professional lives, and they both felt this was something they would help their co-teachers avoid if they were teachers in these classrooms. But they had a pivotal moment in their walk to their offices in which they looked at each other and realized they were researchers, not teachers.

This may sound like the opposite of a participating teacher's perspective, but because it was how the teachers would see Monica and Beth, it was, in fact, a teacher's perspective that was influencing Monica and Beth at this pivotal moment. They realized they were not in the daily life of the classroom, they did not know the complex life surrounding the event they had witnessed that had disturbed them, and so they could not judge. They became early childhood researchers who gave up their critical perspective and their claim to having any worthwhile knowledge, at this moment and about the activities with young children they had observed.

It is interesting to note that Monica and Beth feel they prepared themselves for this 'shift' of theirs in their conversations with each other about multiculturalism. They feel that they unintentionally 'practiced' their nonjudgmental stances in long and hard conversations with each other. They held these conversations in preparation for talks that Beth gave at the University of Jönköping about multicultural education. Furthermore, they both feel that the walks to and from the preschool were often a particularly held space when they would be preparing themselves, individually, to enter the playworld space, time, and mood. Arguably, this shift on the part of Monica and Beth allowed this playworld research project to continue and to produce unexpected and important findings and results in classroom practice.

Perspectives of Children That Changed Our Research Methods and Subjects of Study

A point in the year-long data collection phase of this project when the perspectives of children changed our research methods and/or subjects of study is described in the following. At this point our understanding of the role of playworld researcher changed. This redefined the boundaries of our subject of study, playworlds, and also helped us understand our methods in new ways that we believe will impact future playworld studies.

In many of the playworlds we study, we enter into role intentionally. In one of the playworlds of this project, Beth and Monica filmed a good portion of the playworld but did not intentionally enter into roles. During this playworld, Beth, and sometimes Monica as well, would sit in a corner of the room to film.

Because Beth speaks very little Swedish, as she filmed this playworld, she rarely said anything. Because the room was small, she rarely moved from place to place. She would sometimes say something in English to one of the teachers or to Monica or, very rarely, in response to a child who addressed her.

This playworld was with two- and three-year-old children. Because their play with their teachers was very intense, and very slow, Beth often kept herself awake during these playworld sessions by thinking of other stories at the same time as she was observing the play narrative and filming. As Beth describes this, she simultaneously attended to the play and strengthened her attention by making her mind wander. During this experience she could feel that her body, including her facial features, would become very still with her efforts.

After several months of playing in the playworld with Monica and Beth film-ing, one of the teachers, Tove, told Monica and Beth that one of the children, Maya, has sometimes been standing very still. She would keep her hands still in front of her and look slightly downward without an expression on her face. Maya is usually silent as she stands in this way, but she intermittently turns to the side and speaks a short bit of gibberish to an imaginary person. Tove told Monica and Beth that she was perplexed and asked Maya's mother if she knew what Maya was doing.

Maya's mother explained that Maya often does this, at home. She said that Maya is performing a role and that, when asked, Maya tells her mother that she is Beth. Maya is standing very still, concentrating so hard, holding her camera and occasionally speaking English. We understand this to mean that Beth had been unintentionally in a role in this playworld for a long period of time.

Tove explains that Beth was using the concept of a firmament from Buber (1970), an idea Beth had introduced to some of the teachers earlier in the year: "As long as the firmament of the You is spread over me, the tempests of causality cower at my heels, and the whirl of doom congeals" (p. 59). According to Tove, a firmament was created in this playworld when the first person (a teacher) went into role as the Princess, making the firmament cover all who are participants in this playworld. Beth is a participant in this playworld when she films the play-world, if only because the teachers say they perform differently and often for longer periods of time when she films. Therefore, a researcher in a playworld can be understood to be under the playworld firmament, and hence unavoidably in role, even when she is playing herself and acting so still.

Teacher Participants Rethink and Perform Anew Their Listening to Children and Their Documentation of Children's Exploration

This paper focuses on change in early childhood research, but in the study we found concurrent and resultant change in teacher participants' teaching roles. As noted in the introduction, teachers developed in the playworlds what they describe as an early childhood teaching practice that is more about themselves as whole people than about themselves as teachers.

We believe the teachers reporting that they are exhausted after their participa-tion in playworlds may be evidence that they are becoming involved as 'whole people' (a term that some adult participants in playworlds have used to describe their experience of being in these playworlds) in their teaching in ways that are new to them. However, although evidence of this change is difficult to secure, what we believe to be results of this change in teachers' teaching roles in play-worlds can be seen in several areas.

For instance, the teachers began to speak with each other in new ways in their reflection sessions, covering a broader range of areas in their lives and having more 'fun' together. They now sometimes call these planning sessions "therapy sessions."

FIGURE 9.3 Maya in role as Beth

One teacher had never before been asked to come to a child's home to play but was asked this fourteen times after her group began a playworld. At this time several children also requested more costumes for adults so their teachers could play a broader range of characters. And several teachers reported they could now better understand the children whom they had had the most trouble understanding after they engaged with these children in a playworld.

Furthermore, many teachers characterized playworlds as expanding their toolkit of listening tools. Some teachers pointed out the difficulty of documenting as they used to, from the "outside," while they were involved, with their bodies, in playworlds. They began to experiment with new ways of documenting, which they called from the "inside," reporting their own feelings and experiences after the playworld session was over, in field notes. (They also experimented with using small sports cameras attached to their own or the children's chests.)

Karin, in dual role as pedagogista and researcher, explains that the teachers have for many years tried to be better listeners to the children and that documentation has helped them go back and look at the children's activities. The teachers ask through the documentation, for instance, "Am I really curious about what the children are really saying and doing?" This use of documentation has made the teachers better listeners to children's meaning making when they explore, but in playworlds the teachers have to listen in a new way, yet again. They have to listen to other things and listen to themselves as humans more than they listen to themselves as teachers.

Conclusions

Edith Turner (1992) writes of "a moment when I actually saw a spirit manifestation" (p. 1). You could say that in this research project there were moments when we researchers actually saw—often through the guidance of teachers—play. To paraphrase Turner (1992, p. 1): Participant researchers often "try to participate in the life of the children, but there appear to be limits." And, in response to this shortcoming of traditional early childhood research (1992, p. 12): "We may even have to begin to regard the children's criterion of truth as a fundamental one."

In this research, we found ourselves committed to the children and the teachers in such a way that research became our secondary concern, and the relationships we jointly created with these teachers and children became our primary concern. We came to this position by giving up our privileged position of having the right to be critical from a distance, which is the privileged role of the researcher in traditional research. Paradoxically, we found that by making this shift—by following the lead of the teachers and the children in the playworlds to make this shift—we were able to contribute to both theoretical development in the research field of early childhood and to preschool practice.

As we stated in the introduction to this chapter, our inclusion into early childhood research of the excluded knowledge, knowers, and means of knowing of early childhood constitutes a critique of conventional social science. We replaced the explicit goal of objectivity with the goal of becoming emotionally attached to, and partial to, the teachers and children with whom we were playing. This alternative social scientific method allowed our subject of study to become real in several ways that closely resemble the ways Tinkerbell (and the Velveteen Rabbit) become real, through another genre of imagination and creativity, but we would like to remain firmly within social science. The playworlds research project we have described in this chapter challenges the divide between method and object in conventional social science but remains wedded to empirical evidence and consistent methodology that can influence early childhood educational practice.

In future projects we plan to account for these developments through joint endeavors with the teachers at the preschools who have contributed to this chapter. Our task at hand is to analyze the paradox to which we have pointed: The more we play, the more science we create.

References

Åberg, A., & Lenz Taguchi, H. (2005). *Lyssnandets pedagogik—etik och demokrati I pedagogiskt arbete (The pedagogy of listening—ethics and democracy in education).* Stockholm: Liber.

Aries, P. (1962). *Centuries of childhood.* New York: Alfred A. Knopf.

Baumer, S., Ferholt, B., & Lecusay, R. (2005). Promoting narrative competence through adult-child joint pretense: Lessons from the Scandinavian educational practice of playworld. *Cognitive Development, 20,* 576–590.

Brown, A. (1992). Design experiments: Theoretical and methodological challenges in creating complex interventions in classroom settings. *Journal of the Learning Sciences, 2*(2), 141–178.

Buber, M. (1970). *I and thou.* New York: Simon and Schuster.

Cobb, P., Confrey, J., diSessa, A., Lehrer, R., & Schauble, L. (2003). Design experiments in educational research. *Educational Researcher, 32,* 9–13.

Collins, A., Joseph, D., & Bielaczyc, K. (2004). Design research: Theoretical and methodological issues. *Journal of the Learning Sciences, 13,* 15–42.

Conquergood, D. (2002). Performance studies: Interventions and radical research. *Drama Review, 46*(2), 145–156.

Dahlberg, G., & Lenz Taguchi, H. (1994). *Förskola och skola: om två skilda traditioner och om visionen om en mötesplats.* Stockholm: HLS förlag.

Elkonin, D. B. (2005). The psychology of play. *Journal of Russian and East European Psychology, 43*(1), 1–98.

Engeström, Y. (2008). *The future of activity theory.* A keynote address delivered at the Second Congress of the International Society for Cultural and Activity Research, San Diego, CA, September 9–13.

Fass, P. (2007). *Children of a new world.* New York: New York University Press.

Ferholt, B. (2009). *Adult and child development in adult-child joint play: The development of cognition, emotion, imagination and creativity in playworlds.* San Diego: University of California, San Diego.

Ferholt, B. (2010). A multiperspectival analysis of creative imagining: Applying Vygotsky's method of literary analysis to a playworld. In C. Connery, V. John-Steiner, &

A. Marjanovic-Shane (Eds.), *Vygotsky and creativity: A cultural-historical approach to play, meaning-making and the arts* (pp. 163–180). New York: Peter Lang.

Ferholt, B. (2012). Playworlds and early literary arts education. In C. Korn (Ed.), *Young children and the arts: Nurturing imagination and creativity* (pp. 141–154). New York: Information Age Publishing.

Ferholt, B. (2014). Perezhivanie in researching playworlds. In S. Davis, H. Grainger-Clemson, B. Ferholt, S. Jansson, & A. Marjanovic-Shane (Eds.), *Dramatic interactions in education: Vygotskian and sociocultural approaches to drama, education and research* (pp. 57–75). London: Bloomsbury.

Ferholt, B., & Lecusay, R. (2010). Adult and child development in the zone of proximal development: Socratic dialogue in a Playworld. *Mind Culture and Activity, 17*(1), 59–83.

Freud, A., (1964). *The psychoanalytical treatment of children.* New York: Schocken Books.

Gadamer, H–G. (1997). *Sanning och metod (i urval).* Göteborg: Daidalos.

Groos, K. (1901). *The play of man.* New York: Appleton.

Hakkarainen, P. (1999). Play and motivation. In Y. Engeström, R. Miettinen, & R.-L. Punamäki (Eds.), *Perspectives on activity theory* (pp. 231–249). New York: Cambridge University Press.

Hakkarainen, P. (2004). Narrative learning in the fifth dimension. *Outlines: Critica Social Studies, 6*(1), 5–20.

Hakkarainen, P., & Bredikyte, M. (2008). The zone of proximal development in play and learning. *Cultural-Historical Psychology, 5*(4), 2–11.

Hakkarainen, P., & Ferholt, B. (2013). Imagination and psychological tools in playworlds. In K. Egan and A. Cant. (Eds.), *Wonder-full education* (pp. 203–218). New York: Routledge.

Hofmann, R., & Rainio, A.P. (2007). "It doesn't matter what part you play, it just matters that you're there." Towards shared agency in narrative play activity in school. In R. Alanen & S. Pöyhönen (Eds.), *Language in Action. Vygotsky and Leontievian legacy today* (pp. 308–328). Newcastle upon Tyne: Cambridge Scholars Publishing.

Klein, M., (1986). *The selected Melanie Klein.* New York: The Free Press.

Lenz Taguchi, H. (2010). *Going beyond the theory/practice divide in early childhood education: Introducing an intra-active pedagogy.* London & New York: Routledge.

Lindqvist, G. (1989). *Från fakta till fantasi (From facts to fantasy).* Lund, Sweden: Studentlitteratur.

Lindqvist, G. (1992). *Ensam i vida världen (Lonely in the wide world).* Lund, Sweden: Studentlitteratur.

Lindqvist, G. (1995). The aesthetics of play. A didactic study of play and culture in preschools. Acta Universitatis Upsaliensis. *Uppsala Studies in Education 62.* Stockholm: Almqvist & Wiksell International.

Lindqvist, G. (1996). *Lekens möjligheter (The possibilities of play).* Lund, Sweden: Studentlitteratur.

Lindqvist, G. (2000). *Historia som tema och gestaltning (History as theme and gestalt).* Lund, Sweden: Studentlitteratur.

Lindqvist, G. (2001a). The relationship between play and dance. *Research in Dance Education, 2*(1), 41–53.

Lindqvist, G. (2001b). When small children play: How adults dramatize and children create meaning. *Early Years, 21*(1), 7–14.

Lindqvist, G. (2002). *Lek i skolan (Play in school).* Lund, Sweden: Studentlitteratur.

Lindqvist, G. (2003). Vygotsky's theory of creativity. *Creativity Research Journal, 15*(4), 245–251.

Marjanovic-Shane, A., Ferholt, B., Nilsson, M., Rainio, A.P., Miyazaki, K. (2011). Playworlds: An art of development. In C. Lobman and B. O'Neill (Eds.), *Play and culture.* Play and Culture Studies Vol. 11 (pp. 3–31). Lanham, MD: University Press of America.

Miyazaki, K. (2008). Ibi-play project. Workshop in IBI-Youchien 2008. Oulu University, Kayaani University Consortium, and University of California, San Diego, Laboratory of Comparative Human Cognition.

Miyazaki, K. (2009). Geijutsu kyouiku [Art education]. *Jidou shinrigaku no shinpo [Annual Review of Japanese Child Psychology]*, 2009, 164–186.

Nilsson, M. (2010) Creative pedagogy of play—The work of Gunilla Lindqvist. *Mind Culture and Activity*, 17(1), 14–22.

Objectively. (n.d.) In *Oxford English Dictionary online*. Retrieved from http://www.oed.com

Olsson, L.M. (2009). *Movement and experimentation in young children's learning: Deleuze and Guattari in early childhood education*. New York: Routledge.

Paley, V. (1992) Waking up and finding myself in a classroom *Quarterly Newsletter of Laboratory of Comparative Human Cognition, 14*(3), 65–68.

Piaget, J. (1951). *Play, dreams, and imitation in childhood*. New York: Norton.

Rainio, A.P. (2005). *Emergence of a playworld. The formation of subjects of learning in interaction between children and adults* (Vol. Working Papers 32). Helsinki: Center for Activity Theory and Developmental Work Research.

Rainio, A.P. (2007). Ghosts, bodyguards and fighting fillies: Manifestations of pupil agency in play pedagogy. ACTIO: *International Journal for Human Activity Theory, 1*, 149–160.

Rainio, A.P. (2008a). Developing the classroom as a figured world. *Journal of Educational Change, 9*(4), 357–364.

Rainio, A.P. (2008b). From resistance to involvement: Examining agency and control in playworld activity. *Mind, Culture and Activity, 15*(2), 115–140.

Rainio, A.P. (2009). Horses, girls, and agency: Gender in play pedagogy. *Outlines Critical Practice Studies, 1*, 27–44.

Rainio, A.P. (2010). *Lionhearts of the playworld: An ethnographic case study of the development of agency in play pedagogy*. Helsinki: University of Helsinki, Institute of Behavioral Sciences.

Rainio, A., & Marjanovic-Shane, A. (2013). From ambivalence to agency: Becoming and author, an actor and a hero in a drama workshop. *Learning, Culture and Social Interaction, 2*(2), 111–125.

Rouch, J. (1978). On the vicissitudes of the self: The possession dancer, the magician, the sorcerer, the filmmaker, and the ethnographer. *Studies in the Anthropology of Visual Communication, 5*(1), 2–8.

Sobchack, V.C. (1992). *The address of the eye: A phenomenology of film experience*. Princeton, NJ: Princeton University Press.

Sobchack, V. C. (2004). *Carnal thoughts*. Berkeley: University of California Press.

Turner, E. (1992). *Experiencing ritual*. Philadelphia: University of Pennsylvania Press.

Vygotsky, L.S. (1971). *The psychology of art*. Cambridge, MA: MIT Press.

Vygotsky, L.S. (1978). *Mind in society: The development of higher psychological processes*. Cambridge: Harvard University Press.

Vygotsky, L.S. (1987). Imagination and its development in childhood. In R.W. Rieber and A.S. Carton (Eds.), *The collected works of L.S. Vygotsky* (Vol. 1; pp. 339–350). New York: Plenum Press.

Vygotsky, L.S. (2004). Imagination and creativity in childhood. *Journal of Russian and East European Psychology, 42*(1), 7–97.

Wehner-Godée, C. (2011). *Lyssnandets och seendets villkor: Pedagogisk dokumentation (The conditions of listening and seeing: Pedagogical documentation)*. Stockholm: Stockholms universitetsförlag.

10

IMAGINING CHILDREN'S STRENGTHS AS THEY START SCHOOL

Sue Dockett and Bob Perry

Introduction: The Australian Context

The election of the Rudd-Gillard Labor government in Australia in 2007 prompted a period of intense focus on early childhood education. This led to the development of the first national curriculum framework for early childhood education (Department of Education, Employment, and Workforce Relations, 2009) and the National Quality Framework (Australian Children's Education and Care Quality Authority, 2013). This focus on early childhood education has continued with a change in government.

Underpinning commitments to increase the quality of provision and access to early childhood services have been broader commitments to agendas of social inclusion and disrupting cycles of social and economic disadvantage (Australian Government, 2010). These have been supported by the investment argument for early childhood education. As one example, the then minister for education, Julia Gillard (2009), announced in a speech referring to the 2009–2010 budget commitments for early childhood education:

> The road to a more productive Australia starts as soon as children are born. Early childhood education sets the foundation for learning and wellbeing throughout life. Investment in early childhood education is a longterm investment in the future.

Within this context, transition to school has been positioned as a critical point for children and families on the basis that "improved transition to school" leads to "improved educational, employment, health and wellbeing outcomes" (Council of Australian Governments [COAG], 2009, p. 4). This is regarded as particularly important for some children:

> Children in low-income families are more likely to have poor developmental outcomes, make a difficult transition to school, and have reduced aspiration and to pass this risk on to their children in a cycle of intergenerational disadvantage.
>
> *(COAG, 2009, p. 33)*

The focus on transition is evident across all Australian states and territories, with the emphasis on smoothing or improving transition experiences, particularly for children described as living with disadvantage.

Theoretical Context

Transition is defined as a time of changing roles and identities within a particular context (Bronfenbrenner, 2005; Rogoff, 2003). While the individual attributes of those who are involved are important, so too are the context, the interactions and relationships that are generated, and the time in which, and over which, transition takes place. This position regards transition as both an individual and a social process; while each person experiences the transition to school as an individual, these experiences cannot be understood without reference to their social and cultural contexts. Inherent in this position is regard for children's competencies as evolving and responsive to contexts and recognition that "children do not acquire competencies merely as a consequence of age, but rather through experience, culture, levels of parental support and expectation" (Lansdown, 2005b, p. x).

A smooth transition to school—as opposed to a *difficult* transition—often involves reference to readiness. While a number of current conceptualizations of readiness attend to child, family, community, and school factors, others rely primarily on measures of individual children's skills, knowledge, and abilities (Ackerman & Barnett, 2005; Dockett & Perry, 2013; Snow, 2006). Arguments supporting measures of children's skill level at school entry are based on correlations between such scores and later academic scores at school (Duncan et al., 2007). These are combined with evidence that children living in disadvantaged circumstances generally demonstrate lower levels of school readiness than those in more advantaged circumstances (Crosnoe & Cooper, 2010) and that intervention—often in the form of provision of early childhood education—can ameliorate some of the effects of disparity in levels of readiness (Magnuson & Waldfogel, 2005).

This evidence has been summarized in an Australian report, which concludes:

> The transition to school is likely to be more challenging for children from financially disadvantaged families, Indigenous families, families with children who have a disability, and culturally and linguistically diverse (CALD) families. Children from these backgrounds are also less likely to attend an early childhood education and care services before they start school.
>
> *(Rosier & McDonald, 2011, p. 1)*

One of the consequences of this position is the expectation that children who belong to these groups will struggle with transition; they will experience a difficult transition partly, at least, because they are considered to have backgrounds that do not equip them with sufficient skills or knowledge to prepare them for school (Dockett, 2014). This expectation can be translated into actions that seek to identify the expected problems and then to develop interventions that address these.

Rather than assuming that there is a common set of expectations for starting school, and agreed intervention strategies to ensure all children meet these, alternative approaches consider children's strengths, instead of attending to their perceived deficits, as they start school. Strengths-based approaches do not deny the existence of challenges, but they do recognize that those who know most about the perceived problem are those living it; people are considered experts on their own lives (McCashen, 2005; Saleebey, 2006). Strengths-based approaches to starting school recognize the insights and hopefulness that individuals, their families, and communities bring to the transition and the ways in which these are integral to processes of change.

Strengths-based approaches are embedded within social work and family practice, where they have shifted attention from deficits, problems, and a focus on risk, toward strengths and capacity for growth (Leitz, 2011; Price-Robertson, 2010). Strengths-based approaches are also ecological approaches, recognizing that the networks of social and cultural contexts in which people exist influence their lives, just as individuals influence those contexts (Saint-Jacques, Turcotte, & Pouliot, 2009). Key elements of strengths-based approaches are their focus on the potentials, strengths, interests, and capacities of people, rather than their limits; recognition of the influence of social and cultural contexts; belief in the capacity for change; and acceptance of multiple ways of viewing and understanding the world (Fenton, 2008; Scerra, 2011). Strengths-based approaches are relational, acknowledging the importance of social contexts and relationships; children are likely to demonstrate their strengths and capabilities as they interact with people they know and trust.

When considered in relation to children's transition to school, strengths-based approaches aim not to describe the limits of children's knowledge, skills, or understandings. Rather, they:

- understand that children's learning is dynamic, complex and holistic
- understand that children demonstrate their learning in different ways
- start with what's present, not what's absent.

(Department of Education and
Early Childhood Development [DEECD], 2012, p. 6)

Strengths-based approaches recognize that all children have a range of interests, strengths, and abilities and urge educators to "build a picture of what a child's leaning and development could look like in the future" (DEECD, 2012, p. 6), with appropriate support—in other words, when decisions are not based on responses to a specific measure or expectations about particular family or community backgrounds.

Researching Children's Strengths as They Start School: One Example

Recognizing strengths is a powerful philosophical position, but what does it mean in practice? It is clear that strengths-based approaches go beyond saying positive things about children, requiring educators to consider the contexts in which children and their families live, as well as the ways in which children and their families contribute to building the picture of their strengths (DEECD, 2012).

Acknowledging children's strengths is at the heart of recent discourses about children's rights and children's competence (Christensen & James, 2008; United Nations, 1989). Consequences include the reconceptualization of notions of children and childhood, recognition of children as experts on their own lives; increased efforts to understand children's own perspectives of their lives and experiences; recognition of children's rights to have a say on issues that affect them and for their views to be taken seriously (Christensen & James, 2008; Clark & Moss, 2001; Lansdown, 2005a). Translating strengths-based approaches into practice involves valuing children's experiences, seeking and respecting their perspectives, recognizing their competence to share these perspectives, and being willing to listen and act in response to their perspectives.

Along with a number of researchers around the world (including Broström, 2002; Corsaro, Molinari, & Rosier, 2002; Einarsdóttir, 2010; Fisher, 2009), we have sought children's perspectives of their transition to school. This has involved inviting children's participation in a range of activities, including drawing, photographing, and mapping their experiences, expectations, and perceptions as they start school. In this discussion, we share some of the data generated through children's participation in drawing tasks. While the artifacts produced by these activities are important, they need to be anchored by the conversations around them to promote consideration of the meanings ascribed by the children involved.

A recurring theme in this research has been the focus on the methodology (rationale) for seeking children's participation in specific activities, as well as the methods employed (Dockett, Einarsdóttir, & Perry, 2011). Our research methodology is described as participatory, rights-based research (Beazley, Bessell, Ennew, & Waterson, 2011; Dockett & Perry, 2014). It is characterized by:

- respect for children—both as participants and in what they are asked to do;
- ethical practice—where children are accorded the same rights as adults, with particular attention to voluntary participation;
- systematic and valid approaches to data generation;
- rigorous, appropriate data analysis;

- focus on children's own experiences and contexts; and
- respectful reporting of research that aims to make a positive difference to children's lives.

Underpinning this methodology are commitments to children's rights to be involved in discussions about their transition to school and expectations that, in supportive contexts, they are competent to do so.

Children's Perspectives of Starting School

Across several projects, we have invited children to talk with us about starting school (for example, Dockett & Perry, 2005; Perry & Dockett, 2005; 2011). Sometimes children have been comfortable talking in small groups; other times, they have preferred to talk individually. There are also many instances where children have not wished to talk to us at all, and other instances where they have indicated interest in talking, but changed their minds, and vice versa. As a means of engaging with children during these conversations, we have provided a range of drawing materials and invited children to draw as they talk. Many children have chosen to draw; others have not. Where drawings have been made, we ask permission to scribe children's comments and make a copy of their drawing. The comments and the drawing together form the unit of analysis.

The prompts for drawings and conversations take several forms, including:

- What would you like to know about big school?
- What are you looking forward to at school?
- What do you think school will be like?
- What do new children need to know about this school?
- What was it like when you started school?

As well, one prompt asks children to reflect upon their first year of school, thinking about what things were like at the beginning of the school year and how they had changed by the end of that year (Perry & Dockett, 2005). The prompts facilitate conversation, focusing on what matters for the children involved, their perceptions, experiences, and expectations, and what they wish to share. The tasks are open-ended, and there is no correct response.

The following examples of children's drawings and comments reflect what was important for them at the time. They are drawn from a range of studies, involving children in diverse areas of the state of New South Wales, Australia, including communities characterized by financial disadvantage and high levels of cultural and linguistic diversity. The examples chosen are not representative—rather, they are indicative of strengths, interests, competencies, and potentials of the children involved.

What Do You Think School Will Be Like?

Conversations about children's expectations of school can be promoted by questions about what they think school will be like and what they are looking forward to at school (Figures 10.1–10.2). Children draw on a range of experiences—including those with siblings, transition programs, discussions, popular culture, and media—to build these expectations. Drawings such as these remind us that children start school having had many different encounters with school and what happens at school. These encounters include not only their own experiences, but also those of family members and friends.

What Was It Like When You Started School?

When invited to draw and talk in response to this prompt, many children refer to the affective elements of starting school. As indicated in Figures 10.3–10.4, children experience a wide range of emotions, both describing these and distinguishing quite complex feelings as they start school.

FIGURE 10.1 There will be books, houses that I can play with. Lots of children at big school.

FIGURE 10.2 You have to do coloring in and maths sometimes. You play soccer sometimes. You go to school to learn stuff. At school. It's a beautiful day. Soccer is playing and I'm the scorer.

FIGURE 10.3 I was excited about my new school clothes.

FIGURE 10.4 It was sad to leave Canery [dog] at home.

For some children, regulating their emotions and actions was an important element of starting school (Figures 10.5–10.6). Others emphasized their own approach to school (Figure 10.7), suggesting awareness that their own attitude to starting school influenced their experiences.

Reflections

The focus on affect also was evident in children's responses to the Reflections task, where children were asked to think about how they had changed over their first year

FIGURE 10.5 It was important to be nice and good.

FIGURE 10.6 Not crying at school.

FIGURE 10.7 I wanted it to be fun.

of school. Children's responses (Figures 10.8–10.9) indicate not only an awareness of a range of emotions, but also the subtle differences between emotions—reflected in the distinction between feeling nervous and sad (Figure 10.8).

These images and comments remind us that starting school is a social and emotional experience. It occurs within the context of family and community. These images could be taken as evidence of the immaturity of the children involved—an egocentric focus on what starting school might mean for them, perhaps even reflecting misunderstandings of what school will be like; it may not be the case that there "will be soccer" or "houses to play with." However, the images also demonstrate these children's awareness of their own emotions as well as expectations that these can and will be regulated. For example, stating the importance of "not crying at school" and of "being nice and good" suggests that these children were aware of expectations of the school environment and developing strategies to manage these. From a strengths perspective, they illustrate children's awareness of what is likely to happen as well as their thinking about what they would like to happen. Educators focusing on strengths would be well placed to build upon this awareness by working with the children to identify what strategies and resources they already have to respond to the new school situations, as well as other resources that could be developed or accessed (McCashen, 2005).

FIGURE 10.8 When I started school I was feeling nervous. Now I am feeling sad on the bus.

FIGURE 10.9 When I started school I was shy. Now I am not shy.

Discussion

It is important to note that children's preferences for engaging in tasks such as drawing and talking vary considerably; we cannot assume that all children like or wish to draw or talk about starting school or that all children wish to share their drawings and/or narratives. Indeed, across our studies, a number of children have chosen not to draw: some have drawn and chosen not to allow a copy to be made; some have drawn and then scrawled over the drawing; some have doodled, more than drawn, making patterns as they talked; others have engaged in drawing but demonstrated their ability to shift the conversation to a topic of their own choosing, including little or no reference to the prompt question. In keeping with participatory rights-based research, these responses have been accepted as indicative of what children wished to share with researchers about the topic at that time. In some instances, children have asked to revisit the topic and talk about it some more; in other instances, this has not happened.

When children agree to participate, drawing provides one strategy to reduce the formality of interactions between adults and children, both by reducing the amount of eye contact required and by focusing the conversation around something of interest and relevance to the children involved (Einarsdóttir, Dockett, & Perry, 2009). The informal conversations that accompany activities such as drawing open up opportunities to identify what matters for children and to focus on their strengths, interests, and potentials as they start school.

Across our studies, there is no intention to assess the quality or aesthetics of the drawing. Rather the focus is on the communicative power of the combination of drawing and narrative, where "the meaning of images resides most significantly in the ways that participants interpret those images, rather than as some inherent property of the image themselves" (Stanczak, 2007, p. 11). Hence, the combined act of drawing and talking is construed as an act of meaning-making, rather than representation, prompting focus on children's intentions and children's drawing as a "constructive process of thinking in action" (Cox, 2005, p. 123).

When viewed in this way, activities such as drawing and talking about transition to school provide opportunities to reconceptualize standard forms of readiness or school entry assessment and to consider strengths that may not otherwise be noted. These include children's expectations of school and what school will be like and their perceptions of the experiences they have had or will have at school. Notably, such activities provide opportunities to recognize and value the affective elements of starting school, acknowledging children's awareness of their feelings and responses as well as the strategies they employ to achieve outcomes such as "not crying at school." This is in contrast to many standardized assessments that provide little scope to explore children's hopes, aspirations, or expectations—factors that are likely to impact on their motivation and engagement—of school. Further, the open nature of the task provides opportunities for children to share their strengths and interests—what matters to them—rather than being assessed on what others have determined is important. This is a pivotal element of strengths-based approaches, which look "for opportunities to complement and support existing strengths and capacities as opposed to focusing on, and staying with, the problem or concern" (DEECD, 2012, p. 6).

Conclusion

Children start school with a wide range of skills, knowledge, and understandings. A great deal of research effort has been expended determining what skills set, knowledge base, and set of understandings come together to constitute children's readiness for school. However, comparatively little of this research effort has been directed toward children's perceptions of starting school and investigating what matters for them as they live the experience of transition to school.

Strengths-based approaches are premised on the assumption that each individual has strengths and that building on these strengths leads to worthwhile and sustainable change. In the case of transition to school, such changes are focused on children's learning and engagement with school. Strengths-based approaches also attend to the competencies of those involved—both existing and potential. In practice, this means considering not only what children can do at a given point, but also the potentials each child could reach in an educationally supportive environment. In relation to starting school, strengths-based approaches invite us to move beyond assessments of what children can—or cannot—do as they start school, looking instead to their strengths, capabilities, and potentials. This shifts emphasis from a focus on what a child brings with them to school to a focus on what educators and children can achieve: How can we help all children achieve their potentials?

References

Ackerman, D., & Barnett, W. (2005). *Prepared for kindergarten: What does readiness mean? NIEER Policy Report.* Retrieved from http://nieer.org/resources/policyreports/report5.pdf

Australian Children's Education and Care Quality Authority. (2013). *Guide to the National Quality Standard.* Retrieved from http://files.acecqa.gov.au/files/National-Quality-Framework-Resources-Kit/NQF03-Guide-to-NQS-130902.pdf

Australian Government. (2010). *Social inclusion principles.* Retrieved from http://www.socialinclusion.gov.au/SIAgenda/Principles/Pages/default.aspx

Beazley, H., Bessell, S., Ennew, J., & Waterson, R. (2011). How are the human rights of children related to research methodology? In A. Invernizzi & J. Williams (Eds.), *The human rights of children: From visions to implementation* (pp. 159–178). Farnham, UK: Ashgate.

Bronfenbrenner, U. (2005). The bioecological theory of human development. In U. Bronfenbrenner (Ed.), *Making human beings human: Bioecological perspectives on human development* (pp. 3–15). Thousand Oaks, CA: Sage. (Original work published 2001).

Broström, S. (2002). Communication and continuity in the transition to kindergarten. In H. Fabian & A.-W. Dunlop (Eds.), *Transitions in the early years: Debating continuity and progression for children in early education* (pp. 52–63). London: Routledge Falmer.

Christensen, P., & James, A. (Eds.) (2008). *Researching with children: Perspectives and practices* (2nd ed.). Abingdon, UK: Routledge.

Clark, A., & Moss, P. (2001). *Listening to young children: The mosaic approach.* London: National Children's Bureau.

Corsaro, W.A., Molinari, L., & Rosier, K.B. (2002). Zena and Carlotta: Transition narratives and early education in the United States and Italy. *Human Development, 45*(5), 323–349.

Council of Australian Governments (COAG). 2009. *Investing in the early years—A national early childhood development strategy.* Retrieved from https://www.coag.gov.au/sites/default/files/national_ECD_strategy.pdf

Cox, S. (2005). Intention and meaning in young children's drawing. *International Journal of Art and Design Education, 24*(2), 115–125.

Crosnoe, R., & Cooper, C. (2010). Economically disadvantaged children's transitions into elementary school: Linking family processes, school contexts, and educational policy. *American Educational Research Journal, 47*(2), 258–291.

Department of Education and Early Childhood Development (DEECD). (2012). *Strength-based approach. A guide to writing transition learning and development statements.* Retrieved from www.education.vic.gov.au/earlylearning/transitionschool

Department of Education, Employment, and Workforce Relations. (2009). *Belonging, being and becoming: The early years learning framework for Australia.* Retrieved from http://docs.education.gov.au/system/files/doc/other/belonging_being_and_becoming_the_early_years_learning_framework_for_australia.pdf

Dockett, S. (2014). Transition to school: Normative or relative? In B. Perry, S. Dockett, & A. Petriwskyj (Eds.), *Transitions to school—International research, policy and practice* (pp. 187–200). Dordrecht, Netherlands: Springer.

Dockett, S., Einarsdóttir, J., & Perry, B. (2011). Balancing methodologies and methods in researching with young children. In D. Harcourt, B. Perry, & T. Waller (Eds.), *Researching young children's perspectives: Ethics and dilemmas of educational research with children* (pp. 68–81). Milton Park, UK: Routledge.

Dockett, S., & Perry, B. (2005). Researching with children: Insights from the Starting School Research Project. *Early Childhood Development and Care, 175*(6), 507–521.

Dockett, S., & Perry, B. (2013). Trends and tensions: Australian and international research about starting school. *International Journal of Early Years Education, 21*(2–3), 163–177. doi: 10.1080/09669760.2013.832943.

Dockett, S., & Perry, B. (2014). Participatory rights-based research: Learning from young children's perspectives in research that affects their lives. In O. Saracho (Ed.) *Handbook of research methods in early childhood education: Review of research methodologies* (Vol. 2, pp. 675–710). Charlotte, NC: Information Age.

Duncan, G.J., Dowsett, C.J., Claessens, A., Magnuson, K., Huston, A.C., Klebanov, P., Pagani, L., Feinstein, L., Engel, M., Brooks-Gunn, J., Sexton, H., Duckworth, K., & Jape, C. (2007). School readiness and later achievement. *Developmental Psychology, 43*, 1428–1446. doi: 10.1037/0012–1649.43.6.1428.

Einarsdóttir, J. (2010). Children's experiences of the first year of primary school. *European Early Childhood Education Research Journal, 18*(2), 163–180. doi: 10.1080/13502931003784370.

Einarsdóttir, J., Dockett, S., & Perry, B. (2009). Making meaning: Children's perspectives expressed through drawings. *Early Child Development and Care, 179*(2), 217–232.

Fenton, A. (2008). From strength to strength: An educational research journey using a strengths approach. *International Journal of Pedagogies and Learning, 4*(5), 90–103.

Fisher, J.A. (2009). 'We used to play in Foundation, it was more funner': Investigating feelings about transition from Foundation Stage to Year 1. *Early Years: An International Journal of Research and Development, 29*(2), 131–145.

Gillard, J. (2009). *Jobs, productivity and fairness—A foundation for recovery. Ministerial statement 12 May, 2009.* Retrieved from http://www.budget.gov.au/2009-10/content/ministerial_statements/deewr/html/ms_deewr-03.htm

Lansdown, G. (2005a). *Can you hear me? The right of young children to participate in decisions affecting them.* Working paper 36. Bernard van Leer Foundation, The Hague. Retrieved from http://www.bernardvanleer.org/Can_you_hear_me_The_right_of_young_children_to_participate_in_decisions_affecting_them

Lansdown, G. (2005b). *The evolving capacities of the child.* Florence, Italy: UNICEF. Retrieved from http://www.unicef-irc.org/publications/pdf/evolving-eng.pdf

Leitz, C. (2011). Theoretical adherence to family centered practice: Are strengths-based principles illustrated in families' descriptions of child welfare services? *Children and Youth Services Review, 33*, 888–893. doi: 10.1016/j.childyouth.2010.12.012.

Magnuson, K., & Waldfogel, J. (2005). Early childhood care and education: Effects on ethnic and racial gaps in school readiness, *Future of Children, 15*(1), 169–196.

McCashen, W. (2005). *The strengths approach.* Bendigo, Victoria, Australia: St Luke's Innovative Resources.

Perry, B., & Dockett, S. (2005). 'As I got to learn it got fun': Children's reflections on their first year of school. *Proceedings of Australian Association for Research in Education 2004 Annual Conference,* Sydney. Retrieved from http:///www.aare.edu.au/04pap/doc04324.pdf

Perry, B., & Dockett, S. (2011). 'How 'bout we have a celebration!': Advice from children on starting school. *European Early Childhood Education Research Journal, 19*(3), 373–386.

Price-Robertson, R. (2010). *Supporting young parents.* Communities and Families Clearinghouse Resource Sheet. Retrieved from http://www.aifs.gov.au/cafca/pubs/sheets/ps/ps3.pdf

Rogoff, B. (2003). *The cultural nature of human development.* Oxford: Oxford University Press.

Rosier, K., & McDonald, M. (2011). *Promoting positive education and care transitions for children.* Communities and Families Clearinghouse Resource Sheet. Retrieved from http://www.aifs.gov.au/cafca/pubs/sheets/rs/rs5.html

Saint-Jacques, M., Turcotte, D., & Pouliot, E. (2009). Adopting a strengths perspective in social work practice with families in difficulty: From theory to practice. *Families in Society, 90*(4), 454–461.

Saleebey, D. (Ed.) (2006). *The strengths perspective in social work practice* (5th ed.). Boston: Pearson.

Scerra, N, (2011). *Strengths-based practice: The evidence.* UnitingCare: Children, Young People and Families Research Paper 6. Retrieved from http://www.childrenyoungpeopleandfamilies.org.au/info/social_justice/submissions/research_papers_and_briefs/?a=62401

Snow, K. (2006). Measuring school readiness: Conceptual and practical considerations. *Early Education and Development, 17*(1), 7–41.

Stanczak, G.C. (2007). Introduction: Images, methodologies, and generating social knowledge. In G.C. Stanczak (Ed.), *Visual research methods: Image society, and representation* (pp. 1–21). Thousand Oaks, CA: Sage.

United Nations. (1989). *Convention on the rights of the child.* New York: Author. Retrieved from http://www.unicef.org/crc/crc

11

"TO HAVE OR NOT TO HAVE" AT SCHOOL

Action Research on Early Childhood Education in Galicia (Spain)

Concepción Sánchez-Blanco

Introduction

The subject of this chapter, the impact of poverty on the lives of children, is extremely relevant when we consider the grave economic crisis that is affecting many countries around the world, including Spain. Its pervasive effects are felt within the sector of an impoverished population, and these impacts reverberate in children's schooling throughout their many different educational layers, including in the early childhood years. Poverty in developed countries is a complex issue that needs to be addressed, raising levels of awareness about taken for granted assumptions and pedagogies.

In this chapter, I share an action research project that was carried out in Galicia (Spain) with a class of four-year-olds whose parents experienced significant socio-economic problems. When I started working with a teacher in this school, Lucía (pseudonym), it was evident the class was fractured. Two separate groups emerged, the friends of the classroom and the enemies of the classroom (Brown, 1998, 2008; Kurban & Tobin, 2009). Symbolically, the so-called friends were the children who were involved and could participate in all the tasks that the teacher proposed, while the enemies became the children who did not conform, and this was often manifested in disruptive behaviors. I offer a critical reflection on some of the strategies used by the teacher to think about and discuss social justice and democracy in the classroom.

Context

The economic crisis now occurring in countries that had previously achieved economic prosperity follows a period in time when many citizens had created a comfortable middle-class life and naively viewed poverty as a distant, minority phenomenon they would not encounter. This was often the case for teachers. They tended to forget that the poor or lower socio-economic classes have always been at school since the overt differences or indicators of poverty were not always salient. Relegating poverty at school to the condition of a minor issue, a residual theme, was common (Ferraroti, 2011), and ascribing it to legal or illegal immigration and certain minorities (as is the case in Spain of the ethnic Gypsy population) was prevalent and remains an illegitimate and dangerous theme as it curtails initiatives to seek social equality.

Poverty can impact and be manifested in classrooms in different ways. For example, by attributing moral qualifiers to disruptive classroom childhood behavior, children can be unjustly branded as "naughty" and end up being reprimanded and sanctioned by teachers on a daily basis, spending long periods away from the classroom. In other instances, undesirable children's actions linked to economic problems may well be disguised in classrooms by cloaking the problems as being immature development—indicating behavior as developmental ("they will grow out of it") rather than as a product of their life's circumstances ("the family is having a hard time"). The economic differences and values connected to economic profit have always been present in the classroom.

The Economic Recession as a Backdrop of the Scenario of Our Research

The 2013 UNICEF Report on the situation of childhood in Spain in the period between 2012 and 2013 recognized that child poverty had increased by 10% in just two years, with approximately 2.2 million minors living in homes below the poverty threshold. Certain consistent measures to reduce state debt in the country were put into place by cutting spending on education, health, and social services. The strategies would seem to have the effect of endangering children's rights (Dahlberg & Moss, 2005) since they prevent children from having a suitable standard of living to meet their physical, mental, and social needs (Nutbrown & Clough, 2013, p. 16; Polakow, 2010, pp. 66–82). Moreover, Europe remains a strong economic continent (Bauman, 2005a, p. 53; 2005b), and as such groups of nations join forces to obtain favorable commercial terms from each other. For example, they patrol their common borders to prevent foreigners coming in while needing citizens from less privileged, poor countries to do the heavy, dirty work (Max-Neef, 1982; Smith & Max-Neef, 2011). These scenarios have created new contexts for an ever increasing number of people living below the poverty line.

Theoretical Frameworks

Through different types of strategies and from a very early age in organizations, like schools, children have been able to learn to submit to power relationships and accept these as inevitable. They are also part of hierarchical relationships that are often regarded as natural and substantial not just in interactions between teachers and students but between adults and children or among adults themselves (Bourdieu, 1993). School can change these kinds of relationships if teachers and pupils participate in a democratic environment as manifested every day in the classroom.

Utilizing action research (Elliott, 2007; Somekh, 2005; Somekh & Zeichner, 2009; Kemmis, 2008) and qualitative research methods (Denzin & Lincoln, 2011), this current project represented radical research (Schostak & Schostak, 2008) and aspired to unscramble social relations of exclusion, which occur in the children's classrooms, that are deeply rooted in the economic ethos on which the ideology of capitalism is situated. The deliberation processes on the values implied in Lucía's practices as a teacher and of myself as a researcher have been an essential aspect throughout the development of this research. We are aware of our status and beliefs and needed to pay attention to them so that our particular vision of the world did not impose upon or influence the action research processes (Mac Naughton, Rolfe, & Siraj-Blatchford, 2010, p. 83).

The Action Research Setting and Participants

The action research study took place in a school that is part of the public schools' network in the region of Galicia, Spain, located in the province of A Coruña. This school works with early years' and primary education. Our focus is on early years' education and is conducted with a teacher in a classroom of four-year-olds. The school is located in a rural area, and the nearest town is two kilometers away. The population includes children from different parishes in the council, as well as the urban core. Access to the school from the town center or from the parishes is via local roads. There is free school transport with several routes for students. Children who do *not* use school transport get to school by private family cars. Road traffic and the lack of wide pavements and zebra crossings significantly complicate access for pedestrians. There is no public transportation to the school; therefore, parents with minimal economic resources have limited contact with teachers as they are restricted by travel times (Sánchez-Blanco, 2013).

Defining the Research Context

When I started working with the teacher, Lucía, the class, dangerously, had begun to split into two worlds: "friends" of the classroom and "enemies" of the classroom (Brown, 1998, 2008). The so-called enemies were disruptive during typical classroom activities. However, through their disruptive behavior, it was our view that the children were merely demanding an educational intervention that would take them away from the state of confusion and chaos in their lives. Several children, overwhelmed by the chaos, actually expressed themselves by saying that they did not want any more new children arriving in the classroom. This was dangerous because they were starting to build a rejection of the new and unknown, which, if incorporated as part of their childhood identity, could produce very dangerous values.

As well, there were many families experiencing economic problems in this school. These devastating problems meant families had a dilemma; they had to choose between a community driven by mutual respect and interdependence seeking common good or by economic survival through individualism. For example, in Lucía's classroom, there was one child who would spend all his break times making holes in the college ground, trying to dig out the buried treasure just as he had seen in various pirate films, story tales, and cartoons (Hass Dyson, 1997, pp. 29–46; Melrose, 2012, p. 13). When asked why he was doing this, he indicated that he thought such wealth would bring him all the toys that he desired and had seen in catalogues, in television advertisements, in his peers' homes, and even in his school and classroom, believing this would make his life better. In another instance, we heard about a different child's father who actually took money from the raffle tickets his son was selling for the end-of-year trip as he felt an urgent need to buy gifts for his family at Christmas. Therefore, Lucía's work on democracy became crucial and central to this research study. One of the challenges of this action research was to transform classroom assemblies into places that empower children (Green, 2012), dealing not only with the injustices they face on a daily basis (both at school and at home) but also reviewing classroom rules, making a sort of constitution that gives equitable rights and duties.

Strategies such as working on injustices and democracy represent an antidote against this hopelessness of attaining justice, which can be instilled in children's lives. The teacher's work on democracy could be framed by developing in the children the ability to think critically and analytically, enabling each child to be "an intellectual warrior" who understands the world as it is in relation to what it could be, similar to the claims of Kincheloe (Monchinski, 2011, pp. 159–163). In all of this work, I was personally very optimistic because I believed social change was possible in a social institution as tough as this school. Another reason I was hopeful was that Lucía felt motivated and believed her work with the children was powerful enough to influence other colleagues to begin to critically and radically question life in the school. Deep down, my optimism was about working in this action research with the utopian vision of liberation (Freire & Araujo Freire, 1992; Freire, 2005), and thus it would be credible for this teacher and her students, as well as the families, to benefit from a new approach to participation in the schooling process (Parnell, 2011a; 2011b).

The spirals of reflection in this action research include commitment to social justice: rights and duties in the classroom, building democratic identities from childhood, and "to have or not to have" at school—economic classism and identity. The key moments when data was collected included meetings, play corners, the development of classroom projects, the morning snack, and the playground.

Findings and Discussion

The fear of being poor started to affect several families in Lucía's classroom where, every day, more and more students were being affected by abject poverty.

It stopped being seen as something purely residual—despite these ultra-liberal discussions—by headlining news of tragedies of terrorism, conservation, or climatic disasters that were hiding the fact that financial speculation and economic disasters are the origin of the great evils that afflict the world (Klein, 2008; Žižek, 2010, p. 339). At the start of this research, there were many families in the classroom who thought financial tragedies could never affect them. However, gradually the number of those affected increased, and most became aware that all families were targets in the economic recession.

With this action research, I encouraged Lucía to take all types of newspaper clippings related to poverty and/or economic misfortune into the classroom. This naturally included all experiences the children shared with each other in their assemblies. They could see the images in the newspapers, hear about the stories happening in their world, relate them to their own life experiences, and reflect on larger challenges happening in their community. For example, some children, moved by the impact of the printed images in the newspapers, took significant newspaper clips from the recycling bin to keep, share, and talk about in the assembly with Lucía. One child could identify with all those newspaper stories to the extent that he asked the teacher to take home some remaining newspaper clippings that related to the pictures of a destroyed house. This prompted him to tell Lucía about the holes in the floor of his apartment where he lived with his mother and his brothers and how much he wanted to find the treasure as his family needed a new house. From stories such as this child shared, Lucía was prompted to seek out a movement of solidarity to scale the community up to a new level of engagement.

Intergenerational Solidarity

Historical experience shows that people, when struck by recessions capable of causing such major forms of exclusion, should unite (Sennett, 2012). We must therefore revitalize those uniting forces that already exist as a way to mobilize against the current clamping down on, and cutting of, social rights, especially as this relates directly to the quality and effect on children's educational services. Such mobilization efforts stand to turn each citizen's cause into a common cause—a fight against social injustice (Sen, 2007; 2009). This common-unity (community) encourages us to re-establish an intergenerational solidarity that currently remains buried. As educators we have unwittingly spent years contributing to a culture of competition between youth and older generations. In Spain, youth are experiencing such challenges as a result of the economic crisis. Moreover, many grandparents look after their grandchildren every day; they take on important responsibilities related to childcare and education, and they also help when their own children face economic problems by offering their time and money. But some senior citizens are also activists. Many have participated in demonstrations against the budget cuts in health and education services in Spain. Some have even decided to enter politics and have won local elections. For instance, the new mayor of Madrid, Manuela Carmena, is 69 years old. Thus, considering today's growing fragmentation between generations, revitalizing this intergenerational solidarity is so necessary for feeding change-agency (Waal, 2009).

Freire (2005) reminds us that intolerance is the incapacity to discover that something different is as valuable as we are or sometimes better. This means being different is not inferior. As educators we cannot allow youngsters to see adults as a barrier to their aspirations of independence but rather a highly valuable element in the battle to build an encouraging future for the world. We all have an active role to play in this battle for social justice. Lucía indicated that she was spurred on against these types of hegemonic values and wanted to reinvigorate students' participation in the classroom. She was aware that for some children, it was their grandparents who really took care of their needs and contributed, with their modest pensions, to the meager domestic finances of more than one family. She also knew that they held very valuable information for the school about their grandchildren's lives (Gregory, 2012, pp. 33–41).

Lucía therefore promoted collaboration in the classroom by inviting the grandparents to tell stories about their own childhoods, especially those about their play and life experiences. Knowing how important the stories in the newspaper clippings were to the children, one grandparent told the class about his story and hardship after the civil war in Spain, when he was a child and his family did not have enough money for food and other necessary things. His family did not have running water at home and therefore had to go to wash clothes at a public washing place near the river. Feeling part of the story, one of the children said his mother went every morning to fetch water to wash clothes at a "tap" in the street because it was free and at home they did not have enough money to pay for it. The children realized that many grandparents did not buy toys since their parents needed the money for food, and because of this awareness, they created toys using sticks, stones, bones, and plants. Such narrated experiences, somehow, placed value on the strategies the economically disadvantaged children in the classroom used to supplement the lack of commercial toys in their homes; thus, their discomfort and feelings of inferiority declined. The grandparents' school stories opened the children to the importance of school and the care to not waste school supplies as well as to the value of collectively paying attention to what mattered more.

The cultural elite have subjugated the poor and fragmented them so they have become powerless to fight back. What is needed is collective action for them to resume their dignity. Lucía wanted to turn the classroom into a place where all the children's voices and problems were heard with the same intensity (Iorio, 2006; Iorio & Visweswaraiah, 2010; 2012). In assembly, the classroom would review rules and attend to daily activities, making up a sort of constitution that gave equitable rights and duties. Assemblies would be a very separate place of participation where injustices were reported and actors who were well aware of their rights would be established (Waller & Bitou, 2011) in the search for solutions to problems that ended up being everyone's.

This work is shown in an example one day during assembly when the group discussed if it was legitimate to hit each other. The children concluded that there needed to be a rule about hitting in the classroom because children have rights, such as the right to feel safe in the classroom. However, the contradictions came out when they recognized that sometimes adults had hit them at home. One child who seemed angry felt the need to tell the group about an incident when she saw her father hit her little sister on the behind. This child told her father that he could not hit her sister; this was not fair. Immediately, however, her father turned and hit her in response to her comment. Later, the child reported that her father came to recognize that he had not done the right thing by these actions and indicated that his daughter had made him reflect about his behavior and that he would change. Through such stories and sharing in assemblies, we began to see the assembly time as a credible way to work toward issues of social justice and democracy, especially in the difficult conversations.

Demanding, fighting for, and working for justice must become a global task in social settings like schools where a comfortable life is not enough while others scrape by and/or lose their livelihoods. For justice, human rationality must prevail with technical and economic rationality. Schools must work to destroy this vision of society as a mere combination of consumers able to fragment groups, making them fragile and divisible. As Bauman (2006) suggests, no long-lasting link comes from the activity of consumption but rather through common–unity (community). Numbers, economic tables, and experts' reports, statistics, and surveys cannot take the place of these types of important and human story–related discussions. Education cannot be summed up in experts' reports on quality depending on statistics, evaluations, surveys, and rankings (Yelland, 2005; Yelland & Kilderry, 2005). In this project, when Lucía shared important news clippings with her young children and then opened them up to discussion and possible solutions through assemblies, we are reminded that teachers must recuperate a sense of a civil and ethical mission so that each student and learner can face the problems of his or her personal life (Morin, 2011).

Reflections: Schooling, Childhood, and Economic Classism

Let us not forget that capitalism, by managing poverty through neoliberal policies, may well divide the population by using an essential unifying characteristic: keeping a majority impoverished while a few amass fortunes, remaining camouflaged and/or blurred under the protection of the law that privileges them. A situation of such serious structural violence as we are discussing requests compromised citizens to intervene strategically from social forums such as schools (and not as a knee-jerk reaction). Also take into account that this situation can get worse from the very moment those who are marginalized see themselves as enemies, arousing social confrontation between one another.

Economic Rivalries and Class

We understand that reflection and action on class differences should never be ignored in school settings. Moreover, we urgently need discussions such as Lucía's and the children's to be revived. We should also not forget that economic differences at school, like in any other social setting, have always existed, near and far, leading to social exclusion from an early age. Reviving these discussions and practices was a special task throughout our action research. Many people still believe the apparent social achievement in the Western world has resulted in a more egalitarian society. These have included teachers, who hold such beliefs while working with children under three being contracted by both public and private establishments for reduced salaries. They are forced to complement their existence with additional work for 'under the table pay' (looking after children and/or the elderly, cleaning houses). Such is the impact of childcare marketization (Lloyd, 2012). By eliminating the fight against economic classism from its discussions and practices (which led to a loss of awareness in this respect), schools continued to empower the capitalist class, economic speculators, and the main beneficiaries of the fact that we do not critically think and discuss in terms of class.

Marketization, Children, and Schools for Our Young

We have spent years building an invented model of childhood with certain social economic and political purposes of the market society. These purposes are very much in line with the interests of the large multinationals of children's entertainment, consumerist to exhaustion (Schor, 2004; Linn, 2004), predatory, and limitless corporations, that have consistently demonstrated the splendor of the upper-handed princesses, princes, and superheroes appearing on the multiple screens of mass media (Steinberg & Kincheloe, 1997; Buckingham, 2006).

Such marketization is completely distant from the world's problems and from those everyday flesh-and-bone heroes who fight for a fairer world and who act when many others do nothing (Zimbardo, 2011). This marketization can be regarded as one of the reasons families with significant economic problems buy very expensive toys for their children and create children living lives colonized by brands. Such families offer their children a type of leisure that puts them dangerously into debt because they want to meet the expectations of the invented childhood model.

Schools should not become an accomplice to this model of childhood by empowering this worldview. Thus, our action research was used for Lucía to attack (via her practices) this school of thought that deduces and alienates, as does advertising (Klein, 2008). Thus, through the clippings and assemblies discussions, Lucía remarked how other curricula hindered the development of critical thought and practiced and distanced the children from taking part in the transformation of the world where they live in the direction of social justice (Macrine, McLaren, & Hill,

2010; Kincheloe, 2008). With new eyes, Lucía opened to her own new sense of social justice work in the classroom.

(Her)stories

Through this action research, Lucía realized that history, like science, politics, and economics, can be narrated from the view of the oppressed—their demands, resistances, and battles. Children have a right to know what happened to the oppressed in these environments, including the poor—what their roles were and how they acted and/or should have acted in these great facts that are told in school settings. She also realized that if this work is not developed in a school setting, we are contributing unjustly to silencing the voice of the poorest students in the classroom and/or students who suffer from dearth, difficulties, and financial shortages. In addition, this action research would allow her to reflect with the children, not only on how the poor were subjected to doing all types of servile tasks and on how an ethos of this type would not be reproduced in their daily lives, but also on their actions of resistance. For example, consider the following discussion around birthday celebrations.

Lucía reflected on birthday celebrations that were set in a consumerist ethos and could not be emulated by the poorest (unless this was through the charity of other families who bought everything needed to do so). She realized that by reinforcing the power of the stories that families invented to tell children, lollipops, candies, fried foods, and other frivolities (which initially were so often present in these children's parties) would lose relevance and so would become totally unnecessary. There were many stories inspired by the lives of familiar heroes who had faced difficulties and challenges in their lives and that would be used in turn to revive the idea of the importance of being together to fight against injustice. She therefore fled from this stereotypical magic from the very same entertainment multinationals where the economic prosperity of the characters' lives seduces them to the extent that they can befuddle children's thoughts and produce an escape from daily reality. This seduction makes it difficult to raise awareness of the problems of those who exist and their comprehension. Learning to imagine a fairer world and acting in this direction should be the backbone of school practices as this sort of education must commit to the search for justice (Sánchez-Blanco, 2006; 2009; 2010). Naturally, to see the effects of actions on the present (Mac Naughton, 2005), the stories told about families of children from various generations would be used to feed the desires of "inventing" a world where there was room for us all as actors with the same rights.

Consumerism

We know that as the population gets poorer, the feeling of being a foreigner is emerging with greater force by feeling ejected from the society of consumerism.

It is for this reason that Lucía, aware of this situation in her classroom, strove to build involvements so that children and families felt part of these alternative experiences, ensuing their voices were heard. There were feelings that emerged in children with economic problems by observing some of their classmates' possessions, by listening to their life stories, and by comparing them with their own. They saw how their families had to struggle with all types of difficulties to sometimes access even the most basic elements such as food, clothing, and housing.

Through the discussions, we noted how television played a major role in consumerism. The children all seemed to have televisions, striving to include them in a symbolic universe to which they were materially and actually denied access. Culturally, television seemed an asset that very few could do without, and if they did, it was a last resort. In any case, one could always go watch it elsewhere, albeit in a shop window. In the most impoverished homes, we saw televisions that were plugged in and children who gobbled up their contents as if this was a question of enjoying a desirable life.

Consuming merchandise like the television is not using up and eventually destroying an object (Alba Rico, 2007; 2011), as this object persists and so does its ethos. At this very early age, we noted that children were aware of this merchandise and through this developed awareness; they became aware of other goods, other objects, and other lives. We and the children found large inequalities when comparisons were made between daily lives such as one child having books in the home and another child not; we found that schools need to deal with this liquidation that the television of popular cultures produce (Barber, 2007; Steinberg & Kincheloe, 1997).

There are many children who wish to emulate those with economic power whom they see everywhere, in the street, in mass media, on channels such as the Disney Channel (Giroux & Pollock, 2001), and in and out of school. Several children secretly took home equipment from their classroom and/or their classmates' possessions, which they thought would enable them to enter into this opulent world to which they wanted to belong. Lucía and I discussed how some teachers, unaware of all these issues surrounding poverty, actually label such children as thieves. These teachers lose sight of how often children with economic difficulties suffer deeply from a desire to own many of those things that others possess so as to experience that power for themselves. Overlaying all these multitudes of problems already were stories about the existence of the Magi or Father Christmas that merely fostered prejudice toward the idea that poor people were bad (Sánchez-Blanco, 2006) by implying that good children's behavior led to many rewards.

Looking Within

Lucía, aware of the situation narrated about inequities and material goods, insisted on encouraging the loan of certain classroom objects, such as toys and books, without realizing that this was actually taking away the value of possibilities that poorer families had and what their home environments could offer them. They may not have had pretty dolls, but in exchange they had a grandmother who could spend time with them and tell them a thousand and one stories. One mother said the toys they brought home merely led to a desire for objects that were really not necessary. There was a risk that, with this type of strategy, the toys would become an actual *need* for the children. Lucía would soon discover that knowing how to play without needing toys was the *real* challenge she had to face with this group of children. She also needed to expose the commercial strategies used by multiple screens to guarantee this need for toys whereas the main elements for playing were within the individual child and in others.

Hope in the Classroom

In the classroom, children can learn to protect themselves from social exclusion, tackling any type of vulnerability that unveils itself as a product of this economic-orientated ethos that widely involves us everywhere. The children and Lucía had formed a community with some rules for everyone to have the same rights and where situations of positive discrimination were also understood and shared, such as the right to have rights, in Hannah Arendt's words (Benhabib, 2004). Work was done in this direction. For instance, in the classroom, Lucía set up a weekly calendar of the play areas, which created enough play spaces so that all children could be involved. A great deal of anxiety was placated by being guaranteed equal opportunities to use toys as children hoped that at a certain moment it would be their turn to play with the objects. Lucía placed great importance on the agreed lists of order of intervention, which indicated which child should do such and such task and when; the tasks were usually related to classroom responsibility. With this sort of work, her expectations were covered by hope even in the children's experiences.

Conclusion

By increasing children's desires to have consumer items that others possess, the desire to be "themselves," and to exist without all those objects, fades. Lucía and I found that schools can commit to providing children with a desire to be themselves, to facilitate the construction of identities based on confidence and trust. This is worlds away from the idea that the more you have, the more you are worth. To achieve this desire, some will doubtlessly obtain this excess, albeit through strength when they are older. For example, at the age of five, one child in Lucía's classroom reported at assembly that he had already attempted raids on supermarkets with his older siblings and their friends to steal chocolates and other popular sweets.

However, amid such stories we met children who, on the contrary, could build and revive hope in the worlds of the lower classes. They built a world of possibilities in contrast to a society of excess waste, and they constituted excellent mirrors where the school must look at itself to understand and design ways to work with all children so that having economic problems does not become a source of many twists and turns. These are individuals and families who are able to fight against exclusion (which makes them vulnerable in a capitalist system) using dignity and awareness, whether they are oppressed, beneficial, and/or necessary. With the earliest of ages, schools must lead movements of concentration and emancipation of this type. Protecting children from social exclusion within the school and letting them build strategies to face this work head-on should be part of teachers' daily confrontations. This is the rough encounter involved in our action research with Lucía, attempting to extract all the possibilities that economic difficulties in students can offer, all the learning on the emancipation of awareness. Through this action research we found that awareness about complex issues can be foregrounded and discussed in productive ways.

It is past time to reincorporate the role of economic questions in the processes of exclusion in our research tasks in early education. Implicitly or explicitly, economic questions and exclusions are established in schools from the youngest ages. This task to reintegrate should never fall into oblivion while social injustice continues to govern the world. We cannot ignore that public teaching is mainly what gives a response to the poorest and lowest-level students. As well, with the economic crisis upon us, the number of schoolchildren in this situation increases every day. One of the difficulties to face is the fact that with beliefs and/or assumptions anchored around the illusion of economic prosperity, it is hardly surprising that we encounter centers with families in ill-fated economic situations who refuse to recognize their economic difficulties and consider them a very serious stigma.

Issues of poverty, it seems, have stayed hidden in children's school. It would seem that they might embarrass and undermine school and curricular standardization. This is one of the reasons why some families do not wish to participate in the scions of such problems, pretending nothing is wrong. Others force their children to be quiet in any scenario about their problems, and they are punished in the long run. Both situations come together in the classroom in this study. We found that, in this way, when the school becomes aware of the economic difficulties, the social problems increased because the level of awareness increased. Yet we found that if problems come to light, they can be worked on in active ways. In all these types of situations we cannot forget that children experience the most varied emotions as well as uncovered material needs. Being poor and feeling poor are two sides of a problem against which schools cannot turn their backs.

We must build schools that are able to include and not socially exclude the student body that experiences being poor and feeling poor. And we must start to do this at the beginning of schooling precisely to avoid growing conflict between "haves and have-nots" at school. To this end, we must be able to implement the principles of social justice and equity in our teaching. We do not have to reject our origins but rather connect our past and present-day experiences in hand, mind, and heart together.

Finally, on one occasion in Lucía's classroom, the children were asked in assembly what they would do if they had a magic wand. Some wanted a lot of money, a large house, and many trading cards. These children showed their desire to mimic the wealthy, even using what they considered the language of the powerful. Others, on the other hand, spoke about ending cold and hunger in the world, while some toiled in the school playground, "excavating" to find the treasure that would take them and their family out of poverty. Some talked about the pleasure of helping, playing together, and/or being with their friends. As we see, there are different types of ethos on which the school can act as sites of interrogation, challenge the status quo, and offer young children the opportunity to reflect, make meaning, and see the possibilities that exist in hope.

References

Alba Rico, S. (2007). *Capitalismo y Nihilismo: Dialéctica del Hambre y la Mirada (Capitalism and nihilism)*. Madrid: Akal.

Alba Rico, S. (2011). *Capitalismo, Crisis y Exclusión Social (Capitalism, crisis and social exclusion)*. Retrieved from https://www.youtube.com/watch?v=3FvxUBHFgaA and https://www.youtube.com/watch?v=IJaT6oxwAaE

Barber, B.R. (2007). *How markets corrupt children, infantilize adults, and swallow citizens whole*. New York: Norton & Company.

Bauman, Z. (2005a). *Archipiélago de Excepciones (Archipelago of exception)*. Madrid: Katz/CCCB, 2008.

Bauman, Z. (2005b). *Liquid life*. Cambridge: Polity.

Bauman, Z. (2006). *Liquid fear*. Cambridge: Polity.

Benhabib, S. (2004). *The rights of others. Aliens, residents and citizens*. Cambridge: Cambridge University Press.

Bourdieu, P. (1993). *The Misère du Monde (The weight of the world)*. Paris: Seuil.

Brown, B. (1998). *Unlearning discrimination in the early years*. London: Trentham Books.

Brown, B. (2008). *Equality in action. A way forward with persona dolls*. London: Trentham Books.

Buckingham, D. (2006). Is there a digital generation. In D. Buckingham and R. Willett (Eds.), *Digital generations: Children, young people, and the new media* (pp. 1–13). London: Lawrence Erlbaum.

Dahlberg, M., & Moss, P. (2005). *Ethics and politics in early childhood education*. Abingdon, UK: Routledge Falmer.

Denzin, N.K., & Lincoln, Y.S. (Eds.). (2011). *The Sage handbook of qualitative research* (4th ed.). London: Sage.

Elliott, J. (2007). *Reflecting where the action is. The selected works of John Elliott*. London: Routledge.

Ferraroti, F. (2011). Las Historias de Vida como Método (Life history as a method of research). *Acta Sociológica* (56), 95–119.

Freire, P. (2005). *Pedagogía de la Tolerancia. Organización y notas de Ana María Araújo Freire (Pedagogy of the heart)*. Mexico: FCE/CREFAL.

Freire, P., & Araujo Freire, A.M. (1992). *Pedagogy of hope: Reliving pedagogy of the oppressed.* London: Continuun.

Giroux, H., & Pollock, G. (2001). *The mouse that roared: Disney and the end of innocence* (2nd ed.). Lanham, MD: Rowman & Littlefield.

Green, D. (2012). Involving young children in research. In I. Palaiologou (Ed.), *Ethical practice in early childhood education* (pp. 15–31). Sage: London.

Gregory, E. (2012). The role of siblings and grandparents in the lives of new Londoners. In M.M. Clark & S. Tuckner (Eds.), *Early childhoods in a changing world* (pp. 33–41). New York: Trentham Books.

Hass Dyson, A. (1997). *Writing superheroes: Contemporary childhood, popular culture, and classroom literacy.* New York: Teacher College Press.

Iorio, J.M. (2006). Rethinking conversations. *Contemporary Issues in Early Childhood, 7*(3), 281–289. Retrieved from http://dx.doi.org/10.2304/ciec.2006.7.3.281

Iorio, J.M., & Visweswaraiah, H. (2010). Do daddies wear lipstick and other child-teacher conversations exploring constructions of gender. In T. Jacobson (Ed.), *Gender perspectives in early childhood* (pp. 59–76). St. Paul, MN: Red Leaf Press.

Iorio, J.M., & Visweswaraiah, H. (2012). Crossing boundaries: A variety of perspectives on preschool stories. *Indo-Pacific Journal of Phenomenology, 12* (Special Edition), 1–13.

Kemmis, S. H. (2008). Critical theory and participatory action research. In P. Reason and H. Bradbury-Huang (Eds.), *The Sage handbook of action research. Participative inquiry and practice* (pp. 121–138). London: Sage.

Kincheloe, J.L. (2008). *Critical pedagogy.* (2nd ed.). New York: Peter Lang, 2009.

Klein, N. (2008). *The shock doctrine: The rise of disaster capitalism.* New York: Henry Holt and Company.

Kurban, F., & Tobin, J. (2009). 'They don't like us': Reflections of Turkish children in a German preschool. *Contemporary Issues in Early Childhood, 10*(1), 24–34. Retrieved from http://dx.doi.org/10.2304/ciec.2009.10.1.24

Linn, S.E. (2004). *Consuming kids: The hostile takeover of childhood.* New York: New Press.

Lloyd, E. (2012). The marketisation of early years education and childcare in England. In L. Miller and D. Harvey (Eds.), *Policy issues in the early years* (pp. 107–121). London: Sage.

Mac Naughton, G. (2005). *Doing Foucault in early childhood studies. Applying poststructural ideas.* New York: Routledge.

Mac Naughton, G., Rolfe, S.A., & Siraj-Blatchford, I. (Eds.). (2010). *Doing early childhood research. International perspectives on theory & practice.* (2nd ed.). London: Falmer Press.

Macrine, S., McLaren, P. & Hill, D. (Eds.). (2010). *Revolutionizing pedagogy: Education for social justice within and beyond global neo-liberalism.* New York: Palgrave MacMillan.

Max-Neef, M. (1982). *From the outside looking in: Experiences in 'barefoot economics.'* Uppsala, Sweden: Dag Hammarskjöld Foundation.

Melrose, A. (2012) *Monsters under the bed. Critically investigating early years writing.* New York: Routledge.

Monchinski, T. (2011). Warriors, come out and play. Joe L. Kincheloe and the intellectual warrior. In R. Brock, C.S. Malott, & L.E. Villaverde (Eds.), *Teaching Joe L. Kincheloe* (pp. 155–165). New York: Peter Lang.

Morin, E. (2011). *La Vía. Para el futuro de la humanidad (La Voie. Pour l'avenir de l'humanité).* Madrid: Paidós Estado y Sociedad.

Nutbrown, C., & Clough, P. (2013). *Inclusion in the early years* (2nd ed.). London: Sage.

Parnell, W. (2011a). Experiences of teacher reflection in the studio: Reggio inspired practices. *Journal of Early Childhood Research, 10*(2), 117–133, doi: 10.1177/1476718X11407982

Parnell, W. (2011b). Teacher collaboration experiences: Finding the extraordinary in the everyday moment, *Early Childhood Research and Practice, 13*(2). Retrieved from http://ecrp.uiuc.edu/v13n2/parnell.html

Polakow, V. (2010). Reframing rights: Poverty discourse and children's lives in the United States. In N. Yelland (Ed.), *Contemporary perspectives on early childhood education* (pp. 66–82). London/New York: Open University Press.

Sánchez-Blanco, C. (1997). *La Cooperación en Educación Infantil (Cooperation in early childhood education).* A Coruña, Spain: Universidade da Coruña.

Sánchez-Blanco, C. (2006). *Violencia Física y Construcción de Identidades. Propuestas de Reflexión Crítica para las Escuelas Infantiles (Physical violence and construction of identities).* Barcelona: Graó.

Sánchez-Blanco, C. (2009). *Peleas y daños físicos en Educación Infantil (Fights and physical damage in early childhood education).* Buenos Aires, Argentina: Miño y Dávila.

Sánchez-Blanco, C. (2010) Violence, social exclusion and construction of identities in early childhood education. In J. Schostak & J. Schostak (Eds.), *Researching violence, democracy and the rights of people* (pp. 102–110). London: Routledge.

Sánchez-Blanco, C. (2013). *Infancias Nómadas: Educando el Derecho a la Movilidad (Nomadic childhoods).* Buenos Aires, Argentina: Miño y Dávila.

Schor, J.B. (2004). *Born to buy: The commercialized child and the new consumer culture.* New York: Simon & Schuster.

Schostak, J.F. & Schostak, J.R. (Eds.). (2008). *Radical research. Designing, developing and writing research to make a difference.* London: Routledge.

Sen, A. (2007). *Identidad y Violencia. La Ilusión de un Destino (Identity and violence: The illusion of destiny).* Buenos Aires, Argentina: Katz.

Sen, A. (2009). *The idea of justice.* London: Penguin Press.

Sennett, R. (2012). *Together. The rituals, pleasures and politics of cooperation.* New Haven, CT: Yale University Press.

Smith, Ph. B., & Max-Neef, M. (2011). *Economics unmasked: From power and greed to compassion and the common good.* Cambridge, UK: UIT Cambridge Ltd.

Somekh, B. (2005). *Action research: A methodology for change and development.* London: Open University Press.

Somekh, B., & Zeichner. K. (2009). Action research for educational reform. Remodelling action research theories and practices in local contexts. *Educational Action Research, 17*(1), 5–21.

Steinberg, SH.R., & Kincheloe, J.L. (Eds.).(1997). *Kinderculture: The corporate construction of childhood.* Boulder, CO: Westview Press.

Teasley, C., Sánchez-Blanco, C., & De Palma, R. (2012). Postcolonial perspective, social integration and cultural diversity vis-à-vis neoliberal policies and practices in Galician schooling. *Power and Education, 4*(3), 303–314. Retrieved from http://dx.doi.org/10.2304/power.2012.4.3.303

UNICEF (2013). *La Infancia en España. 2012–2013. El Impacto de la Crisis en los Niños (Children in Spain. The impact of the crisis on children).* Madrid: UNICEF. Retrieved from http://www.unicef.es/sites/www.unicef.es/files/Infancia_2012_2013_final.pdf

Waal, Frans de (2009). *The age of empathy: Nature's lessons for a kinder society.* New York: Three Year Press.

Waller, T., & Bitou, A. (2011). The sociology of childhood: Children's agency and participation in telling their own stories. In T. Waller, J. Whitmarsh, & K. Clarke (Eds.), *Making sense of theory & practice in early childhood. The power of ideas* (pp. 101–114). New York: Open University Press/McGraw-Hill.

Yelland, N.J. (2005). Curriculum practice and pedagogies with ICT in the information age. In N.J. Yelland (Ed.), *Critical issues in early childhood* (pp. 224–242). Buckingham, UK: Oxford University Press.

Yelland, N.J., & Kilderry, A. (2005). Postmodernism, passion and potential for future childhoods. In N.J. Yelland (Ed.), *Critical issues in early childhood* (pp. 243–248). Buckingham, UK: Oxford University Press.

Zimbardo, Ph. (2011) *HIP (Heroic Imagination Project).* Retrieved from http://blog.ted.com/2011/02/03/phil-zimbardo-and-the-heroic-imagination-project-ted-blog-exclusive-video/ and http://heroicimagination.org

Žižek, S. (2010). *Living in the end times.* London: Verso.

12

ONE TEST IS NOT ENOUGH

Getting to Really Know Your Students

Sandra L. Osorio

> *"Bueno niños y niñas por favor saquen sus libros y habren a la página 298. Hoy vamos a leer el cuento* El gran bigote *por Gary Soto."* [OK, boys and girls, everyone please take out their basal readers and turn to page 324. Today we will have to read Big Bushy Mustache *by Gary Soto.] All twenty-two of my second grade bilingual students took out their orange basal readers and opened to the page. As a class we read the strategy focus for this particular story "prediction" that was on the first page. The strategy focus statement read "Los problemas empiezan cuando Ricky tiene que interpretar un papel en la obra de teatro de la escuela. Al leer el cuento, trata de* **predecir** *cómo se solucionarán los problemas" [Problems start when Ricky gets a part in a school play. As you read, try to* **predict** *how the problems will be solved.]*

This was a typical day during literacy instruction in my own second grade classroom as I worked with my Spanish-English bilingual students and our required reading curriculum, a basal reader. My students were expected to read one story in the basal reader each week as well as complete the worksheets that accompanied the stories. This particular story was the only one out of 20 stories in the two anthologies with a Latino-looking character. I soon realized that the story line and the way the curriculum was set up by the teacher's manual did not invoke meaningful connections. During literacy instruction I was the one in control, following the directions from the teacher's manual and making sure students understood how to use the designated strategy to aid in the comprehension of the story.

As a result of accountability pressures, my school standardized their literacy instruction, meaning that a particular reading program has to be adopted for use school wide. Some district personnel felt that in order to meet the standards, every child needed to receive the same instruction with the intent that each child was granted equal access to the same curriculum. Having one type of curriculum for students did not guarantee equal access to learning because each student had individual literacy and language skills that would influence how they learned. My bilingual students, who were negotiating between two different languages, have various cultural backgrounds and different "funds of knowledge" (González, Moll, & Amanti, 2005) that were not being taken into consideration with this scripted curriculum, and this is further evidenced in the benchmark testing administered to my students throughout the year.

Looking at the benchmark tests as well as the reading curriculum required by my district, I felt I was not meeting the needs of my students. Without abandoning the school's policy and required reading curriculum, I decided to introduce students to more multicultural literature through discussion groups, specifically choosing Latino children's literature that was written by Latino authors for Latino children. I felt this would allow my students to make more personal connections and have meaningful connections around literature. In this chapter I share how a test labeled two of my students, Carlos and Alejandra, as not being proficient readers because they did not reach the required benchmark score throughout the year. When I looked beyond their test results, I realized they had many complexities to their identities as readers.

Research Setting

This research was conducted at Lincoln Elementary School located in the Midwestern United States. The town's population included approximately 41,000 people with 60% identifying as Caucasian and 5% as Latino or Hispanic in origin (United States Census Bureau, 2010). The school's population included 443 students, with 275 students on a subsidized lunch program and 164 students identified as Latinos (Illinois State Board of Education, 2010). Many Latino students were on subsidized lunch. The Latino population had been steadily increasing since the bilingual program had relocated into the building in 2003.

There were more than 100 students in the bilingual program in this particular year. The bilingual program consisted of one kindergarten, a first grade classroom, and a second grade comprising all native Spanish speakers. In fourth and fifth grade, however, native Spanish speakers were integrated with all other students and were pulled away from the classroom for Spanish and English as a Second Language (ESL) services. This research study was conducted in my own Spanish-bilingual second grade classroom, and this was my second year with the same students—I had been their first grade teacher as well.

My classroom was made up of 20 native Spanish-speaking students, all of whom were second-generation Latina/o students. All but six of the students were born in the area where the school was located. Sixteen of the students were of

Mexican descent, one student was of Mexican and Guatemalan descent, and three were of Guatemalan descent. Literacy instruction in my classroom was all in Spanish, and the philosophy behind this was to have students develop a strong base in their native language to facilitate literacy development in English (August & Hakuta, 1997; August & Shanahan, 2006; Ramírez, 2000).

Carlos performed to classroom expectations in his academic subject matters. He scored lowest on the school reading benchmark test because he could not read fluently and fast enough. Still, many other children looked to him for friendship and companionship. They enjoyed his company, and he benefitted because others liked to help him succeed. All the children always wanted to be with him, even during reading. He was not extremely talkative but would talk and answer questions during classroom activities.

Alejandra had a difficult time with comprehension in many academic subject areas. Math was especially hard for her when it came to using complex problem-solving skills such as in word problems. She did have a below average score on the school reading benchmark test. At the same time, Alejandra found herself surrounded by many friends in class, and others wanted to be in her group or play with her at recess. When it came to whole group activities, she would stay quiet. In first grade, her mother placed her in an all–English classroom in this same school, resulting in crying every day during the first two weeks of school. In her own words, Alejandra expressed, "No entiende nada" [I did not understand anything]. After two weeks, the decision was made to place her back into the bilingual program, and she has remained there. Her mother placed a high importance on learning to read, write, and speak English; Alejandra shared that her mother made her do homework and read each night in English along with her Spanish assignments. To note, interestingly, Alejandra had a large family network in our particular town.

My Lens as Researcher

As a child who grew up bilingual, I had similar experiences as the students I taught. As a bilingual student, I felt that many times my teachers misunderstood me. Many assumed I was deficient because I spoke another language at home. All my experiences of having low expectations placed on me greatly influenced my research interests as well as my daily teaching practices. I wanted to make sure that other bilingual children were not seen from this deficit-based lens. Working as a Spanish-bilingual teacher for over seven years, I strived to be a teacher who acknowledges the resources bilingual children bring with them to school and builds upon these resources.

Theoretical Framework

Funds of knowledge perspective (Moll & Greenberg, 1990; Moll & Diaz, 1987) takes advantage of the families' household and community resources as a primary means of organizing classroom instruction. Moll, Amanti, Neff, and Gonzalez (1992) looked at students' working-class Mexican households in Tucson, Arizona, and found that families knew things, such as farming and animal management, construction, and building, as well as trade, business, and finance, to name a few (Moll & Greenberg, 1990). They developed the term "funds of knowledge" and defined it as the historically accumulated and culturally developed bodies of knowledge and skills essential for household or individual functioning and skill (González, Moll, & Amanti, 2005). It is a way to look at all households, including those of working-class or poor communities, in terms of their strengths and resources. This framework informs my study.

My Research Approach: Literature Discussion Groups

Literature discussion groups informed by Martínez-Roldán and López-Robertson (1999/2000) were offered and maintained in the spring semester 2012, from January to May. Students were introduced to this format of literature discussions during our 2010 to 2011 school year, when I had decided to implement this practice in addition to the required curriculum. Students were reintroduced to this format through whole class literature discussions. Once I had modeled and felt that students practiced enough, I then placed them in small literature discussion groups of four to five students. The group members were not assigned any particular roles, and there was no set leader; instead students were given sentence starters to write down their ideas on sticky notes as they prepared for discussion. Each group of literature discussions was five days long, including two days of preparation for the discussions and three days of group discussion facilitated by me. Of particular note, my role was one of facilitator rather than leader.

I made it clear to my students that I was not the one who would be 'running' the discussion. They were there to share *their* own ideas, and I was there to support them in that process. After the first day of discussion, I chose one section from the book for students to reread, and I gave a thinking prompt as a way to scaffold and support. This section could be a place in the story where there was some misunderstandings by students or a section I thought was important to (and for) them. At the beginning of the second day's discussion, this section was the starting point of that day's discussion, and so on.

I selected the books for literature discussion groups using criteria similar to Martínez-Roldán and López-Robertson (1999/2000): (a) stories I felt were interesting and would appeal to my students, (b) stories that seemed to allow students to see aspects of their lives reflected positively, and (c) books that I felt my students could connect to. The majority of the books I selected were bilingual, written in both English and Spanish, and my students were expected to read in Spanish whenever that was an option. Ultimately, they could also read it in English if they so chose. During their discussions students were allowed to use either one of their languages to share their meaning-making process, which resulted in the majority using Spanish as a means of communicating.

Students were given a choice among all the book titles for each rotation, which was usually between four or five book titles. At the beginning of each rotation,

I gave a 'book talk' where I shared selective passages of each of their book choices. Students were then given time to browse the books and fill out a ballot in which they ranked their top book choices. Students were placed in their first choice whenever possible. If their first choice was unavailable, they were certainly placed in their second choice of book group.

Students prepared for discussions by reading the story and marking the book with sticky notes. On each sticky note students were expected to write, so they would remember what they wanted to say in the discussion group. They were taught to follow a sentence starter logic I taught them, such as "I'm thinking . . ." or "What I am noticing in the story is . . ." These sentence starters were used as a reminder for them to start the conversation when in discussion groups. This method helped discussion groups formulate rich conversations.

Personal Narratives

During one small group's discussion of the book *Trencitas/Braids* by Kathleen Contreras, Alejandra shared that she had never met her grandmother on her father's side because her grandmother had died in Mexico. She also shared how her mother sometimes felt sad when talking to family in Mexico. Alejandra said, "Mi mamá un día habló con su papá en México y la hizo llorar. Nosotras estábamos bien espantadas porque desde afuera, hasta adentro, hasta nuestro cuarto, se escuchaba que estaba llorando. Cuando terminó le preguntamos qué te pasó y ella no dijo nada." [One day my mom was talking to her dad and he made her cry. We were scared because from outside to inside, to our room, we could hear her crying. When she was done we asked her what happened and she said nothing.]

Further, during the discussion of the book *Del Norte al Sur/From North to South*, Alejandra shared how her mother does not like the United States. This sentiment came after Lucia had commented how she would prefer to live in Mexico than in the United States. The discussion then continued about a feeling that Mexicans were not wanted here in the United States. Alejandra then shared some of the fears she had of having her family separated. Alejandra was born in the United States, so she knows she can stay in the United States. Her parents and older sister were not born in the United States, so she lives with the daily fear that someday they might be taken away from her.

The small group continued to talked about how they came to develop their own opinions, including about messages they had seen on television shows, such as *Primer Impacto*, a Spanish news series. Lucia said, "Sí, en las noticias están pasando mucho de todo eso en *Primer Impacto*, que traten de no salir los mexicanos." [Yes, in the news they are showing lots of that on *First Impact*, that they try to take out the Mexicans.] Alejandra nodded her head and said, "Uh hun los Mexicanos." [Uh hun the Mexicans.] Then, Lucia enthusiastically stated, "Porque los policías están tratando de parar a todos los mexicanos y van a tratar de mandarlos . . ." [Because police are trying to stop all Mexicans and are going to send them . . .], which Alejandra finished the thought for her, "A su estado" [To their state]. Lucia then went on to say something that most of the group members nodded their head and agreed with: "Están tratando de mandar a México porque no quieren a los mexicanos, quieren puros americanos acá." [They are trying to send them to Mexico because they don't like Mexicans, they want just Americans here.]

As a teacher I was somewhat surprised my students felt this way. While this would be expected from adults, I did not expect to hear it from a seven-year-old, so I asked, "¿Y cómo se sienten ustedes con eso, ustedes siendo mexicanos y americanos?" [And, how do you feel being both Mexican and American?] I wanted to know how they felt because they were from Mexican descent but had been born in the United States and were therefore United States citizens. Alejandra responded to my question by saying, "Yo me siento mal porque mi mamá dice que si la van a deportar, buen si la llegan a llevar a México que no sabe a quién llevarse. Porque se necesita lleva a Perla pero no sabe si dejarnos a nosotros dos. Dice mi mamá que si llegan a parar puede que ya nunca nos vea porque ellos se van y puede que nos dejen a nosotros hijas con otra familia." [I feel bad because my mom says that if they deport her, well if they take her to Mexico, that she doesn't know who to take. Because she has to take Perla but she doesn't know about leaving us two. My mom says if they stop her, it can be as if she will never see us again because they will have to leave. It will be as if they will leave us children with another family.]

In the previous conversation, I took serious note of the fact that my students talked about how some of them felt that Mexicans were not wanted here in the United States. This is a complicated issue for many of my students since the majority of them are Mexican Americans. This conversation between Alejandra and Lucia demonstrates the complex lives of my students at even a young age; especially as they are dealing with issues of deportation and family separation, which are usually reserved for adult conversations and preoccupation.

Students in my classroom have to deal with the separation of family members and with the complexities of being of a different culture. This is a difficult reality of their lives. Their participation in literature discussion gave them a way to express some of these feeling and realize many of their classmates had similar experiences. In these previous brief examples, we see a glimpse of what can occur when you get students involved in literature discussions around books that reflect particular aspects of their lives. The fact that my students could see themselves in the book allowed them to share a good deal of personal narratives related to their experiences, such as the experiences of loss, fear, and identity. These are all topics that are not normally part of the second grade curriculum, but as seen from the stories shared by these students, these books provided a context for language exploration and for the children to connect books to their own lives.

Leaders Emerge

During the discussion with the *Trencitas/Braids* group, Alejandra seemed to take on the teacher role when the teacher was not present. I had walked away from the group to attend to some other students working at a center and told the

discussion group to reread the final part of the book that we would be discussing later. All four children had been reading the story aloud together when
Alejandra stopped and said, "Punto, recuerde los puntos y los commas." [Period,
remember the periods and the commas.] She was reminding her classmates that
they had to pause at the periods and commas whenever reading. She also told
her classmates, "Ya vamos a seguir" [We are now going to continue . . .] when
an argument had broken out between other members of the group about how
softly they were to be reading. When they had also finished reading she said,
"¿Preguntas?" [Questions?] in an effort to give her classmates a way into the
discussion as I sometimes demonstrated. This was all enacted when I was not
present. This was a characteristic of Alejandra's that I had not seen demonstrated
through the activities using the basal reader. When reading while using the
required basal reader process, Alejandra was usually quiet, not answering questions or taking part in the class discussion.

Again, during a different discussion using *Pepita Habla Dos Veces/Pepita Talks Twice*,
I made it clear that I was not 'running' the discussion by choosing to stay silent for
over ten seconds. I wanted students to have the conversation while I was present only
to support them in their efforts. Sofia said, "¿Carlos?" as if nudging him to speak and
'run' the discussion. I stated, "Yo estoy tratando de no hablar, voy a dejar que ustedes
discutan y yo escucho, hágale pues." [I am trying not to talk, I am going to let you
discuss and I will listen, go ahead.] Then Carlos took the initiative and said, "Otra
pagina, ummm, vaz hacer tu pregunta?" [The other page, ummm, are you going to
ask your question?] This was directed to Guillermo, who had placed a sticky note on
the next page, and Carlos invited Guillermo to share his question with the group.
Carlos then called on Sofia to share her thoughts on Guillermo's question. Carlos
also finished Sofia's response, when she started, "Es que como que alguna gente
habla en ingles como . . ." [It's like when some people speak English . . .] and Carlos
finished with ". . . y otras en español" [. . . and others in Spanish]. This showed how
others in the group often turned to Carlos to lead the discussion when the teacher
was not doing it. Carlos was willing to take on this role and become the leader, a role
he had not previously chosen during activities using the basal reader series.

These examples show how my two students welcomed the ability to be placed
in a leadership role. With this new discussion format both Alejandra and Carlos
were able to show the abilities they had to aid and lead the discussion of the group.
This is particularly evident when Alejandra and Carlos took on similar practices
to my teaching. These students were able to create spaces that encouraged clear
communication around book comprehension, mechanics of reading, and connections of the literature to social experiences. These elements reflect exemplars of
reading practices whether in English or Spanish.

Connection to Characters' Narratives

I found that one of the biggest influences on a student's level of engagement with
a story was their personal identification with a particular character's narrative.

In many of the literature discussion groups, I noticed students were much more engaged than previously with the basal readers. These literature books were made available in their native language, and the story line related to their lives. In the discussion groups, I saw that when students were highly engaged, the conversation was more fluid without much input from me as teacher.

In the discussion of *Del Norte al Sur/From North to South*, Alejandra shared various stories about her family's different experiences as related to their undocumented status. Alejandra also spoke to the example of the police stopping her father while driving back from Chicago. She reported that her mother had told her not to listen to what the officer was saying. After they were allowed to leave, they were followed to the house by the officer. Once home, her father was questioned again. While Alejandra was not of undocumented status, her parents and oldest sister were, and this fact affected her day-to-day activities, including the fear she felt every day. Of particular note, I found her the most engaged and with the longest responses during the third rotation of *Del Norte al Sur/From North to South*. She had personal experiences that related to the story and felt safe in this particular discussion group to share them.

Carlos was also very engaged during the book discussion of *Pepita Habla Dos Veces/Pepita Talks Twice*. Carlos shared different personal narratives related to his bilingualism. He talked about how he knows more English than his father, "Yo ya sé más que mi papá en inglés" [I know more English than my dad], but not his mother, "Mi mamá ella sabe casi todo en inglés, ella ya sabe escribir en inglés, yo no sé cómo escribe cursive en ingles" [My mom know almost everything in English, she knows how to write in English, I don't know how to write in cursive in English.] He spoke of having to speak English when playing outside his home because most of his friends were African American or white, "Este yo, casi todos mis amigos son como morenitos, pero a veces otros no, otros son blancos y otros así (apunta a su propia piel), pero hablan puro inglés y le tengo que hablar en inglés." [I, almost all my friends are black, but some are not, others are white and others like this (points to his brown skin), but they speak English so I have to speak to them in English.] This story related directly to experiences Carlos had on a daily basis.

Personal identification with particular characters' narratives was illustrated in both Alejandra's and Carlos's experiences with literature discussion groups. Alejandra connected the text to her family's experiences and her ultimate fears of loss, while Carlos, through the text, negotiated relationships, in particular his friendships, through recognition of variation of skin color and language uses. Again, the literature discussion group functioned as a way to develop communication necessary for fostering strong reading practices.

Educational Implications

Taking into account a school's obligation to meet the needs of all their students, specifically the growing population of Latino students in schools, this study has implications for teaching practices in early childhood classrooms specifically for children whose speak a language other than English. One critical implication is that every student comes into the classroom with a wealth of knowledge. Many times this wealth of knowledge cannot be measured because it is not considered to be part of the typical school literacy practices. Often, the reading instruction students receive does not draw or extend on the resources they bring to school; this is specifically reflective of Latino students (Moll, Diaz, Estrada, & Lopes, 1992).

Research indicates the importance of creating a context valuing students' backgrounds, including their lives, language, and identities (Darder, 1995; Garcia, 2001; Nieto, 2002; Soto, 1997). Nieto (2002) shows that when students felt their background was valued, it actually promoted their learning. The current study illustrates that when a student is allowed to share personal narratives related to the literature discussion groups, the teacher is able to understand students from another perspective, including identity and life experience. This occurred when the students made personal connections to the story line of the text. Based on this work, I note the importance of teachers knowing their students and choosing books that reflect aspects of the students' lives. Also, I realize that students need space to express their ideas and thoughts, specifically their personal narratives.

The personal narratives produced in the literature discussion groups showed that the students' use of native language was a resource. Being in a setting where their native language was encouraged, students were able to draw on their linguistic knowledge as a tool to develop reading practices applicable to Spanish and English: for example, when the literature discussion group focuses on the pause at the period (at the end of the sentence). The use of relevant literature connects a student's background and native language, recognizing and valuing the students' experiences as a way to promote student learning.

Another important implication is giving students space to discuss socio–political issues in groups (Fain, 2008)—spaces that are safe and offer resources, such as texts and discussion formats, that connect to different aspects of their lives. The issues that surfaced in the literature discussions groups were initiated by the students and reflective of their lives. In order to create spaces for these discussions, teachers need to be willing to give up some of their power and change their teaching practices. When the teacher takes the role of facilitator, conversation partner, and learner, the students are able to make more meaningful connections while covering the day's learning. This constructs a context that is now more personal and directly related to the students' experiences. Martínez-Roldán (2005) suggests that when there is a strong focus on the teaching of procedures or protocols, then the focus is taken away from the meaning-making process of students. I find this to be true in my research.

Additional Thoughts

Every student offers his or her unique story and brings his or her own knowledge to learning. By utilizing literature discussion groups, the students illustrated their complexity and rich identities (Nieto, 2002). My research demonstrated the students' ability to have meaningful and detailed conversations, comprehend text by connecting to personal experiences, engage as leaders, and communicate with peers clearly—all characteristics contributing to students as readers. Further, when the students authentically expressed themselves and their intense personal stories, demonstrated leadership when given the opportunity, and connected to a character's narratives in relevant ways, my classroom came alive with meaning making for both the children and myself. The literature discussion groups ignited an interest in other classroom practice considerations. In particular, I wonder how I might use my experience with the literature discussion groups as a way to rethink practices throughout the day's experiences so children use native language as a resources and locate their stories within social awareness and advocacy.

References

August, D., & Hakuta, K. (Eds.) (1997). *Improving schooling for language-minority children: A Research agenda.* Washington, DC: National Academy Press.

August, D., & Shanahan, T. (Eds.) (2006). *Developing literacy in second-language learners: Report of the National Literacy Panel on Language Minority Children and Youth.* Mahwah, NJ: Erlbaum.

Darder, A. (1995). Buscando America: The contribution of critical Latino educators to the academic development and empowerment of Latino students in the U.S. In C. Sleeter & P. McLaren (Eds.), *Multicultural education, critical pedagogy, and the politics of difference* (pp. 319–347). Albany, NY: SUNY Press.

Fain, J.G. (2008). "Um, they weren't thinking about their thinking": Children's talk about issues of oppression. *Multicultural Perspectives, 10,* 201–208.

Garcia, E.E. (2001). *Hispanic education in the United States: Raices y alas.* New York: Rowman & Littlefield.

González, N., Moll, L., & Amanti, C. (2005). *Funds of knowledge: Theorizing practices in households, communities, and classrooms.* Hillsdale, NJ: Lawrence Erlbaum.

Illinois State Board of Education. (2010). *2010 state report card.* Retrieved from http://www.isbe.net/assessment/report_card.htm

Martínez-Roldán, C.M. (2005). The inquiry acts of bilingual children in literature discussions. *Language Arts, 83,* 22–32.

Martínez-Roldán, C.M., & López-Robertson, J.M. (1999/2000). Initiating literature circles in a first-grade bilingual classroom. *Reading Teacher, 53,* 270–281.

Moll, L.C., Amanti, C., Neff, D., & Gonzalez, N. (1992). Funds of knowledge for teaching: Using a qualitative approach to connect homes and schools. *Theory into Practice, 31,* 132–141.

Moll, L.C., & Diaz, S. (1987). Change as the goal of educational research. *Anthropology and Education Quarterly, 18,* 300–311.

Moll, L.C., Díaz, S., Estrada, E., & Lopes, L. (1992). Making contexts: The social construction of lessons in two languages. In M. Saravia-Shore & S.F. Arvizu (Eds.), *Cross-cultural literacy: Ethnographies of communication in multiethnic classrooms* (pp. 339–366). New York: Garland.

Moll, L.C., & Greenberg, J. (1990). Creating zones of possibilities: Combining social contexts for instruction. In L.C. Moll (Ed.), *Vygotsky and education* (pp. 319–348). Cambridge, UK: Cambridge University Press.

Nieto, S. (2002). *Language, culture, and teaching: Critical perspectives for a new century*. Mahwah, NJ: Erlbaum.

Ramírez, J.D. (2000, April). Bilingualism and literacy: Problem or opportunity? A synthesis of reading research on bilingual students. *A Research Symposium on High Standards in Reading for Students from Diverse Language Groups: Research, Practice and Policy: Proceedings*. Washington, DC: Office of Bilingual Education and Minority Language Affairs, U.S. Department of Education.

Soto, L.D. (1997). *Language, culture, and power: Bilingual families and the struggle for quality education*. Albany, NY: SUNY Press.

United States Census Bureau. (2010). State and county quickfacts. Retrieved from http://quickfacts.census.gov/qfd/states/17000.html

CONTRIBUTORS

Karin Alnervik is an Assistant Professor of Early Childhood Education in the School of Education and Communication at Jönköping University. Her research is primarily in the field of preschool didactics and her interest focuses pedagogical documentation, children's exploration, and peer learning.

Ysaaca D. Axelrod is an Assistant Professor in Teacher Education and Curriculum Studies at the University of Massachusetts, Amherst. She received her Ed.D. from Teachers College at Columbia University. Prior to receiving her doctorate, she was a kindergarten teacher in the Bay Area in California. Her research interests include: language and literacy development of young children, particularly emergent bilinguals; the intersections between identity, language ideologies, and language development; and ethnographic research in classrooms.

Paige M. Bray, Ed.D., is an Associate Professor of Early Childhood Education at the University of Hartford. Her research includes co-constructed inquiry, the use of meta-cognitive tools, and collaborative participatory research approaches to working with communities, families, and teachers. The Parent Inquiry Initiative is a sustained example of methodological choices reflecting a long-held value of practitioner knowledge and commitment to mutual use and benefit—research with, not on, collaborators. A teacher of early childhood children (three- to eight-year-olds) and adults, she remains committed to teaching and utilizing the classroom as a transformative space for integrating research, theory, and practice.

Sue Dockett is Professor in Early Childhood Education, Charles Sturt University, Australia. Prior to entering tertiary education, Sue worked as an educator in prior-to-school settings as well as the early years of school. Since 1988, Sue has been involved in early childhood teacher education and research. Much of her research agenda is focused on educational transitions, particularly transitions to school and the expectations, experiences, and perceptions of all involved. With Bob Perry, Sue has published widely, both nationally and internationally, in the area of transition to school. Integral to the investigations of educational transitions is a commitment to incorporating children's perspectives. Much of Sue's current collaborative work is focused on refining and critiquing these approaches as well as conceptual and theoretical analysis of what is meant by engaging children and young people's voices within research agendas.

Sandy Farquhar is Director of ECE in the Faculty of Education, University of Auckland, New Zealand. Her book *Ricoeur, Identity and Early Childhood* (2010) develops a series of narratives about the way in which young children's identities are played out in policy and curriculum documents. She has co-edited two special issues on philosophy of early childhood education for *Educational Philosophy and Theory*. Other publications include *Lost in Translation: The Power of Language* (2011) and *Narrative Identity and Early Childhood Education* (2012). Sandy is a convenor of the interdisciplinary narrative and metaphor special interest network at the University of Auckland.

Beth Ferholt is an Assistant Professor in the Department of Early Childhood and Art Education at Brooklyn College, City University of New York. Her areas of research broadly stated are learning, development, and imagination. Her research builds upon the tradition of cultural-historical activity theories. Consistent foci of her research include the methodological project of challenging the divide between method and object in conventional social science; playworlds; the concept of perezhivanie, which is useful in challenging divides between emotion and cognition and individual and environment; and practices of early childhood education in which children are understood as culture and knowledge creators.

Emmanuelle N. Fincham holds an M.A. in Early Childhood Education and Special Education and is a toddler teacher at the Rita Gold Center at Teachers College, Columbia University. At Teachers College, she is also a doctoral student and an instructor in the Early Childhood Preservice Master's program. Emmanuelle engages in teacher research in the classroom, using autoethnographic and narrative methods to examine the possibilities of teaching young children with a gaze informed by feminist poststructural theory.

Stefania Giamminuti was previously an early childhood teacher in an International School in Rome (Italy). She is currently a Lecturer in Early Childhood education, Curtin University (Perth, WA). Stefania was awarded her Ph.D. with Distinction at the University of Western Australia in 2010. She is the recipient of the 2010 Early Career Award of the Western Australian Institute for Educational Research and a recipient of the Early Childhood Australia Doctoral Thesis Award for 2010. A recipient of the Creswick Foundation Fellowship for 2006, Stefania spent six months engaging in Ph.D. research in the municipal infant–toddler centers and schools of Reggio Emilia, Italy.

Allison Sterling Henward is Assistant Professor of Early Childhood at the University of Hawaii at Manoa. Her research is focused on the social and cultural nature of childhood with a focus on children's use and production of media culture. She has published numerous articles on the way children understand and use media in preschool classrooms in a variety of contexts. Her research is also concerned with the social and cultural nature of early childhood programs with a particular focus on social class as a variable in early childhood curriculum and instruction.

Anders Jansson holds a Ph.D. from Stockholm University and was an assistant professor of Educational Science at Jönköping University during the Playworld project and is currently an assistant professor of Special Education at Stockholm University. His research focuses on issues regarding teaching–learning processes and development, especially creativity and narrativity, grounded in Vygotskian theory and activity theory, and related research methods such as formative intervention and educational formative experiments conducted in collaboration with teachers. In relation to his research he is interested in the development of teaching and learning in various subjects and communicative modalities in accomplishing an inclusive education.

Richard T. Johnson is Professor in the Curriculum Studies Department, College of Education, University of Hawaii. With a background of early childhood education, he supervises students in the field and works closely with schools, teachers, and staff.

Erin M. Kenney, M.Ed., holds a Master's Degree in Early Childhood Education from the University of Hartford. She is currently pursuing a Ph.D. in developmental psychology at the University of New Hampshire. Erin has worked with children, parents, and families for 12 years in multiple capacities including work as a mentor, tutor, teacher, and childcare administrator. She has served as research assistant, project manager, and most recently co-principal investigator for the Parent Inquiry Initiative at the University of Hartford.

Peter Moss is an Emeritus Professor at the Institute of Education University of London. His interests include early childhood education and care; the workforce in children's services; the relationship between care, gender, and employment; the relationship between early childhood and compulsory education; social pedagogy; and democracy in children's services. He coordinates an international network on leave and related work/life policies. Recent books include: *Transformative Change and Real Utopias in Early Childhood Education*; *Early Childhood and Compulsory Education: Reconceptualising the Relationship*; and *Radical Education and the Common School: A Democratic Alternative* (with Michael Fielding), which won first prize in 2012 in the annual book award of the Society for Educational Studies.

Monica Nilsson is an Associate Professor of Early Childhood Education at the School of Education and Communication (HLK) at Jönköping University in Sweden. Monica Nilsson's research is primarily in the field of preschool didactics. Her research builds upon the tradition of cultural-historical activity theories. Her research interest and methodological approach is development of preschool practices in close collaboration with preschools. Her foci has been on playworlds, a Vygotskian inspired form of adult-child joint play, and on pedagogy of listening, the pedagogical philosophy that originated in the preschools in Reggio Emilia, Italy, and a meeting of these two practices.

Sandra L. Osorio is an Assistant Professor at Illinois State University in the School of Teaching and Learning. She earned her Ph.D. in curriculum and instruction from the University of Illinois at Urbana-Champaign, under the direction of Dr. Anne Haas Dyson. She is a former bilingual educator who worked with children from diverse racial, ethnic, and linguistic backgrounds for over seven years. Her own personal narrative growing up bilingual and having a deficient-based identity placed upon her because of her linguistic differences has served as a source of motivation to become an educator and researcher.

Bob Perry is Professor in the Research Institute for Professional Practice, Learning and Education at Charles Sturt University, Albury-Wodonga, Australia. Bob's current research interests include powerful mathematics ideas in preschool and the first years of school; ethical tensions in researching with children; transition to school, with particular emphasis on starting school within families with complex support needs, preschool education in remote Indigenous communities, and transition to school for Indigenous families. Bob shares his life with his partner, Sue Dockett, and their son, Will, both of whom ensure that he keeps his feet firmly on the ground.

Concepción Sánchez-Blanco is Tenured Professor in the Faculty of the Educational Sciences at the University of A Coruña (Spain). She belongs to the Investigation and Innovation in Education Group, formed in 2007 by faculty members from the Department of Pedagogy and Curriculum Studies at the same university. She shares a common interest in the pursuit of social justice through qualitative inquiry in educational research. Her specific research is centered on early childhood education, social values, the hidden curriculum, social exclusion, and learning about democracy and social justice at this level.

Marek Tesar is a Lecturer in Childhood Studies and Early Childhood Education at the Faculty of Education at the University of Auckland. His research is concerned with early years teacher subjectivities and the construction of childhoods. He has published journal articles and book chapters in this area, and his doctorate received prestigious national and international awards.

INDEX